EXSANGUINE™

EXSANGUINE™

SCRIPT BY JOSHUA SCOTT EMMONS AND TIM SEELEY
ART BY TIM SEELEY COLORS BY CARLOS BADILLA
LETTERS BY JOSHUA SCOTT EMMONS AND CRANK!
COVER AND CHAPTER BREAK ART BY TIM SEELEY WITH DAVE STEWART

DARK HORSE BOOKS

EDITORS SCOTT ALLIE AND DANIEL CHABON
ASSISTANT EDITOR SHANTEL LAROCQUE
DESIGNER KAT LARSON
PUBLISHER MIKE RICHARDSON

PRESIDENT AND PUBLISHER MIKE RICHARDSON   EXECUTIVE VICE PRESIDENT NEIL HANKERSON   CHIEF FINANCIAL
OFFICER TOM WEDDLE   VICE PRESIDENT OF PUBLISHING RANDY STRADLEY   VICE PRESIDENT OF BOOK TRADE SALES
MICHAEL MARTENS   VICE PRESIDENT OF BUSINESS AFFAIRS ANITA NELSON   EDITOR IN CHIEF SCOTT ALLIE
VICE PRESIDENT OF MARKETING MATT PARKINSON   VICE PRESIDENT OF PRODUCT DEVELOPMENT DAVID SCROGGY
VICE PRESIDENT OF INFORMATION TECHNOLOGY DALE LAFOUNTAIN   SENIOR DIRECTOR OF PRINT, DESIGN, AND
PRODUCTION DARLENE VOGEL   GENERAL COUNSEL KEN LIZZI   EDITORIAL DIRECTOR DAVEY ESTRADA   SENIOR
BOOKS EDITOR CHRIS WARNER   EXECUTIVE EDITOR DIANA SCHUTZ   DIRECTOR OF PRINT AND DEVELOPMENT CARY
GRAZZINI   ART DIRECTOR LIA RIBACCHI   DIRECTOR OF SCHEDULING CARA NIECE   DIRECTOR OF INTERNATIONAL
LICENSING TIM WIESCH   DIRECTOR OF DIGITAL PUBLISHING MARK BERNARDI

PUBLISHED BY DARK HORSE BOOKS
A DIVISION OF DARK HORSE COMICS, INC.
10956 SE MAIN STREET
MILWAUKIE, OR 97222

FIRST EDITION: AUGUST 2013
ISBN 978-1-61655-158-2

10 9 8 7 6 5 4 3 2 1
PRINTED IN CHINA

INTERNATIONAL LICENSING: (503) 905-2377
ADVERTISING SALES: (503) 905-2237
COMIC SHOP LOCATOR SERVICE: (888) 266-4226

EX SANGUINE VOLUME 1

THIS VOLUME COLLECTS ISSUES #1 THROUGH #5 OF *EX SANGUINE*.

CHAPTER ONE
THE HOLLOW MAN

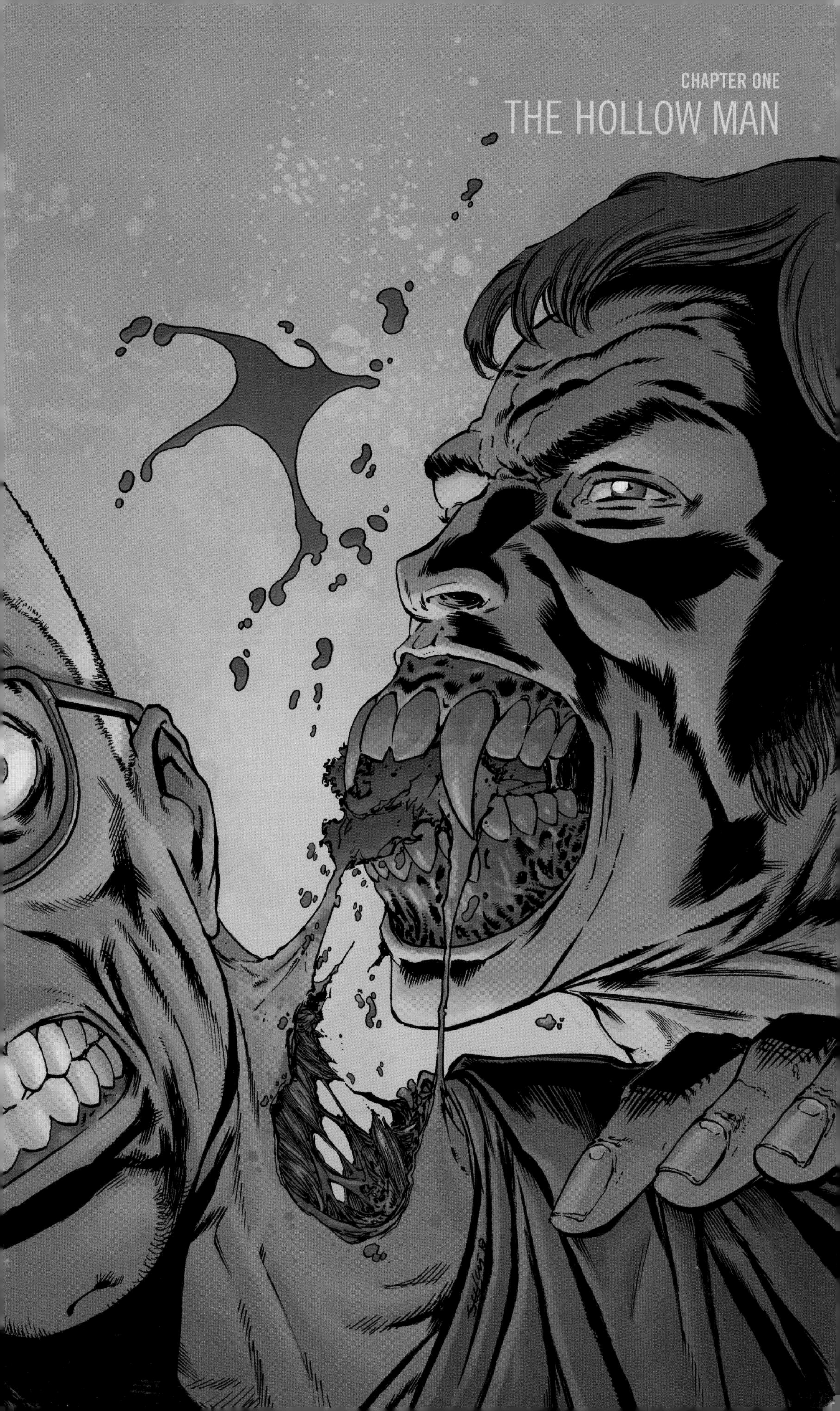

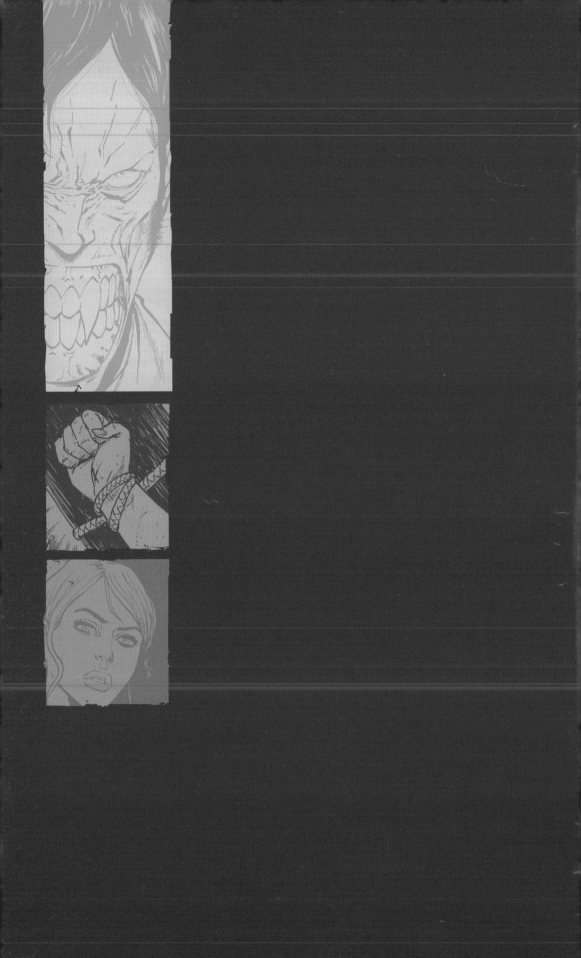

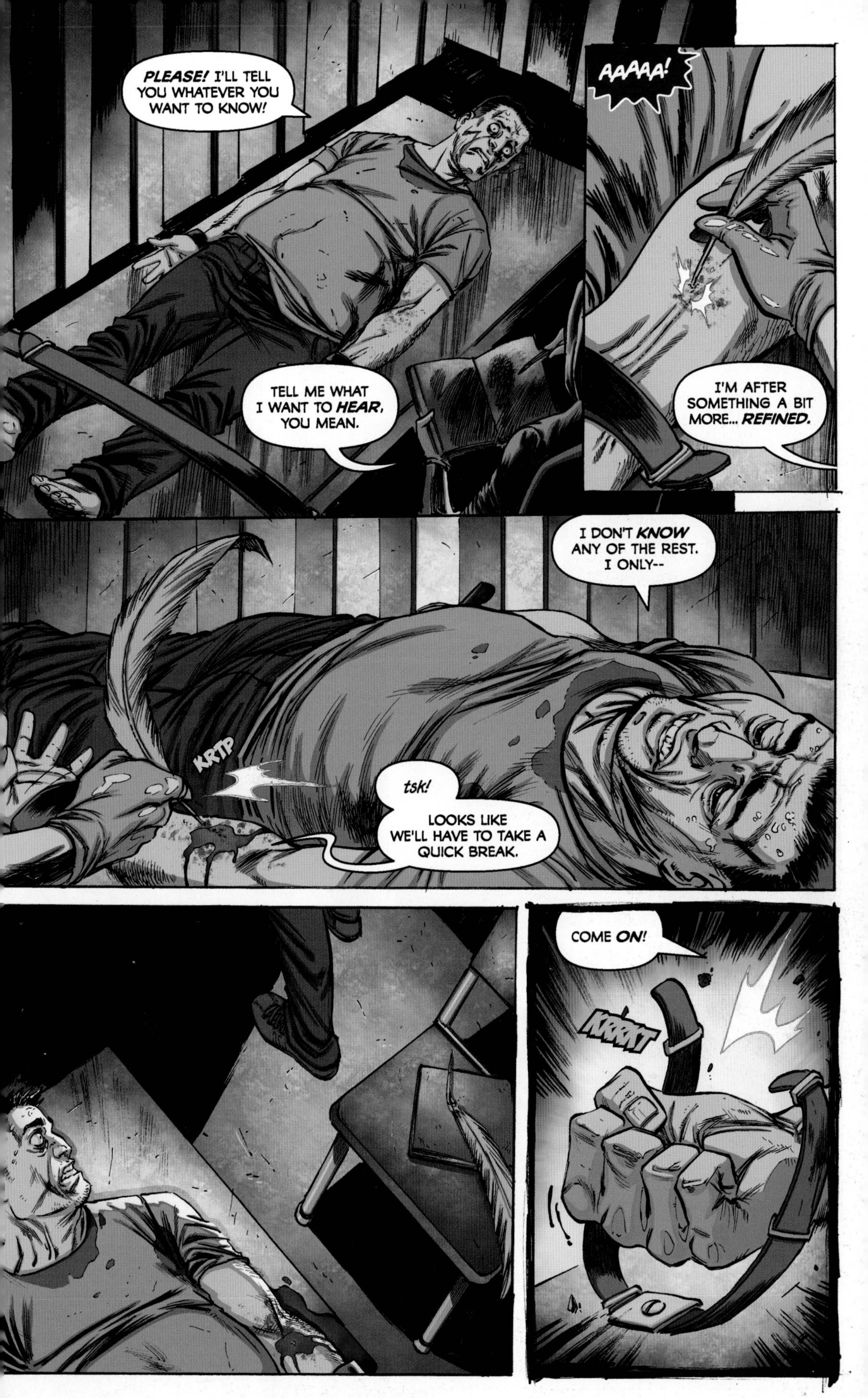
PLEASE! I'LL TELL YOU WHATEVER YOU WANT TO KNOW!
AAAAA!
TELL ME WHAT I WANT TO HEAR, YOU MEAN.
I'M AFTER SOMETHING A BIT MORE... REFINED.
I DON'T KNOW ANY OF THE REST. I ONLY--
KRTP
tsk!
LOOKS LIKE WE'LL HAVE TO TAKE A QUICK BREAK.
COME ON!
KRRRKT

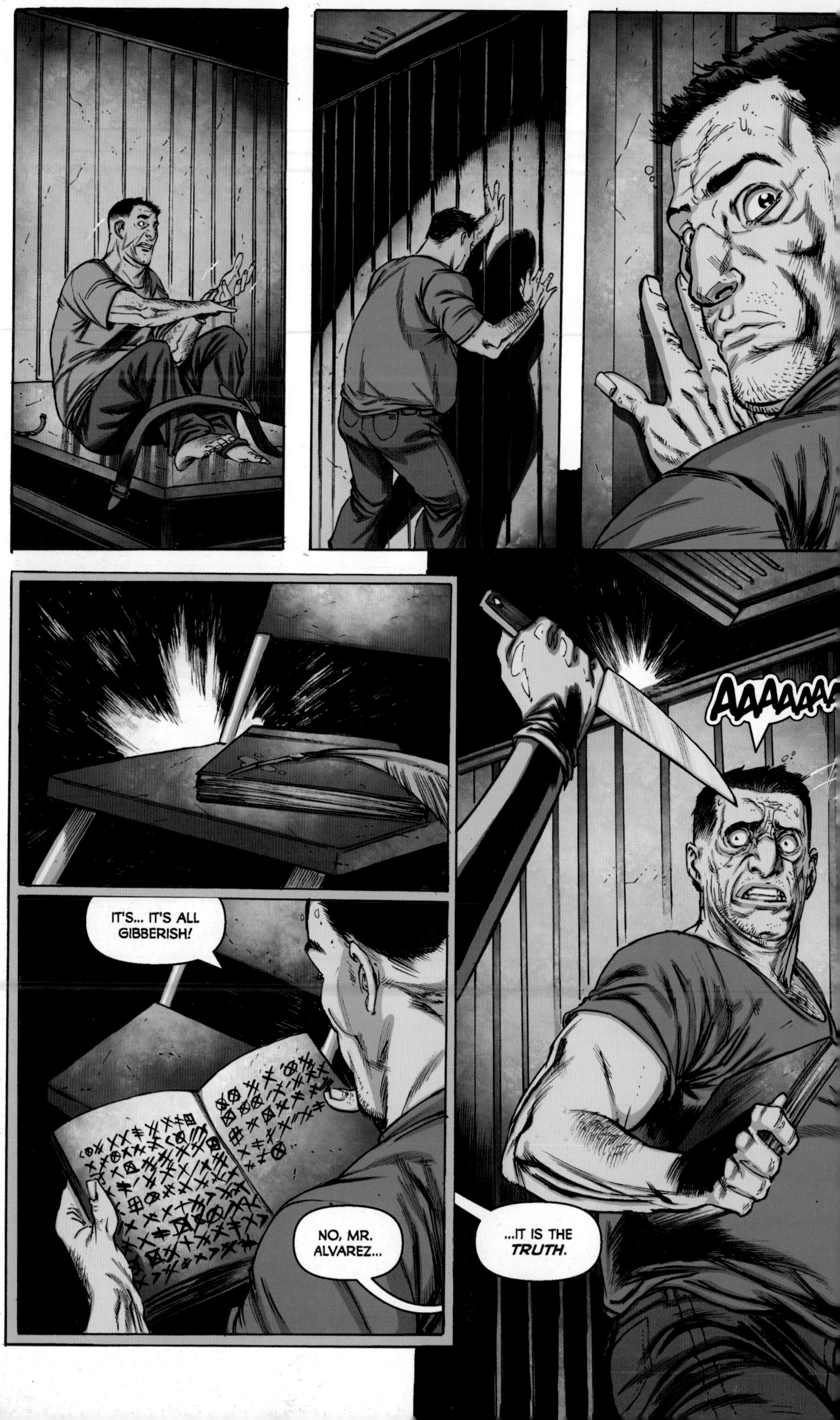
AAAAAA
IT'S... IT'S ALL GIBBERISH!
NO, MR. ALVAREZ...
...IT IS THE *TRUTH*.

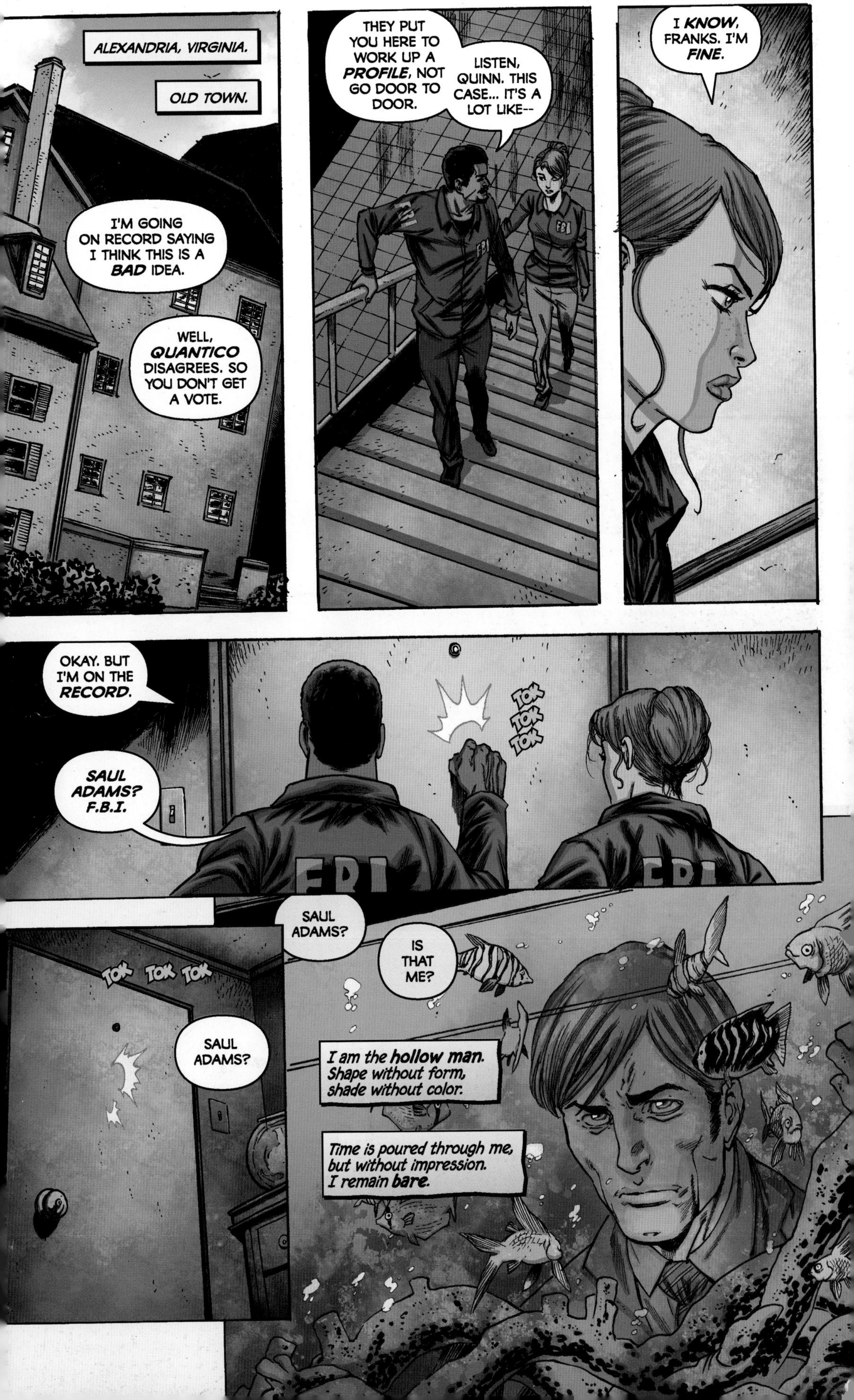
ALEXANDRIA, VIRGINIA.
OLD TOWN.
I'M GOING ON RECORD SAYING I THINK THIS IS A BAD IDEA.
WELL, QUANTICO DISAGREES. SO YOU DON'T GET A VOTE.
THEY PUT YOU HERE TO WORK UP A PROFILE, NOT GO DOOR TO DOOR.
LISTEN, QUINN. THIS CASE... IT'S A LOT LIKE--
I KNOW, FRANKS. I'M FINE.
OKAY. BUT I'M ON THE RECORD.
SAUL ADAMS? F.B.I.
TOK TOK TOK
TOK TOK TOK
SAUL ADAMS?
SAUL ADAMS?
IS THAT ME?
I am the hollow man. Shape without form, shade without color.
Time is poured through me, but without impression. I remain bare.

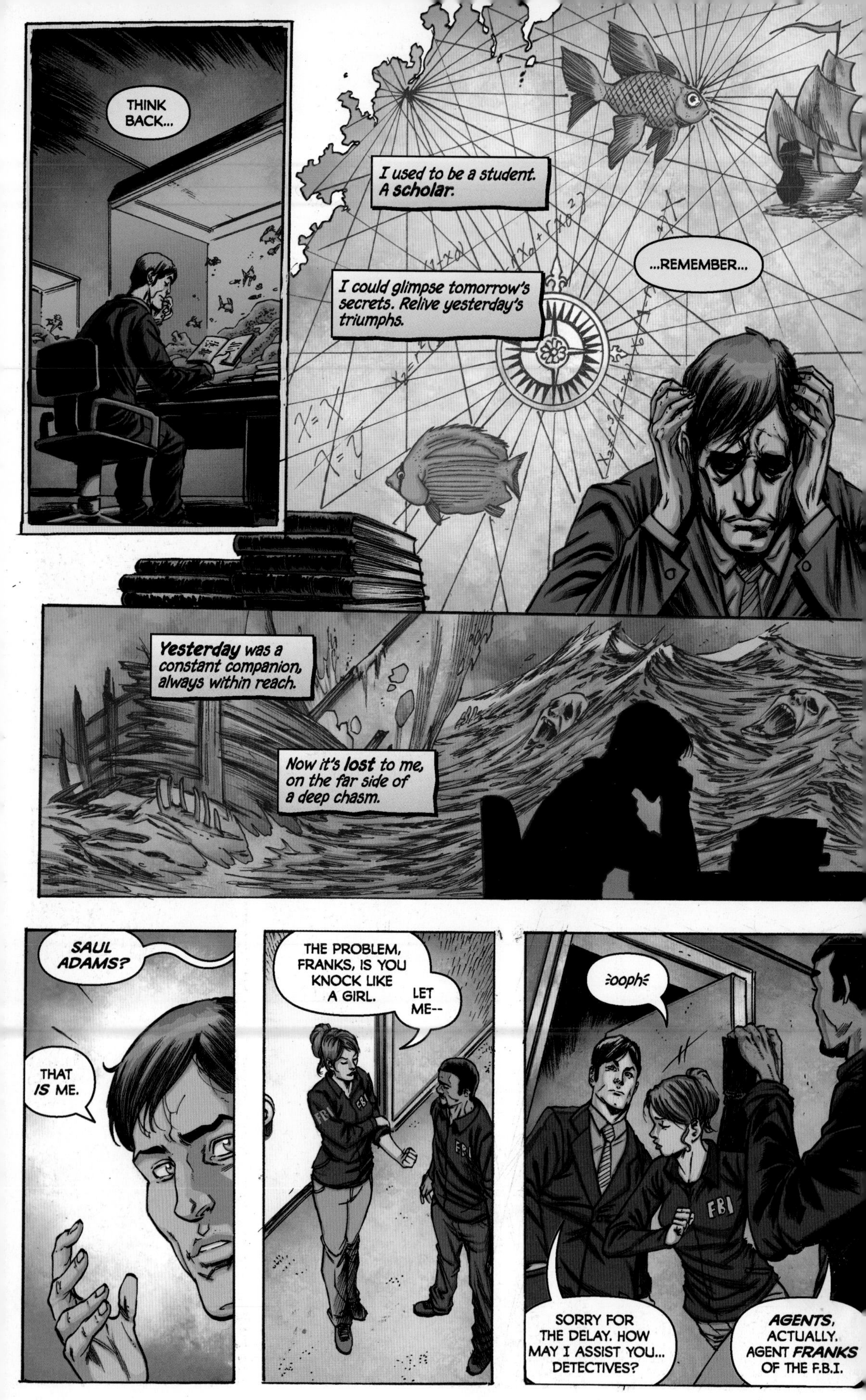
THINK BACK...
I used to be a student. A scholar.
I could glimpse tomorrow's secrets. Relive yesterday's triumphs.
...REMEMBER...
Yesterday was a constant companion, always within reach.
Now it's lost to me, on the far side of a deep chasm.
SAUL ADAMS?
THAT IS ME.
THE PROBLEM, FRANKS, IS YOU KNOCK LIKE A GIRL.
LET ME--
ooph
SORRY FOR THE DELAY. HOW MAY I ASSIST YOU... DETECTIVES?
AGENTS, ACTUALLY. AGENT FRANKS OF THE F.B.I.

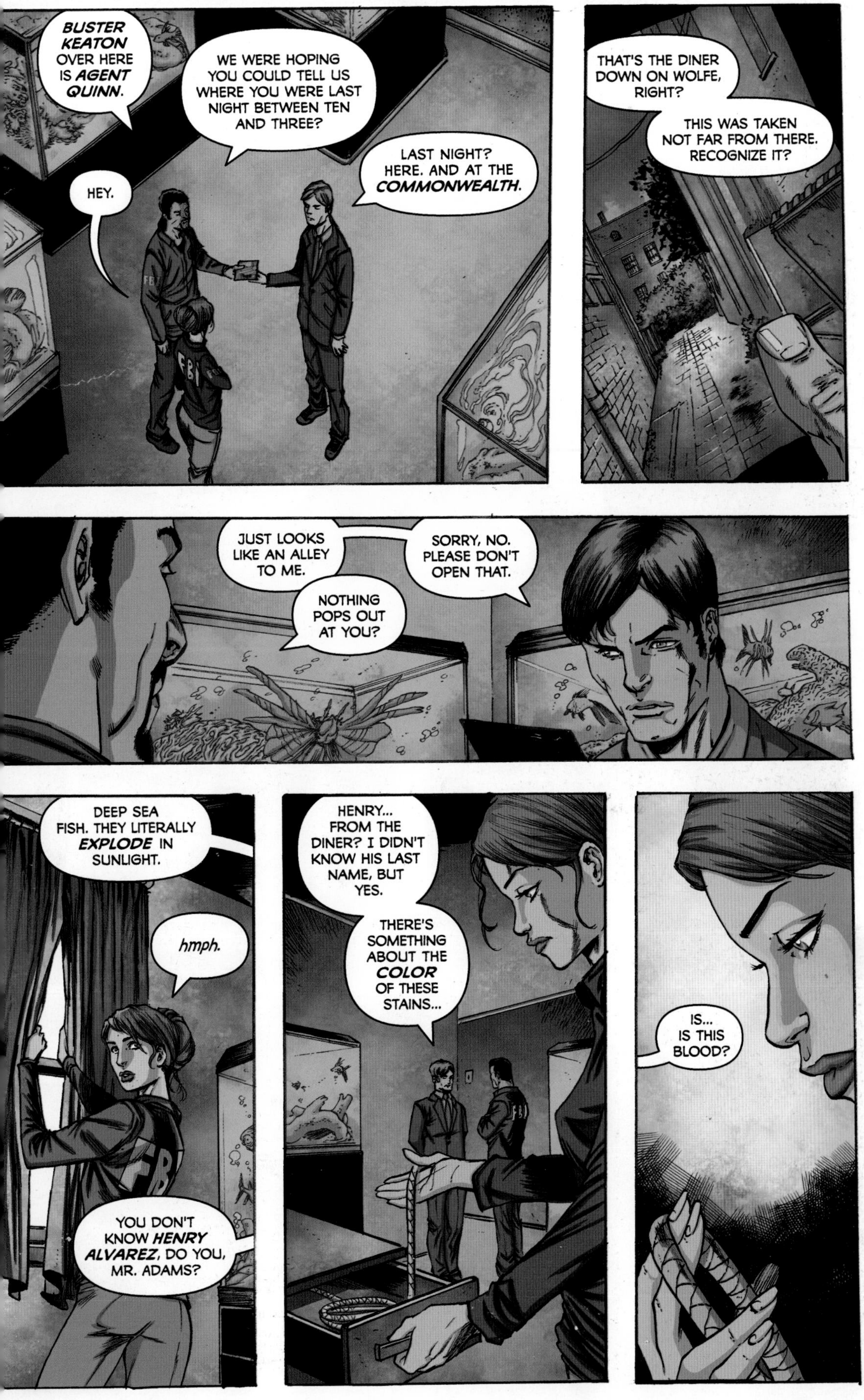
BUSTER KEATON OVER HERE IS AGENT QUINN.
WE WERE HOPING YOU COULD TELL US WHERE YOU WERE LAST NIGHT BETWEEN TEN AND THREE?
HEY.
LAST NIGHT? HERE. AND AT THE COMMONWEALTH.
THAT'S THE DINER DOWN ON WOLFE, RIGHT?
THIS WAS TAKEN NOT FAR FROM THERE. RECOGNIZE IT?
JUST LOOKS LIKE AN ALLEY TO ME.
SORRY, NO. PLEASE DON'T OPEN THAT.
NOTHING POPS OUT AT YOU?
DEEP SEA FISH. THEY LITERALLY EXPLODE IN SUNLIGHT.
hmph.
YOU DON'T KNOW HENRY ALVAREZ, DO YOU, MR. ADAMS?
HENRY... FROM THE DINER? I DIDN'T KNOW HIS LAST NAME, BUT YES.
THERE'S SOMETHING ABOUT THE COLOR OF THESE STAINS...
IS... IS THIS BLOOD?

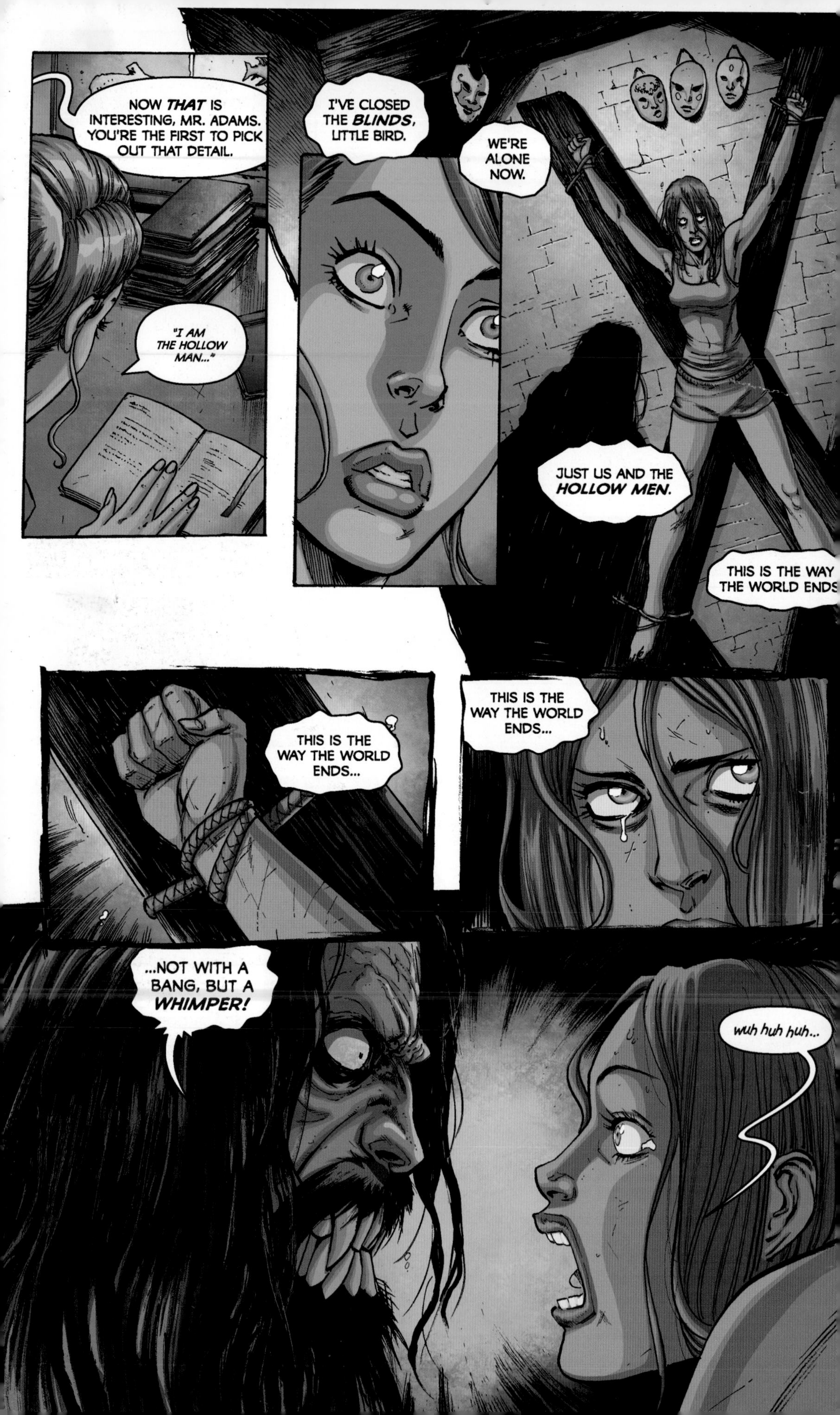
NOW *THAT* IS INTERESTING, MR. ADAMS. YOU'RE THE FIRST TO PICK OUT THAT DETAIL.
"I AM THE HOLLOW MAN..."
I'VE CLOSED THE *BLINDS*, LITTLE BIRD.
WE'RE ALONE NOW.
JUST US AND THE *HOLLOW MEN*.
THIS IS THE WAY THE WORLD ENDS
THIS IS THE WAY THE WORLD ENDS...
THIS IS THE WAY THE WORLD ENDS...
...NOT WITH A BANG, BUT A *WHIMPER!*
wuh huh huh...

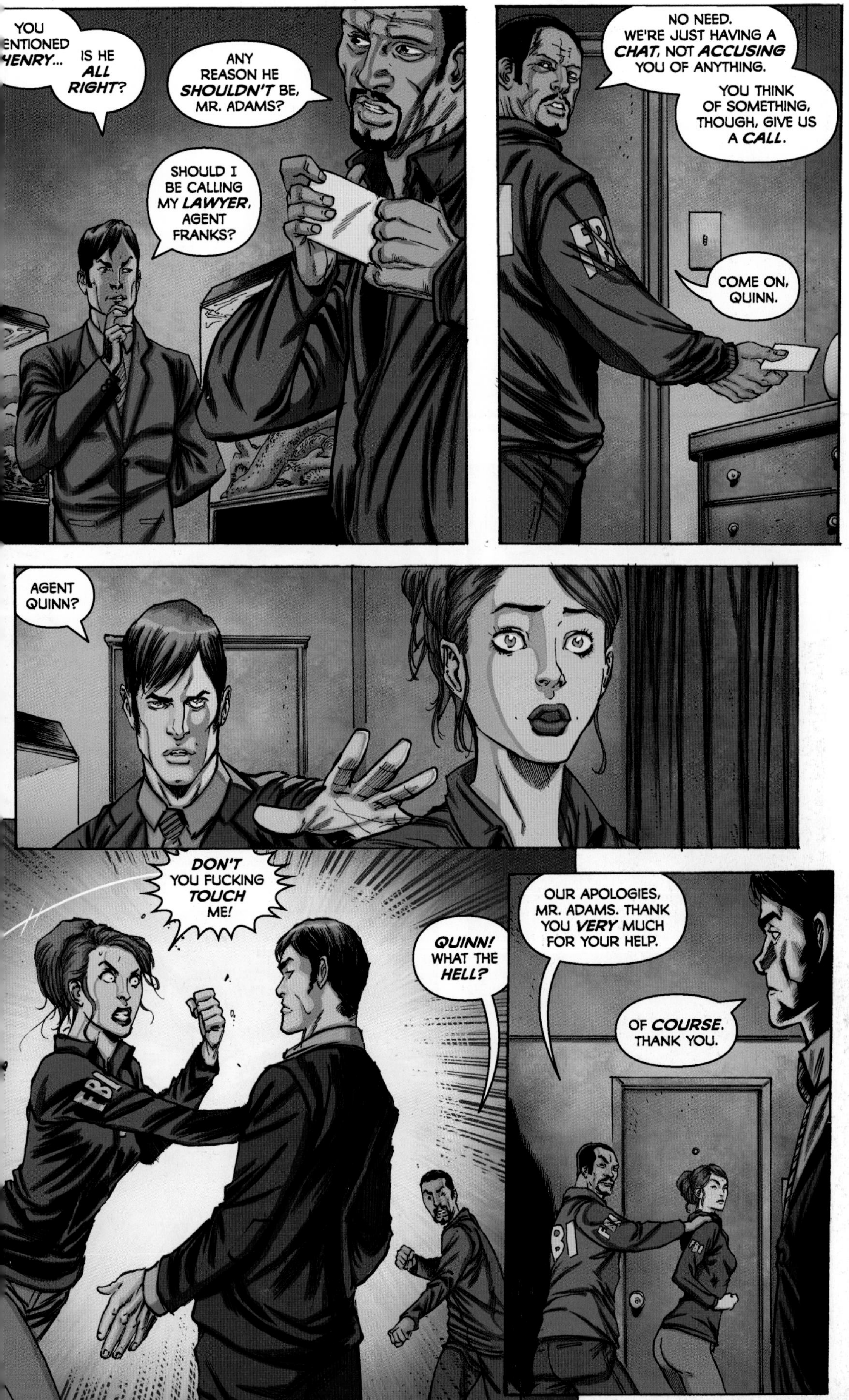

YOU ENTIONED HENRY...
IS HE ALL RIGHT?
ANY REASON HE SHOULDN'T BE, MR. ADAMS?
SHOULD I BE CALLING MY LAWYER, AGENT FRANKS?
NO NEED. WE'RE JUST HAVING A CHAT, NOT ACCUSING YOU OF ANYTHING.
YOU THINK OF SOMETHING, THOUGH, GIVE US A CALL.
COME ON, QUINN.
AGENT QUINN?
DON'T YOU FUCKING TOUCH ME!
QUINN! WHAT THE HELL?
OUR APOLOGIES, MR. ADAMS. THANK YOU VERY MUCH FOR YOUR HELP.
OF COURSE. THANK YOU.

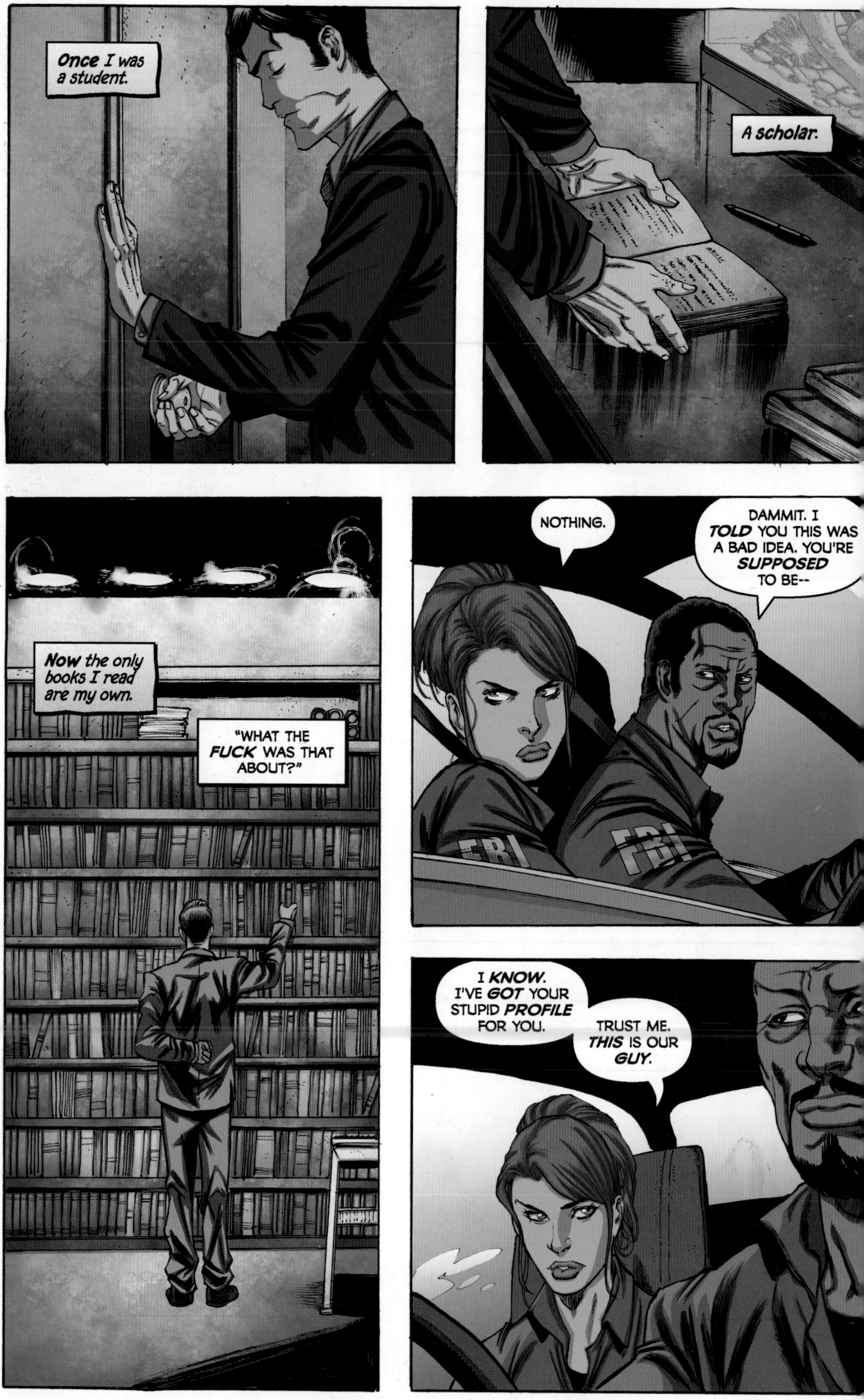
Once I was a student.
A scholar.
Now the only books I read are my own.
"WHAT THE FUCK WAS THAT ABOUT?"
NOTHING.
DAMMIT. I TOLD YOU THIS WAS A BAD IDEA. YOU'RE SUPPOSED TO BE--
I KNOW. I'VE GOT YOUR STUPID PROFILE FOR YOU.
TRUST ME. THIS IS OUR GUY.

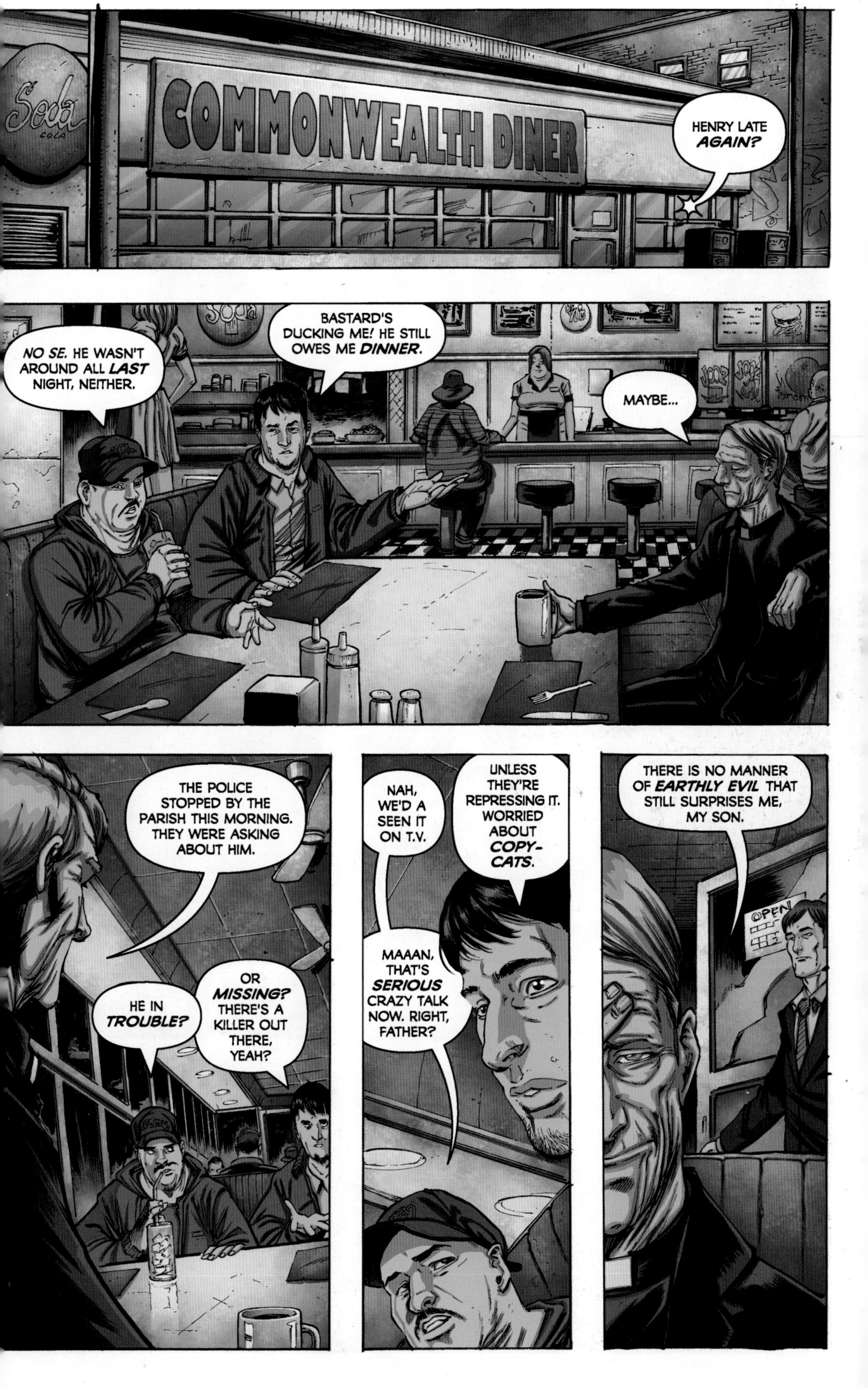

COMMONWEALTH DINER
Soda COLA
HENRY LATE AGAIN?
NO SE. HE WASN'T AROUND ALL LAST NIGHT, NEITHER.
BASTARD'S DUCKING ME! HE STILL OWES ME DINNER.
MAYBE...
THE POLICE STOPPED BY THE PARISH THIS MORNING. THEY WERE ASKING ABOUT HIM.
HE IN TROUBLE?
OR MISSING? THERE'S A KILLER OUT THERE, YEAH?
NAH, WE'D A SEEN IT ON T.V.
UNLESS THEY'RE REPRESSING IT. WORRIED ABOUT COPY-CATS.
MAAAN, THAT'S SERIOUS CRAZY TALK NOW. RIGHT, FATHER?
THERE IS NO MANNER OF EARTHLY EVIL THAT STILL SURPRISES ME, MY SON.
OPEN

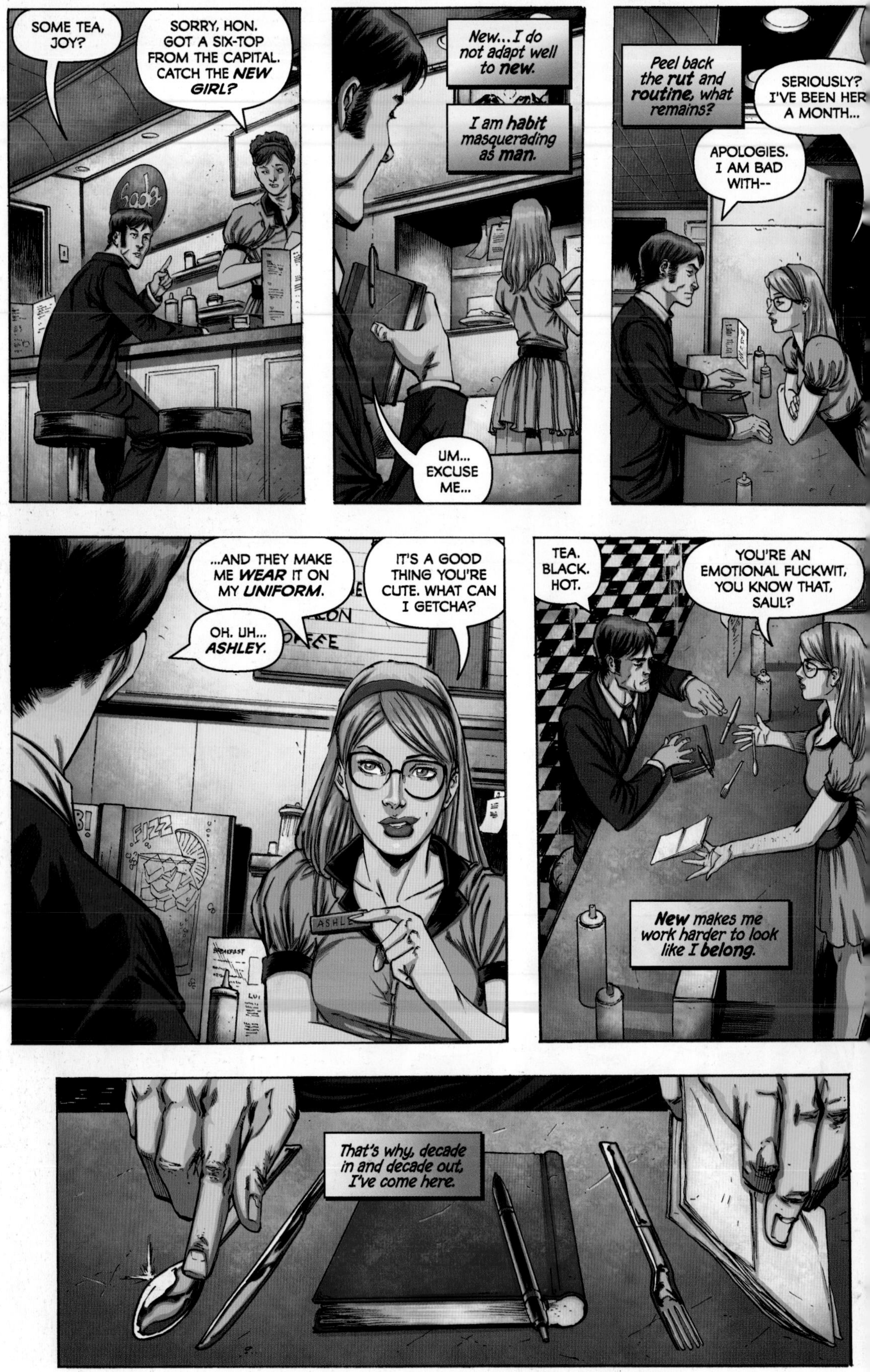
SOME TEA, JOY?
SORRY, HON. GOT A SIX-TOP FROM THE CAPITAL. CATCH THE NEW GIRL?
New...I do not adapt well to new.
I am habit masquerading as man.
UM... EXCUSE ME...
Peel back the rut and routine, what remains?
SERIOUSLY? I'VE BEEN HER A MONTH...
APOLOGIES. I AM BAD WITH--
OH. UH... ASHLEY.
...AND THEY MAKE ME WEAR IT ON MY UNIFORM.
IT'S A GOOD THING YOU'RE CUTE. WHAT CAN I GETCHA?
FIZZ
TEA. BLACK. HOT.
YOU'RE AN EMOTIONAL FUCKWIT, YOU KNOW THAT, SAUL?
New makes me work harder to look like I belong.
That's why, decade in and decade out, I've come here.

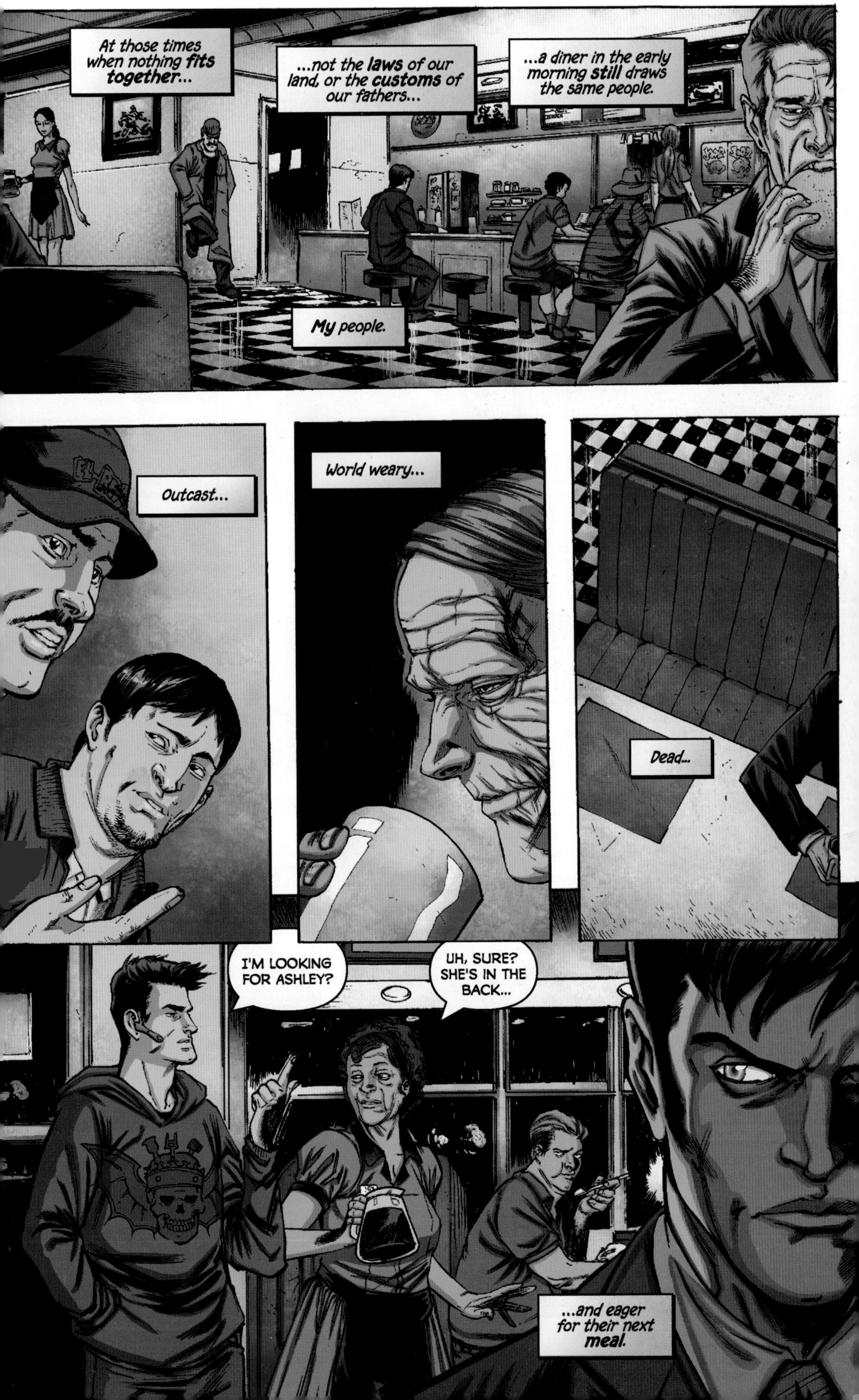
At those times when nothing fits together...
...not the laws of our land, or the customs of our fathers...
...a diner in the early morning still draws the same people.
My people.
Outcast...
World weary...
Dead...
I'M LOOKING FOR ASHLEY?
UH, SURE? SHE'S IN THE BACK...
...and eager for their next meal.

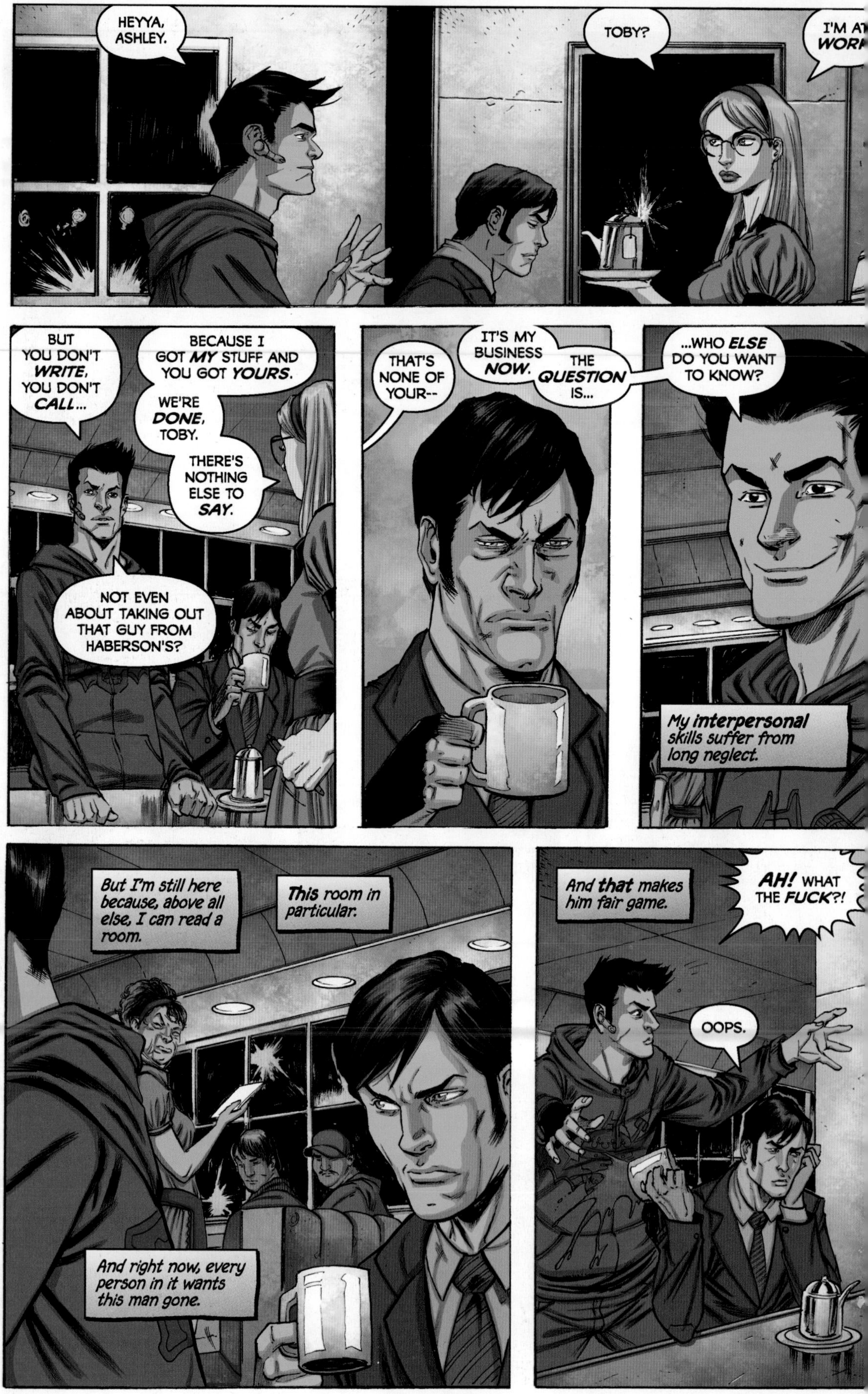
HEYYA, ASHLEY.
TOBY?
I'M AT WORK
BUT YOU DON'T WRITE, YOU DON'T CALL...
BECAUSE I GOT MY STUFF AND YOU GOT YOURS.
WE'RE DONE, TOBY.
THERE'S NOTHING ELSE TO SAY.
NOT EVEN ABOUT TAKING OUT THAT GUY FROM HABERSON'S?
THAT'S NONE OF YOUR--
IT'S MY BUSINESS NOW.
THE QUESTION IS...
...WHO ELSE DO YOU WANT TO KNOW?
My interpersonal skills suffer from long neglect.
But I'm still here because, above all else, I can read a room.
This room in particular.
And right now, every person in it wants this man gone.
And that makes him fair game.
AH! WHAT THE FUCK?!
OOPS.

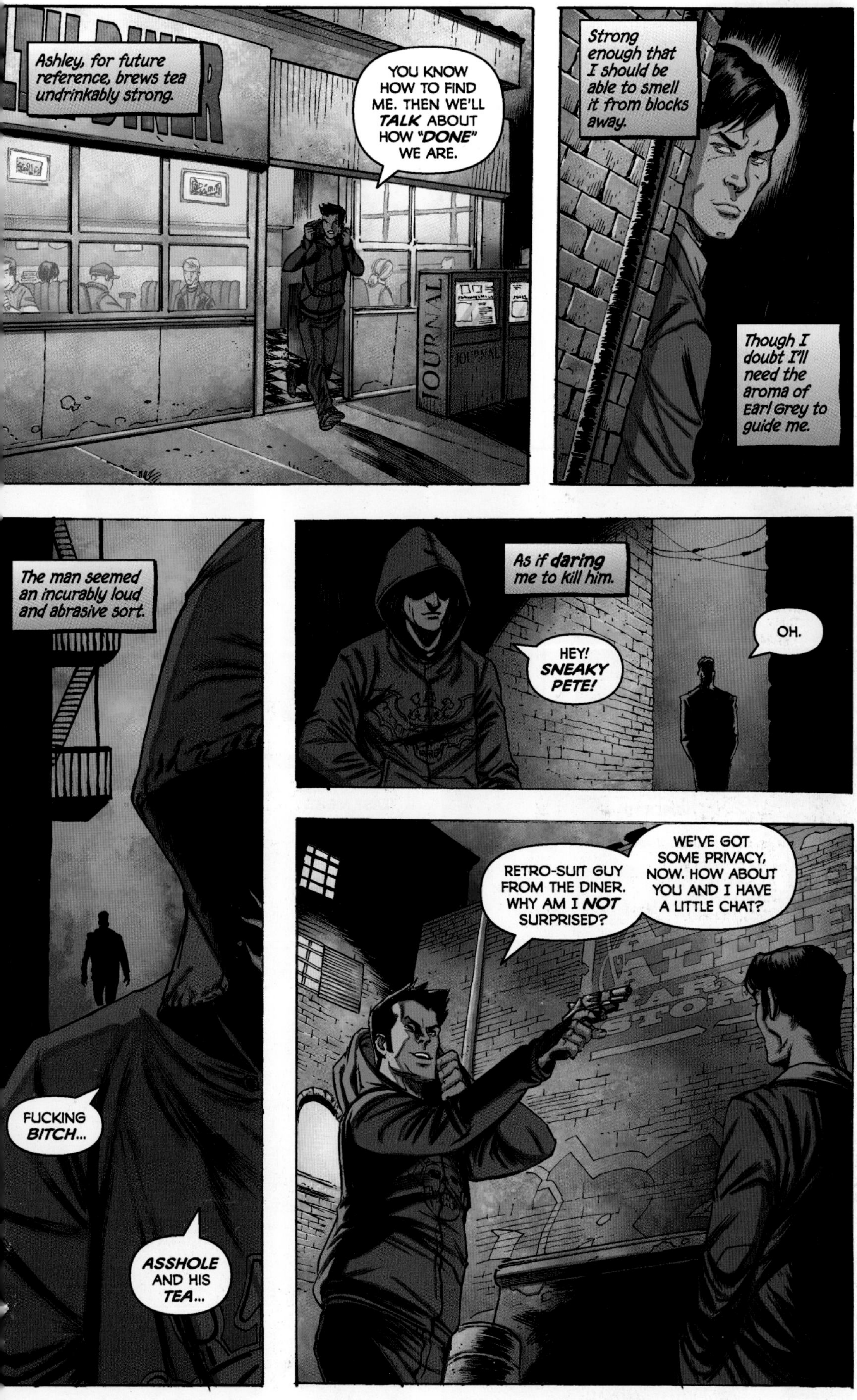
Ashley, for future reference, brews tea undrinkably strong.
YOU KNOW HOW TO FIND ME. THEN WE'LL TALK ABOUT HOW "DONE" WE ARE.
Strong enough that I should be able to smell it from blocks away.
Though I doubt I'll need the aroma of Earl Grey to guide me.
The man seemed an incurably loud and abrasive sort.
FUCKING BITCH...
ASSHOLE AND HIS TEA...
As if daring me to kill him.
HEY! SNEAKY PETE!
OH.
RETRO-SUIT GUY FROM THE DINER. WHY AM I NOT SURPRISED?
WE'VE GOT SOME PRIVACY, NOW. HOW ABOUT YOU AND I HAVE A LITTLE CHAT?

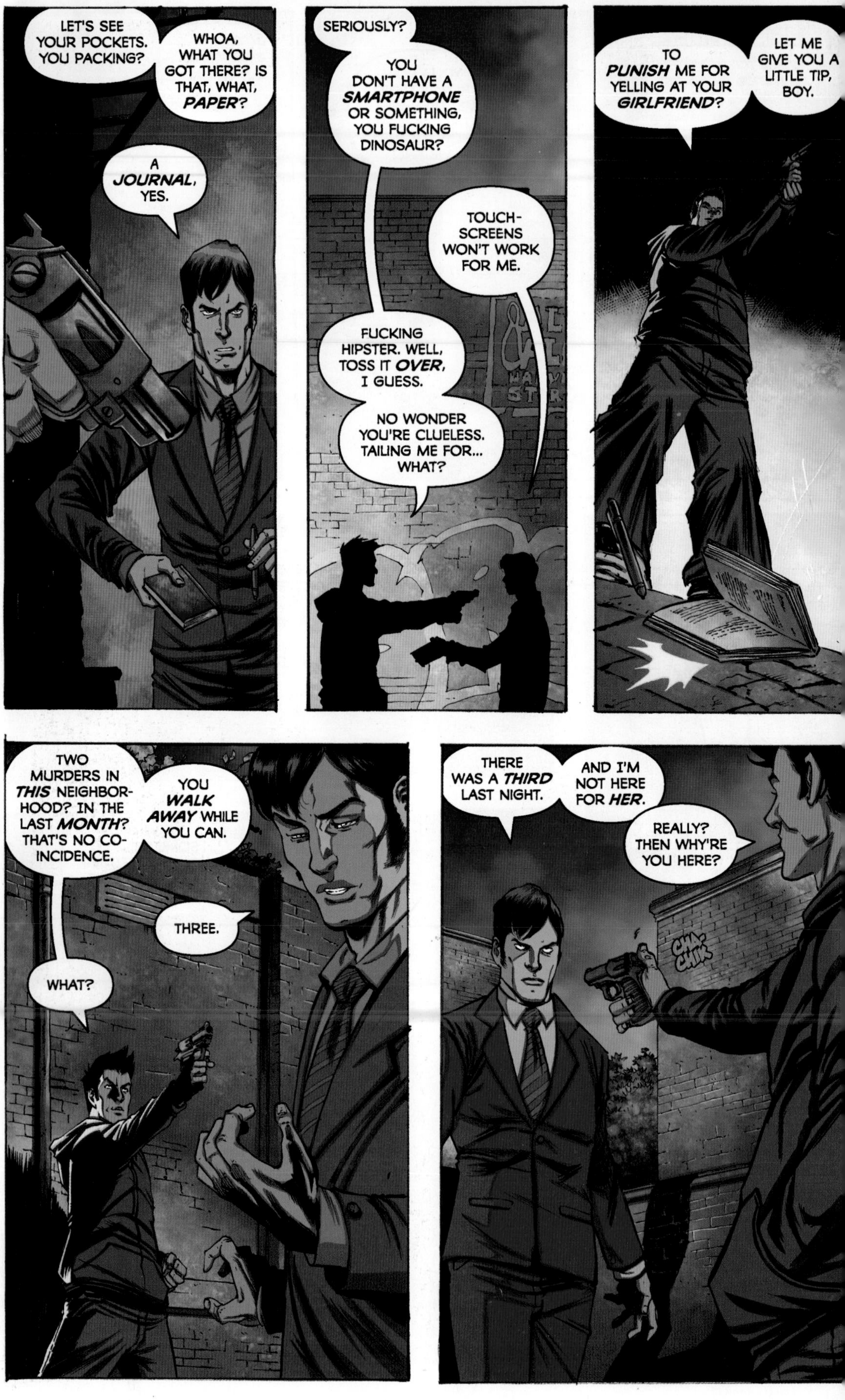
LET'S SEE YOUR POCKETS. YOU PACKING?
WHOA, WHAT YOU GOT THERE? IS THAT, WHAT, PAPER?
A JOURNAL, YES.
SERIOUSLY?
YOU DON'T HAVE A SMARTPHONE OR SOMETHING, YOU FUCKING DINOSAUR?
TOUCH-SCREENS WON'T WORK FOR ME.
FUCKING HIPSTER. WELL, TOSS IT OVER, I GUESS.
NO WONDER YOU'RE CLUELESS. TAILING ME FOR... WHAT?
TO PUNISH ME FOR YELLING AT YOUR GIRLFRIEND?
LET ME GIVE YOU A LITTLE TIP, BOY.
TWO MURDERS IN THIS NEIGHBOR-HOOD? IN THE LAST MONTH? THAT'S NO CO-INCIDENCE.
YOU WALK AWAY WHILE YOU CAN.
THREE.
WHAT?
THERE WAS A THIRD LAST NIGHT.
AND I'M NOT HERE FOR HER.
REALLY? THEN WHY'RE YOU HERE?
CHAK CHIK

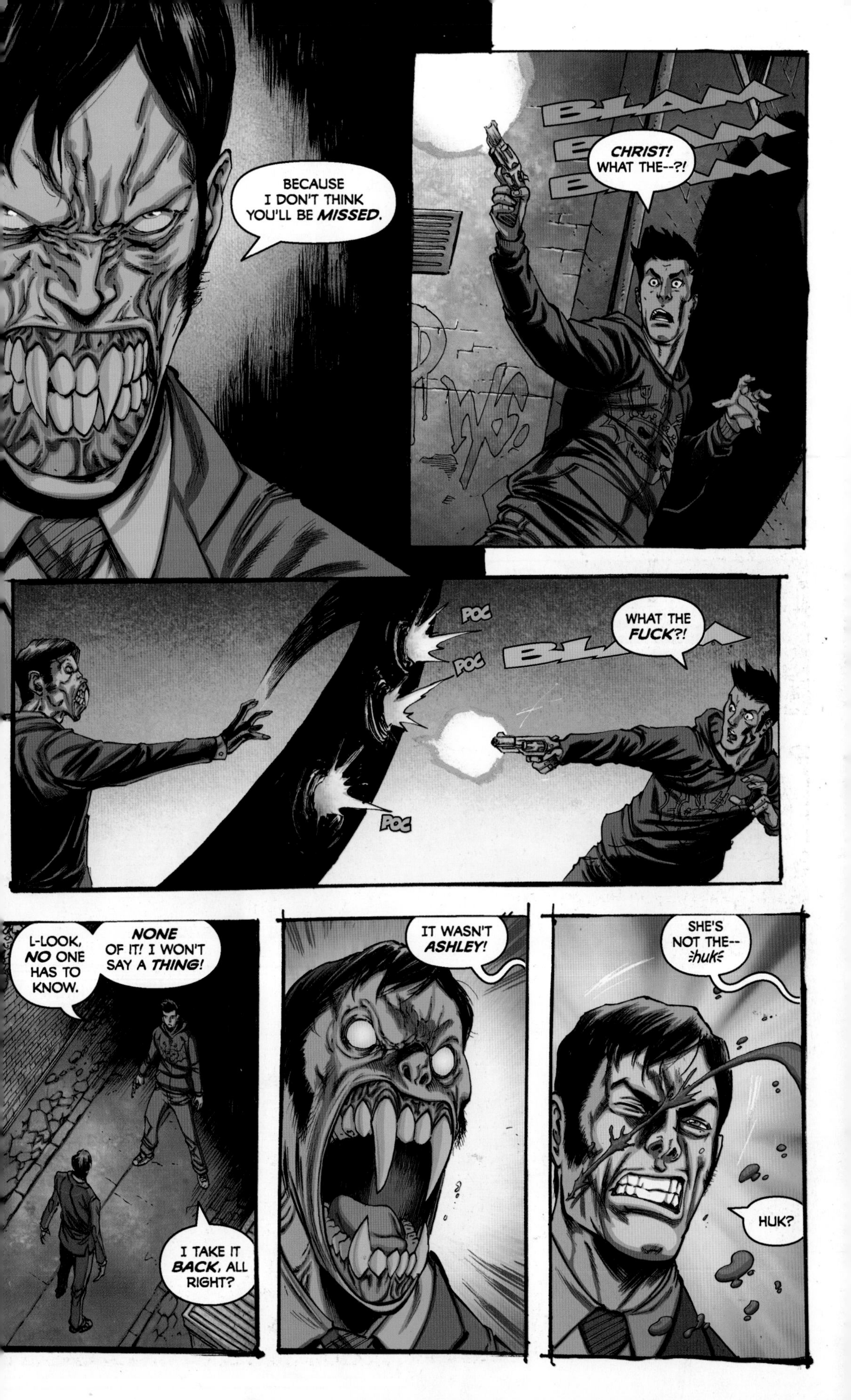
BECAUSE I DON'T THINK YOU'LL BE MISSED.
BLAM BLAM BLAM
CHRIST! WHAT THE--?!
POC
POC
BLAM
WHAT THE FUCK?!
POC
L-LOOK, NO ONE HAS TO KNOW.
NONE OF IT! I WON'T SAY A THING!
I TAKE IT BACK, ALL RIGHT?
IT WASN'T ASHLEY!
SHE'S NOT THE-- huk
HUK?

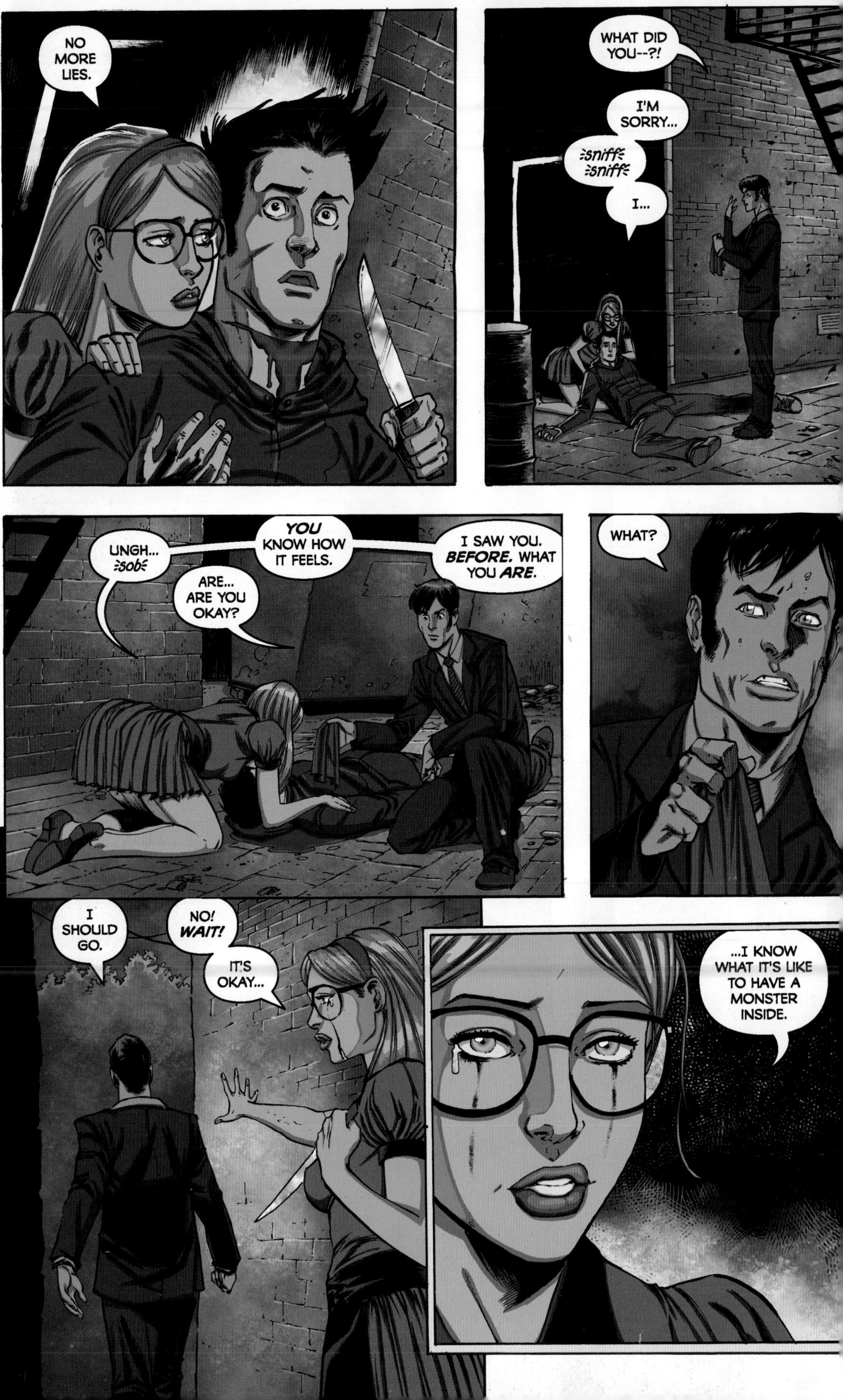

NO MORE LIES.
WHAT DID YOU--?!
I'M SORRY...
sniff *sniff*
I...
UNGH... *sob*
YOU KNOW HOW IT FEELS.
I SAW YOU. BEFORE. WHAT YOU ARE.
ARE... ARE YOU OKAY?
WHAT?
I SHOULD GO.
NO! WAIT!
IT'S OKAY...
...I KNOW WHAT IT'S LIKE TO HAVE A MONSTER INSIDE.

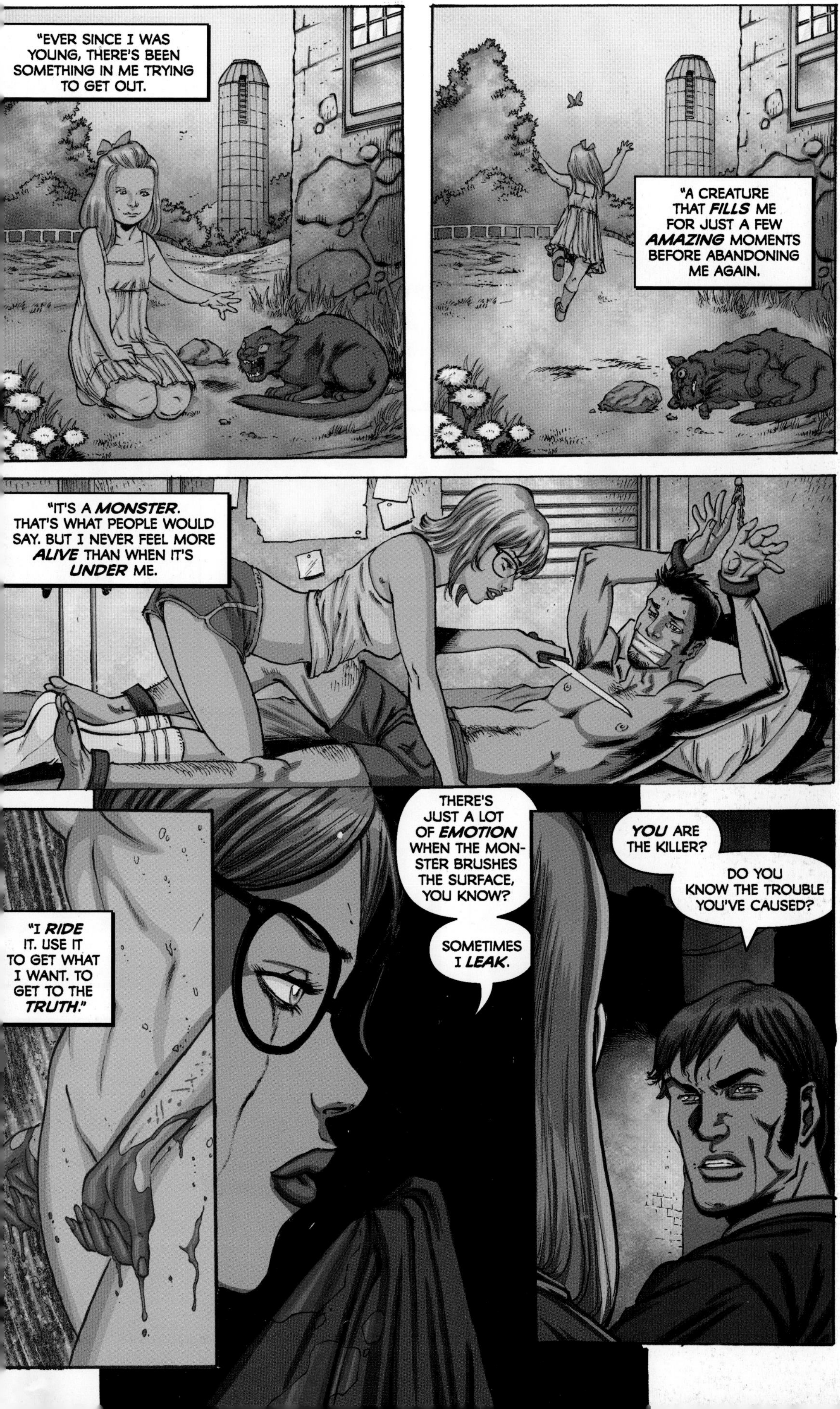
"EVER SINCE I WAS YOUNG, THERE'S BEEN SOMETHING IN ME TRYING TO GET OUT.
"A CREATURE THAT FILLS ME FOR JUST A FEW AMAZING MOMENTS BEFORE ABANDONING ME AGAIN.
"IT'S A MONSTER. THAT'S WHAT PEOPLE WOULD SAY. BUT I NEVER FEEL MORE ALIVE THAN WHEN IT'S UNDER ME.
"I RIDE IT. USE IT TO GET WHAT I WANT. TO GET TO THE TRUTH."
THERE'S JUST A LOT OF EMOTION WHEN THE MONSTER BRUSHES THE SURFACE, YOU KNOW?
SOMETIMES I LEAK.
YOU ARE THE KILLER?
DO YOU KNOW THE TROUBLE YOU'VE CAUSED?

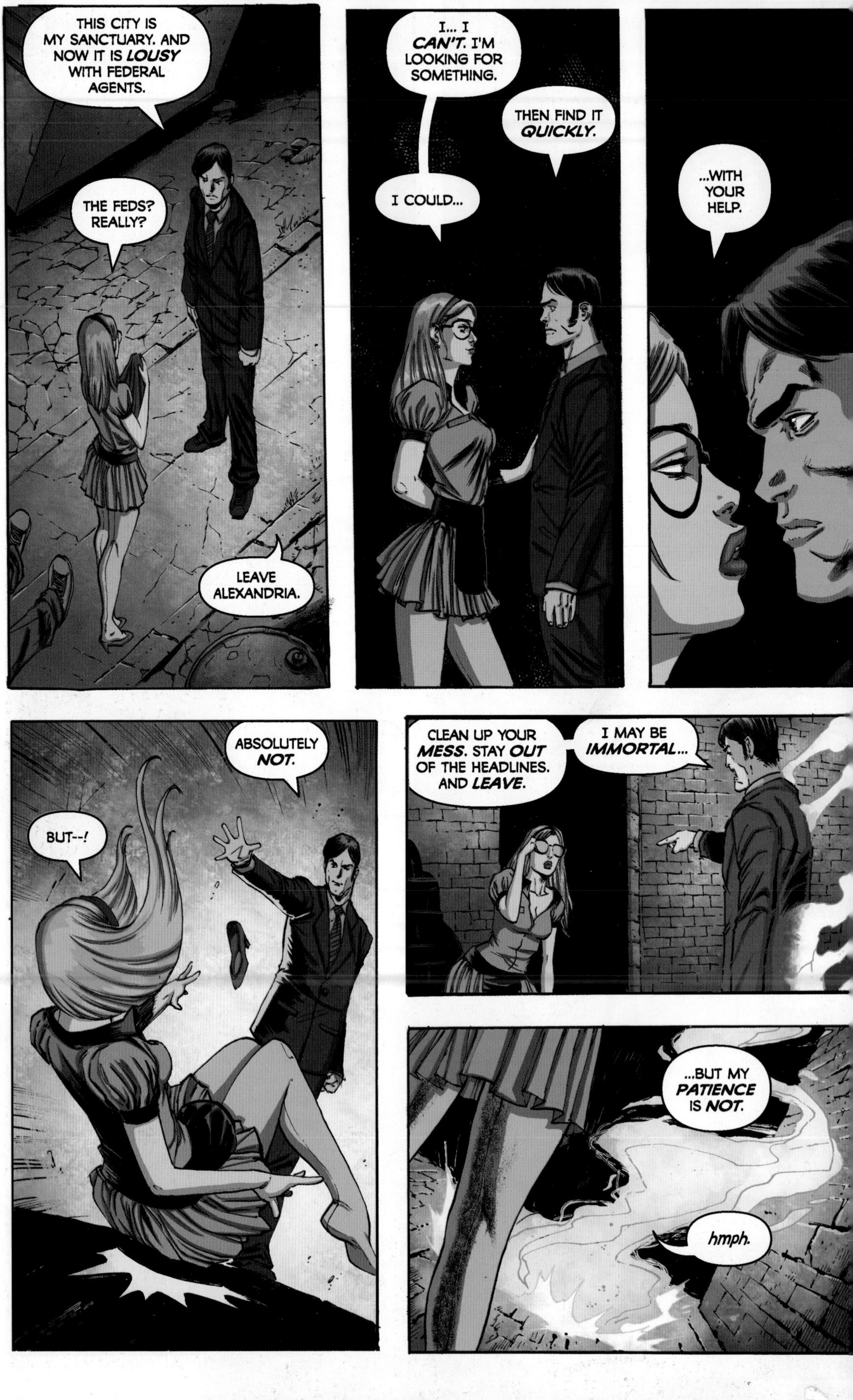
THIS CITY IS MY SANCTUARY. AND NOW IT IS *LOUSY* WITH FEDERAL AGENTS.
THE FEDS? REALLY?
LEAVE ALEXANDRIA.
I... I *CAN'T*. I'M LOOKING FOR SOMETHING.
I COULD...
THEN FIND IT *QUICKLY*.
...WITH YOUR HELP.
ABSOLUTELY *NOT*.
BUT--!
CLEAN UP YOUR *MESS*. STAY *OUT* OF THE HEADLINES. AND *LEAVE*.
I MAY BE *IMMORTAL*...
...BUT MY *PATIENCE* IS *NOT*.
hmph.

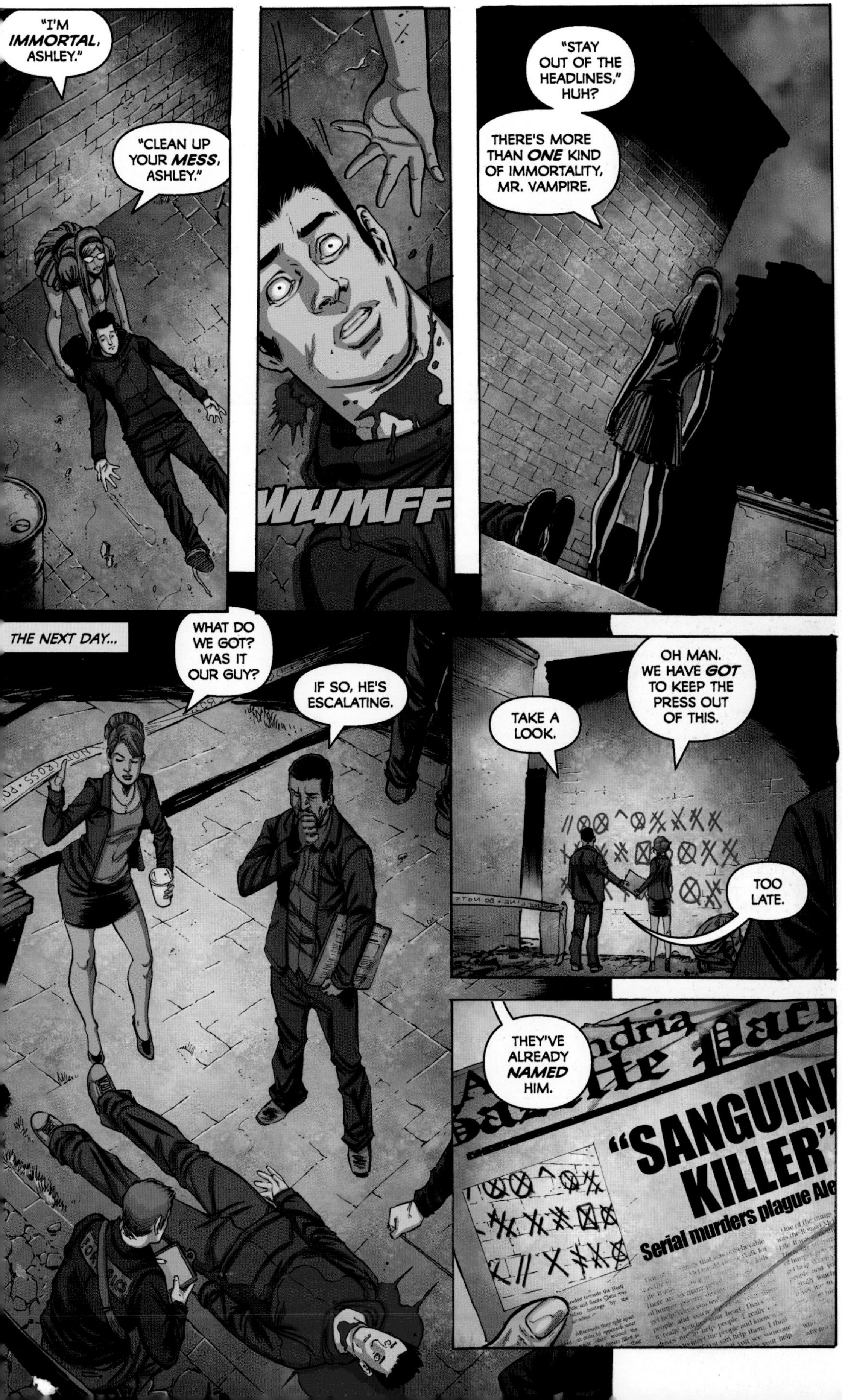
"I'M *IMMORTAL*, ASHLEY."
"CLEAN UP YOUR *MESS*, ASHLEY."
WUMFF
"STAY OUT OF THE HEADLINES," HUH?
THERE'S MORE THAN *ONE* KIND OF IMMORTALITY, MR. VAMPIRE.
THE NEXT DAY...
WHAT DO WE GOT? WAS IT OUR GUY?
IF SO, HE'S ESCALATING.
TAKE A LOOK.
OH MAN. WE HAVE *GOT* TO KEEP THE PRESS OUT OF THIS.
TOO LATE.
THEY'VE ALREADY *NAMED* HIM.
"SANGUIN
KILLER"
Serial murders plague Ale

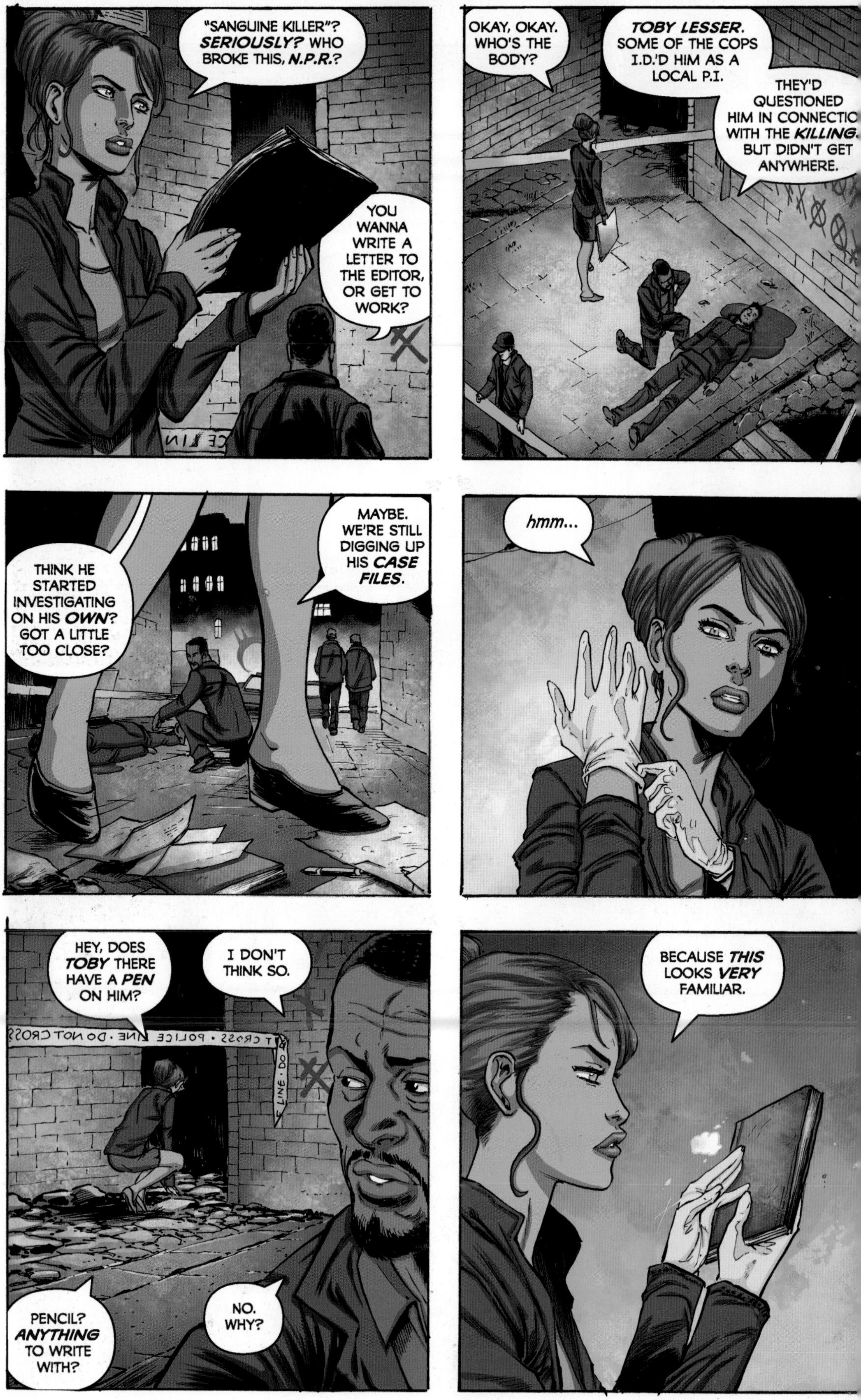
"SANGUINE KILLER"? SERIOUSLY? WHO BROKE THIS, N.P.R.?
YOU WANNA WRITE A LETTER TO THE EDITOR, OR GET TO WORK?
OKAY, OKAY. WHO'S THE BODY?
TOBY LESSER. SOME OF THE COPS I.D.'D HIM AS A LOCAL P.I.
THEY'D QUESTIONED HIM IN CONNECTIO WITH THE KILLING. BUT DIDN'T GET ANYWHERE.
THINK HE STARTED INVESTIGATING ON HIS OWN? GOT A LITTLE TOO CLOSE?
MAYBE. WE'RE STILL DIGGING UP HIS CASE FILES.
hmm...
HEY, DOES TOBY THERE HAVE A PEN ON HIM?
I DON'T THINK SO.
PENCIL? ANYTHING TO WRITE WITH?
NO. WHY?
BECAUSE THIS LOOKS VERY FAMILIAR.

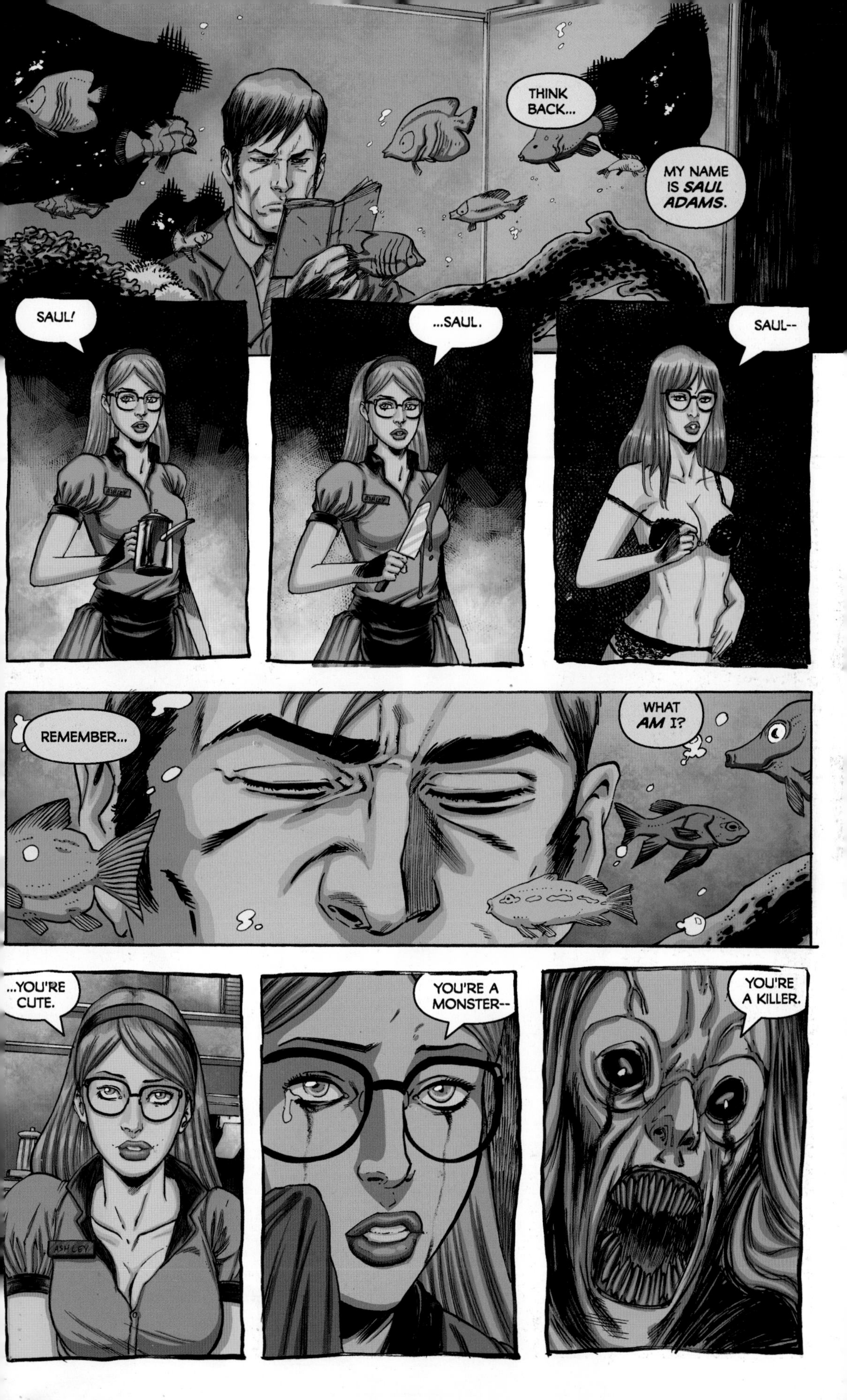
THINK BACK...
MY NAME IS SAUL ADAMS.
SAUL!
...SAUL.
SAUL--
ASHLEY
REMEMBER...
WHAT AM I?
...YOU'RE CUTE.
ASHLEY
YOU'RE A MONSTER--
YOU'RE A KILLER.

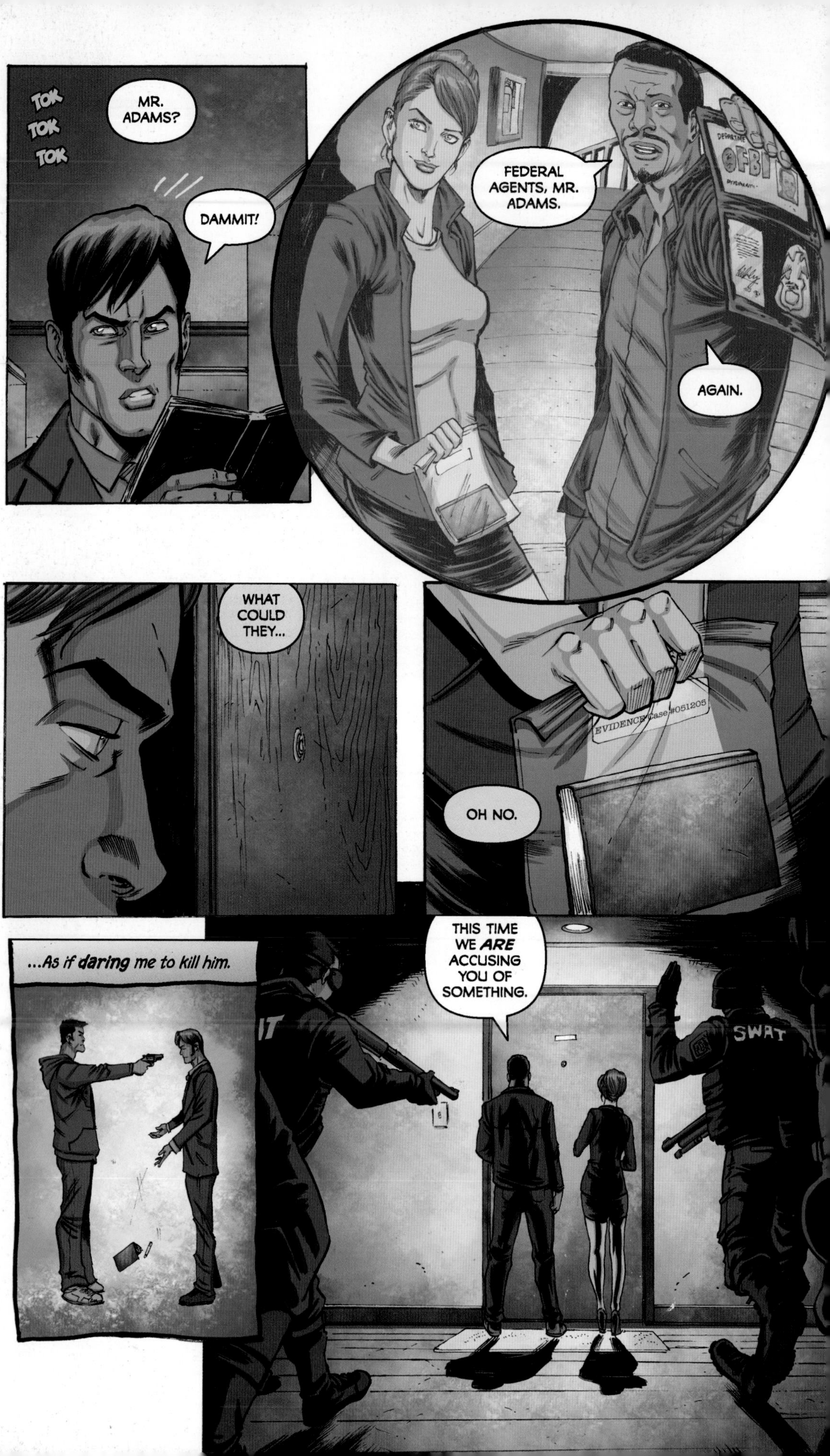
TOK
TOK
TOK
MR. ADAMS?
DAMMIT!
FEDERAL AGENTS, MR. ADAMS.
AGAIN.
WHAT COULD THEY...
EVIDENCE Case #051205
OH NO.
...As if *daring* me to kill him.
THIS TIME WE *ARE* ACCUSING YOU OF SOMETHING.
SWAT

CHAPTER TWO
PENTHOUSE

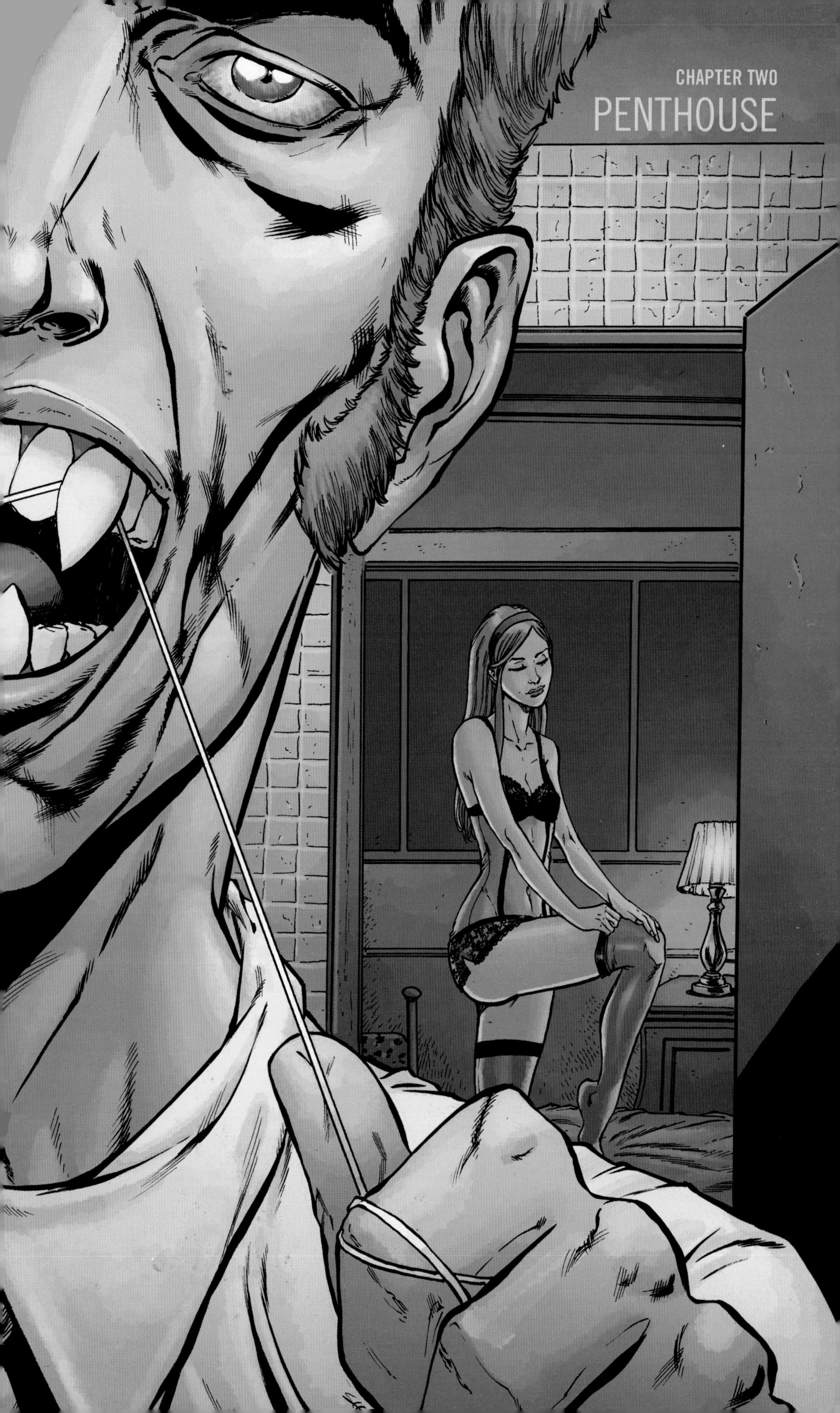

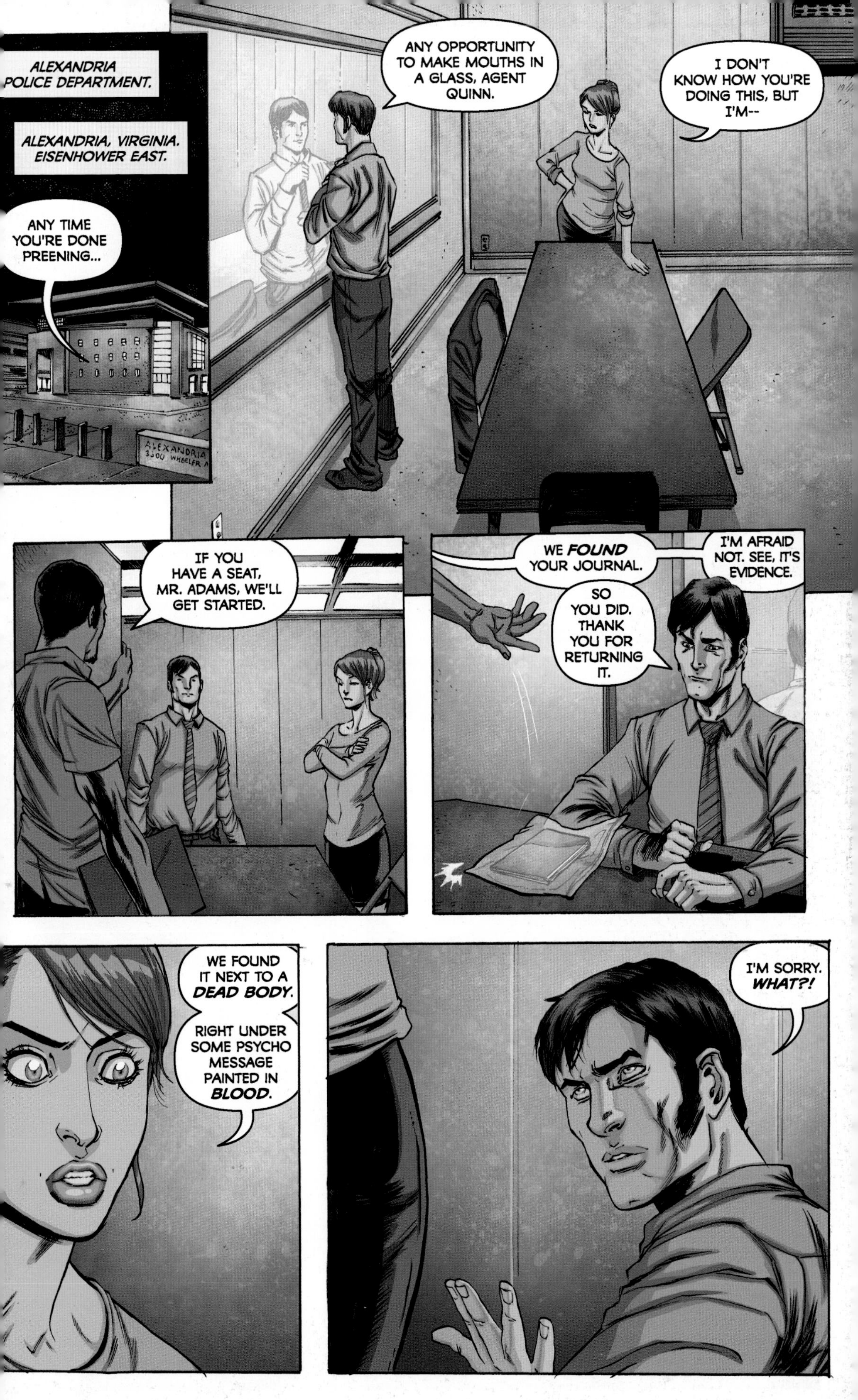
ALEXANDRIA POLICE DEPARTMENT.
ALEXANDRIA, VIRGINIA. EISENHOWER EAST.
ANY TIME YOU'RE DONE PREENING...
ALEXANDRIA
ANY OPPORTUNITY TO MAKE MOUTHS IN A GLASS, AGENT QUINN.
I DON'T KNOW HOW YOU'RE DOING THIS, BUT I'M--
IF YOU HAVE A SEAT, MR. ADAMS, WE'LL GET STARTED.
WE *FOUND* YOUR JOURNAL.
SO YOU DID. THANK YOU FOR RETURNING IT.
I'M AFRAID NOT. SEE, IT'S EVIDENCE.
WE FOUND IT NEXT TO A *DEAD BODY*.
RIGHT UNDER SOME PSYCHO MESSAGE PAINTED IN *BLOOD*.
I'M SORRY. *WHAT?!*

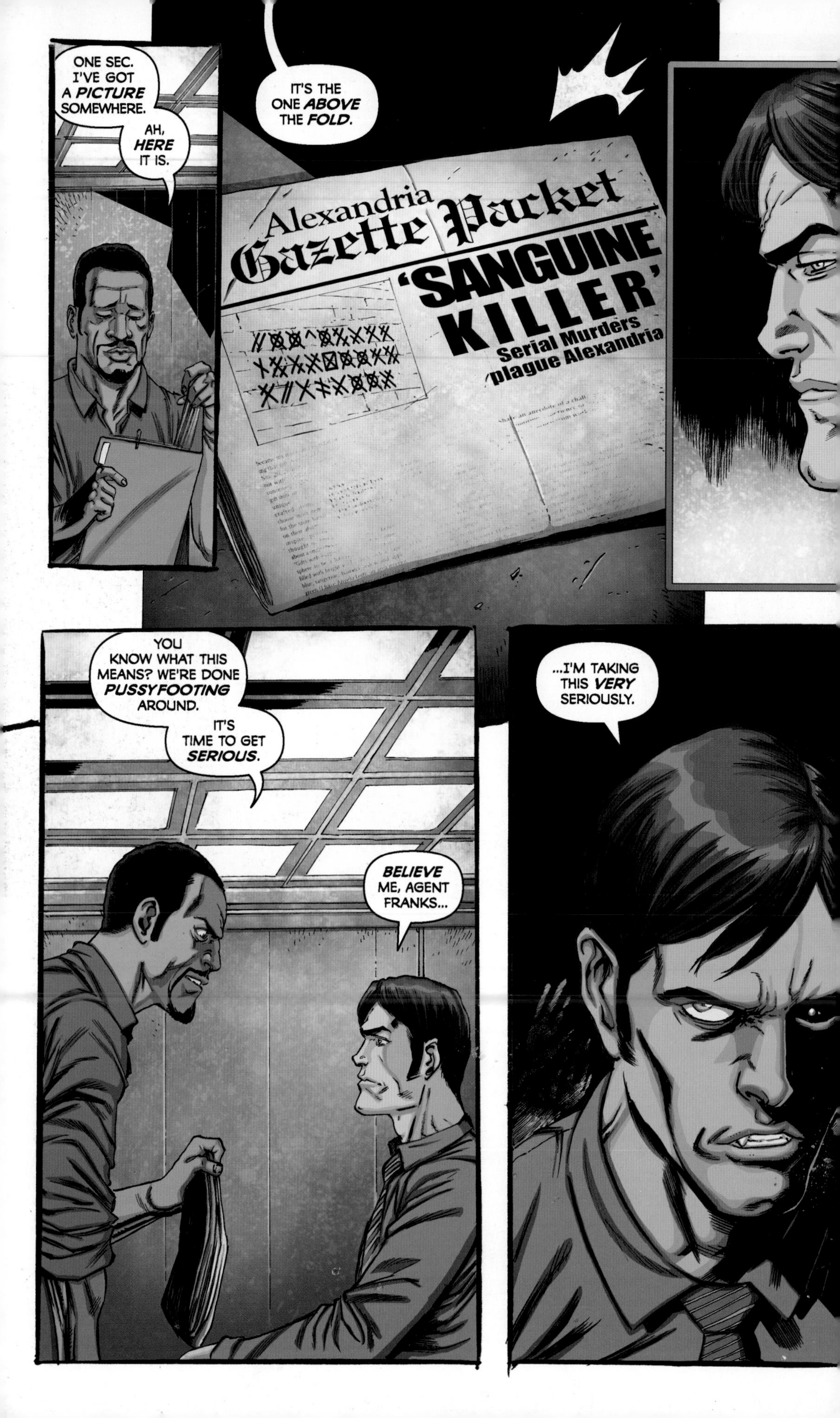
ONE SEC. I'VE GOT A *PICTURE* SOMEWHERE.
AH, *HERE* IT IS.
IT'S THE ONE *ABOVE* THE *FOLD*.
Alexandria Gazette Packet
'SANGUINE KILLER'
Serial Murders plague Alexandria
YOU KNOW WHAT THIS MEANS? WE'RE DONE *PUSSYFOOTING* AROUND.
IT'S TIME TO GET *SERIOUS*.
BELIEVE ME, AGENT FRANKS...
...I'M TAKING THIS *VERY* SERIOUSLY.

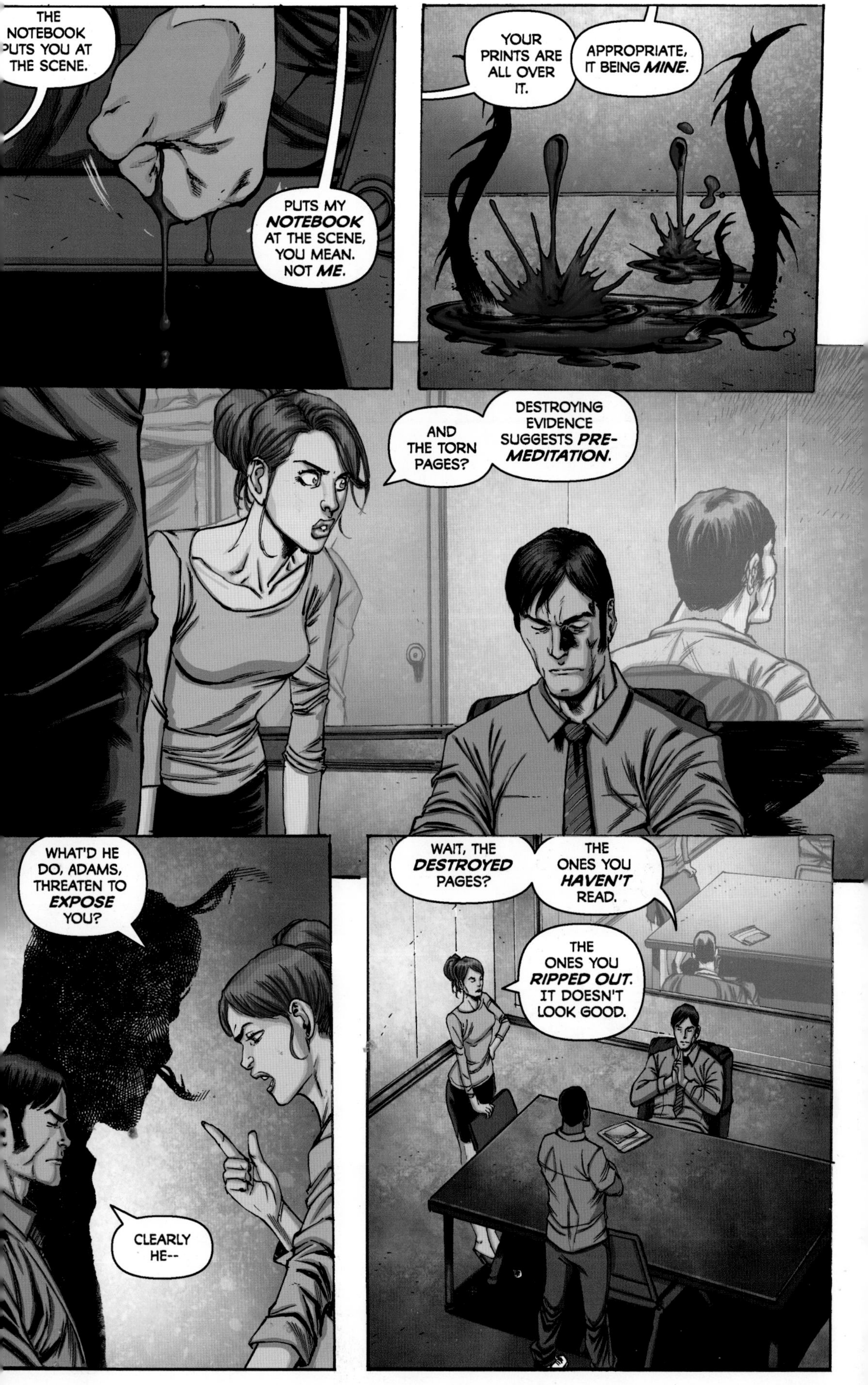
THE NOTEBOOK PUTS YOU AT THE SCENE.
PUTS MY NOTEBOOK AT THE SCENE, YOU MEAN. NOT ME.
YOUR PRINTS ARE ALL OVER IT.
APPROPRIATE, IT BEING MINE.
AND THE TORN PAGES?
DESTROYING EVIDENCE SUGGESTS PRE-MEDITATION.
WHAT'D HE DO, ADAMS, THREATEN TO EXPOSE YOU?
CLEARLY HE--
WAIT, THE DESTROYED PAGES?
THE ONES YOU HAVEN'T READ.
THE ONES YOU RIPPED OUT. IT DOESN'T LOOK GOOD.

DID YOU WANT TO BOOK ME FOR VANDALIZING A JOURNAL?

YOU WANT TO TREAT THIS LIKE A GAME...?

AGENT FRANKS? A MOMENT?

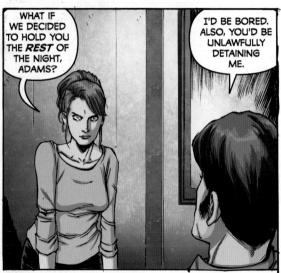

WHAT IF WE DECIDED TO HOLD YOU THE *REST* OF THE NIGHT, ADAMS?

I'D BE BORED. ALSO, YOU'D BE UNLAWFULLY DETAINING ME.

MAYBE. IT'D GIVE US TIME TO SET UP A BIG PERP WALK, THOUGH.

LOTS OF PRESS *BRIGHT* AN[D] EARLY IN TH[E] *MORNIN*[G].

THANK YOU VERY MUCH FOR YOUR TIME, MR. ADAMS. YOU'RE FREE TO GO.

NO WAY AROUND IT.

NO *WAY* WE'RE JUST LETTING HIM WALK!

MR. ADAMS HERE HAS AN ALIBI FOR HIS WHEREABOUTS LAST EVENING.

ALWAYS A PLEASUR[E] AGENTS. PLEASE TAK[E] CARE.

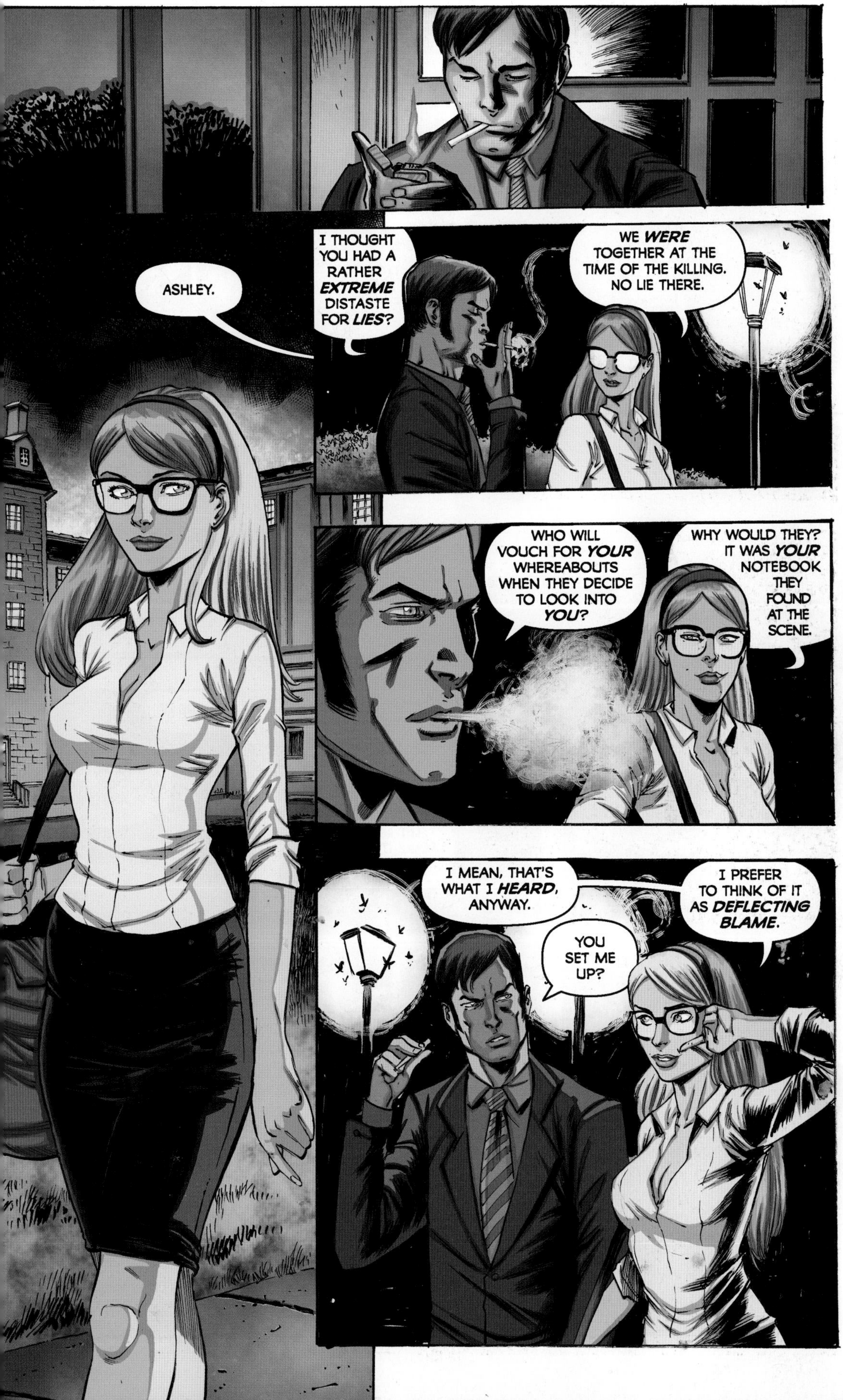
ASHLEY.
I THOUGHT YOU HAD A RATHER EXTREME DISTASTE FOR LIES?
WE WERE TOGETHER AT THE TIME OF THE KILLING. NO LIE THERE.
WHO WILL VOUCH FOR YOUR WHEREABOUTS WHEN THEY DECIDE TO LOOK INTO YOU?
WHY WOULD THEY? IT WAS YOUR NOTEBOOK THEY FOUND AT THE SCENE.
I MEAN, THAT'S WHAT I HEARD, ANYWAY.
YOU SET ME UP?
I PREFER TO THINK OF IT AS DEFLECTING BLAME.

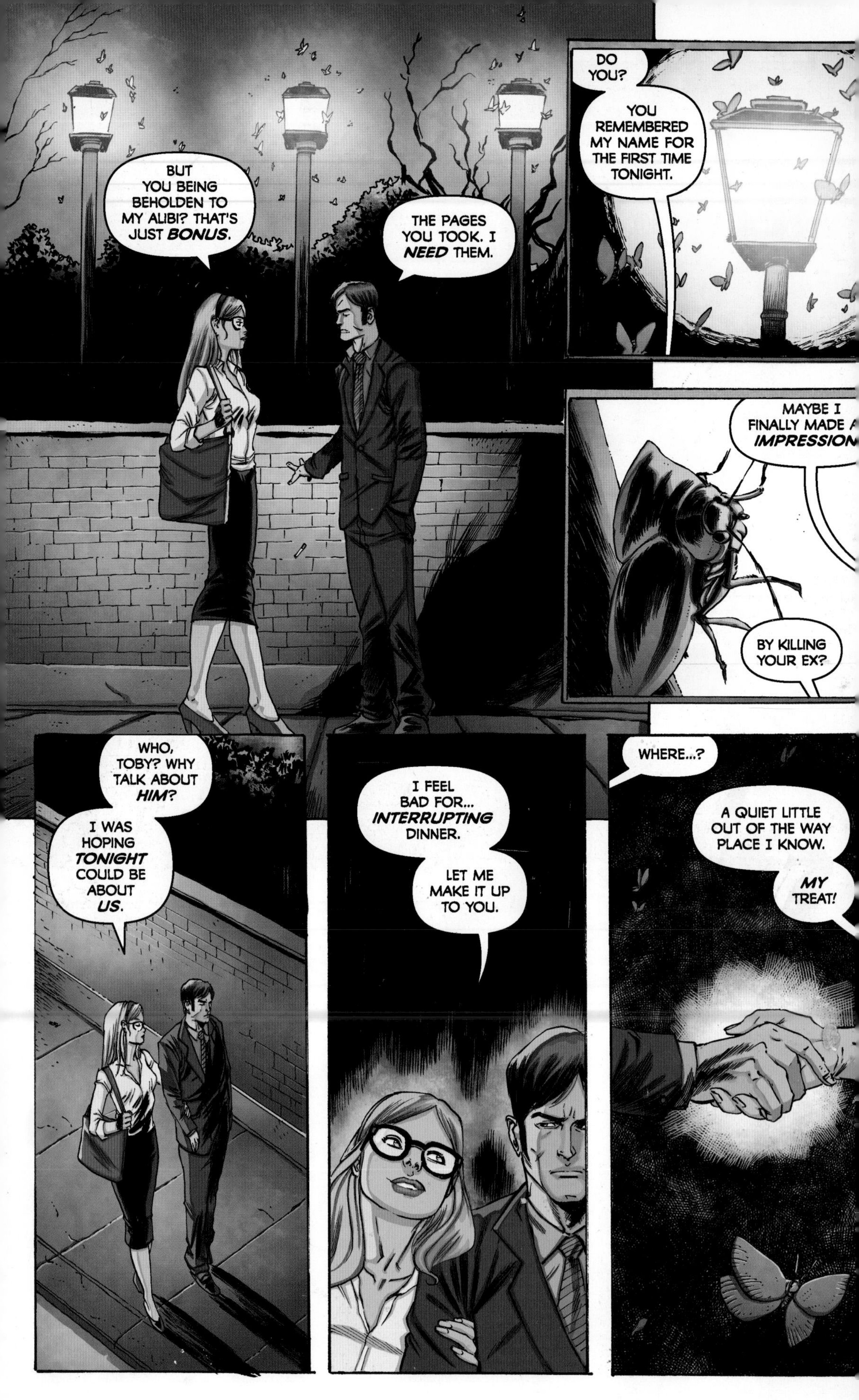
BUT YOU BEING BEHOLDEN TO MY ALIBI? THAT'S JUST **BONUS**.
THE PAGES YOU TOOK. I **NEED** THEM.
DO YOU?
YOU REMEMBERED MY NAME FOR THE FIRST TIME TONIGHT.
MAYBE I FINALLY MADE A **IMPRESSION**
BY KILLING YOUR EX?
WHO, TOBY? WHY TALK ABOUT **HIM**?
I WAS HOPING **TONIGHT** COULD BE ABOUT **US**.
I FEEL BAD FOR... **INTERRUPTING** DINNER.
LET ME MAKE IT UP TO YOU.
WHERE...?
A QUIET LITTLE OUT OF THE WAY PLACE I KNOW.
MY TREAT!

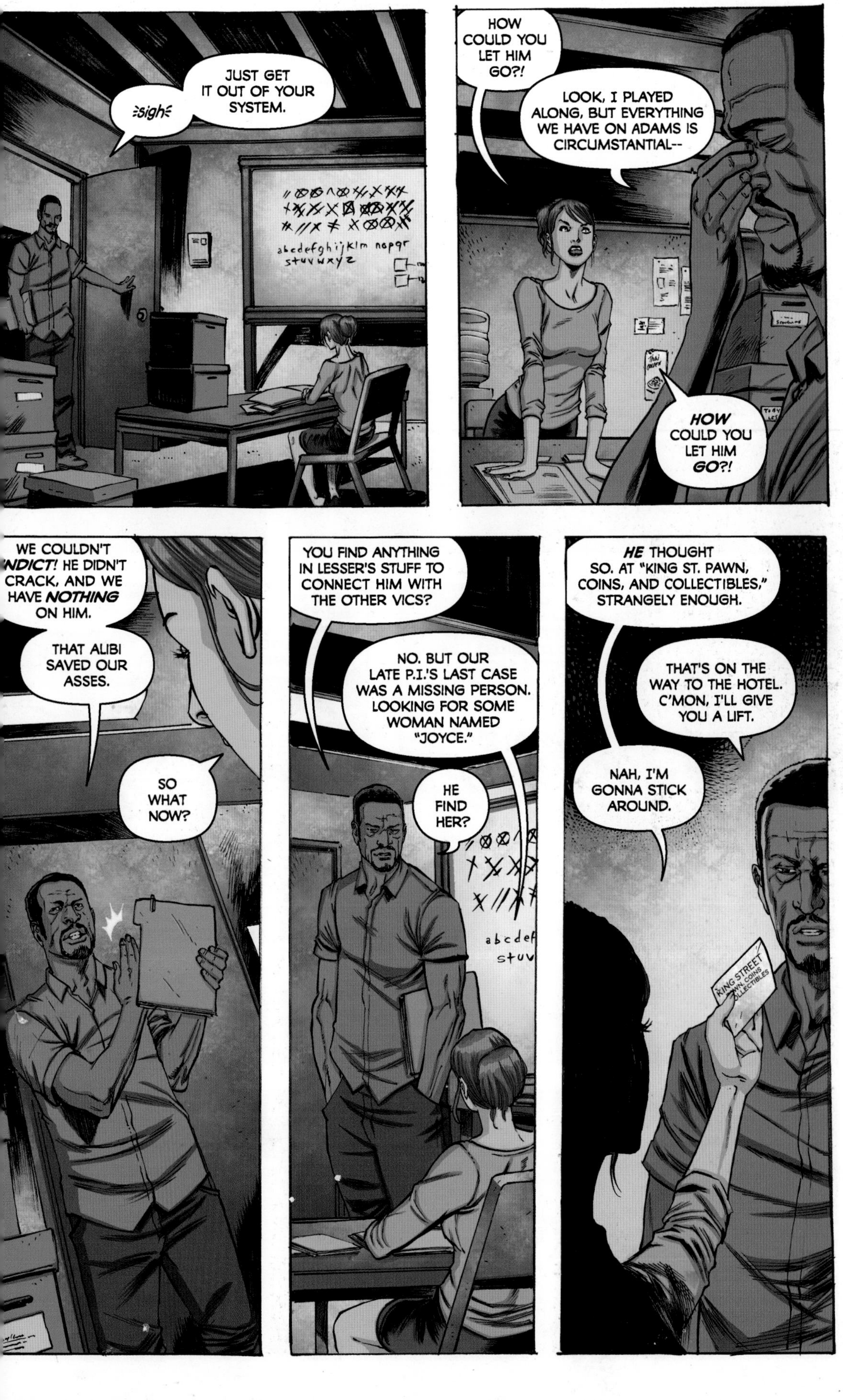

JUST GET IT OUT OF YOUR SYSTEM.
sigh
abcdefghijklm nopqr stuvwxyz
HOW COULD YOU LET HIM GO?!
LOOK, I PLAYED ALONG, BUT EVERYTHING WE HAVE ON ADAMS IS CIRCUMSTANTIAL--
HOW COULD YOU LET HIM GO?!
WE COULDN'T NDICT! HE DIDN'T CRACK, AND WE HAVE NOTHING ON HIM.
THAT ALIBI SAVED OUR ASSES.
SO WHAT NOW?
YOU FIND ANYTHING IN LESSER'S STUFF TO CONNECT HIM WITH THE OTHER VICS?
NO. BUT OUR LATE P.I.'S LAST CASE WAS A MISSING PERSON. LOOKING FOR SOME WOMAN NAMED "JOYCE."
HE FIND HER?
HE THOUGHT SO. AT "KING ST. PAWN, COINS, AND COLLECTIBLES," STRANGELY ENOUGH.
THAT'S ON THE WAY TO THE HOTEL. C'MON, I'LL GIVE YOU A LIFT.
NAH, I'M GONNA STICK AROUND.

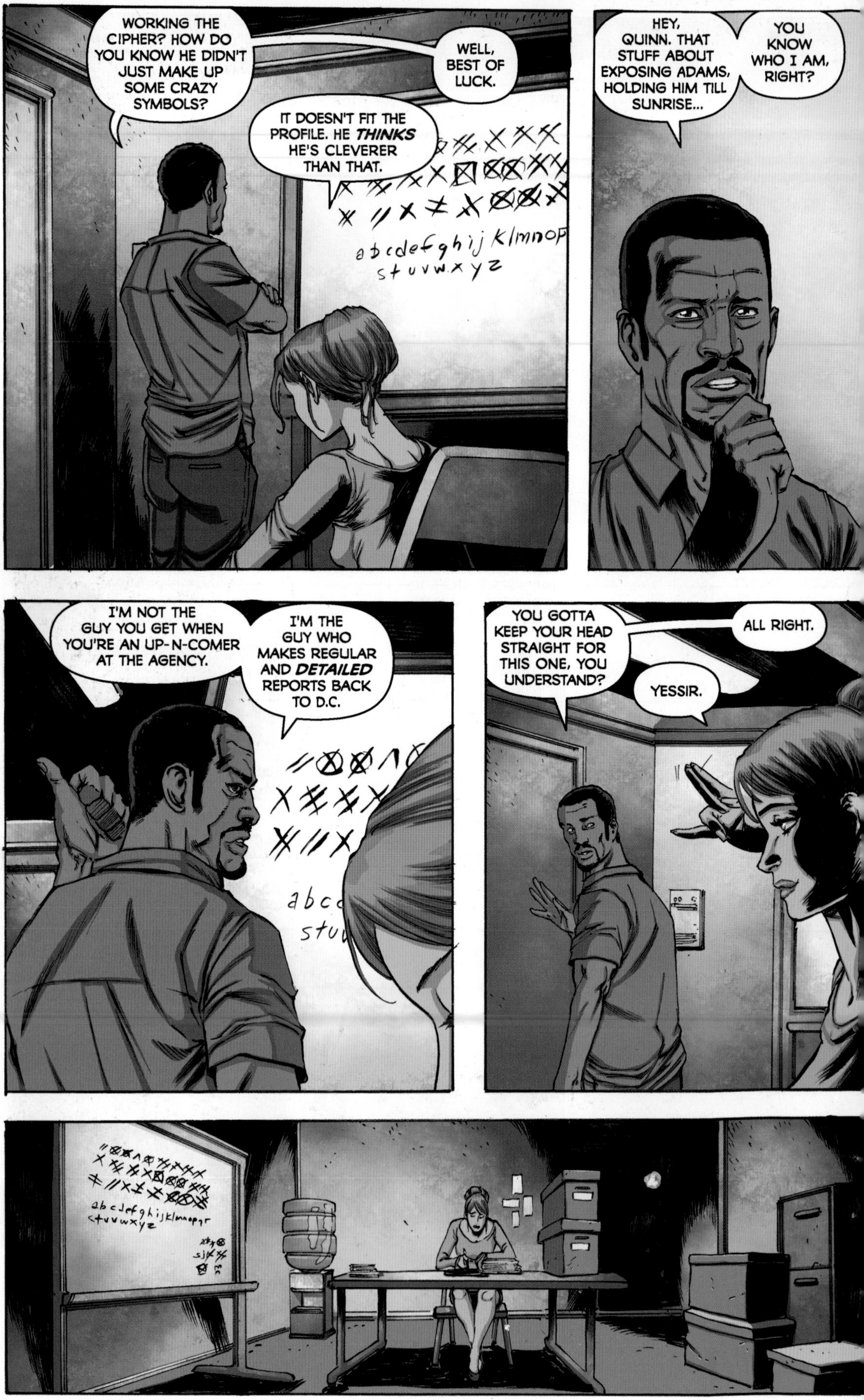
WORKING THE CIPHER? HOW DO YOU KNOW HE DIDN'T JUST MAKE UP SOME CRAZY SYMBOLS?
IT DOESN'T FIT THE PROFILE. HE *THINKS* HE'S CLEVERER THAN THAT.
WELL, BEST OF LUCK.
abcdefghij klmnop
stuvwxyz
HEY, QUINN. THAT STUFF ABOUT EXPOSING ADAMS, HOLDING HIM TILL SUNRISE...
YOU KNOW WHO I AM, RIGHT?
I'M NOT THE GUY YOU GET WHEN YOU'RE AN UP-N-COMER AT THE AGENCY.
I'M THE GUY WHO MAKES REGULAR AND *DETAILED* REPORTS BACK TO D.C.
YOU GOTTA KEEP YOUR HEAD STRAIGHT FOR THIS ONE, YOU UNDERSTAND?
YESSIR.
ALL RIGHT.

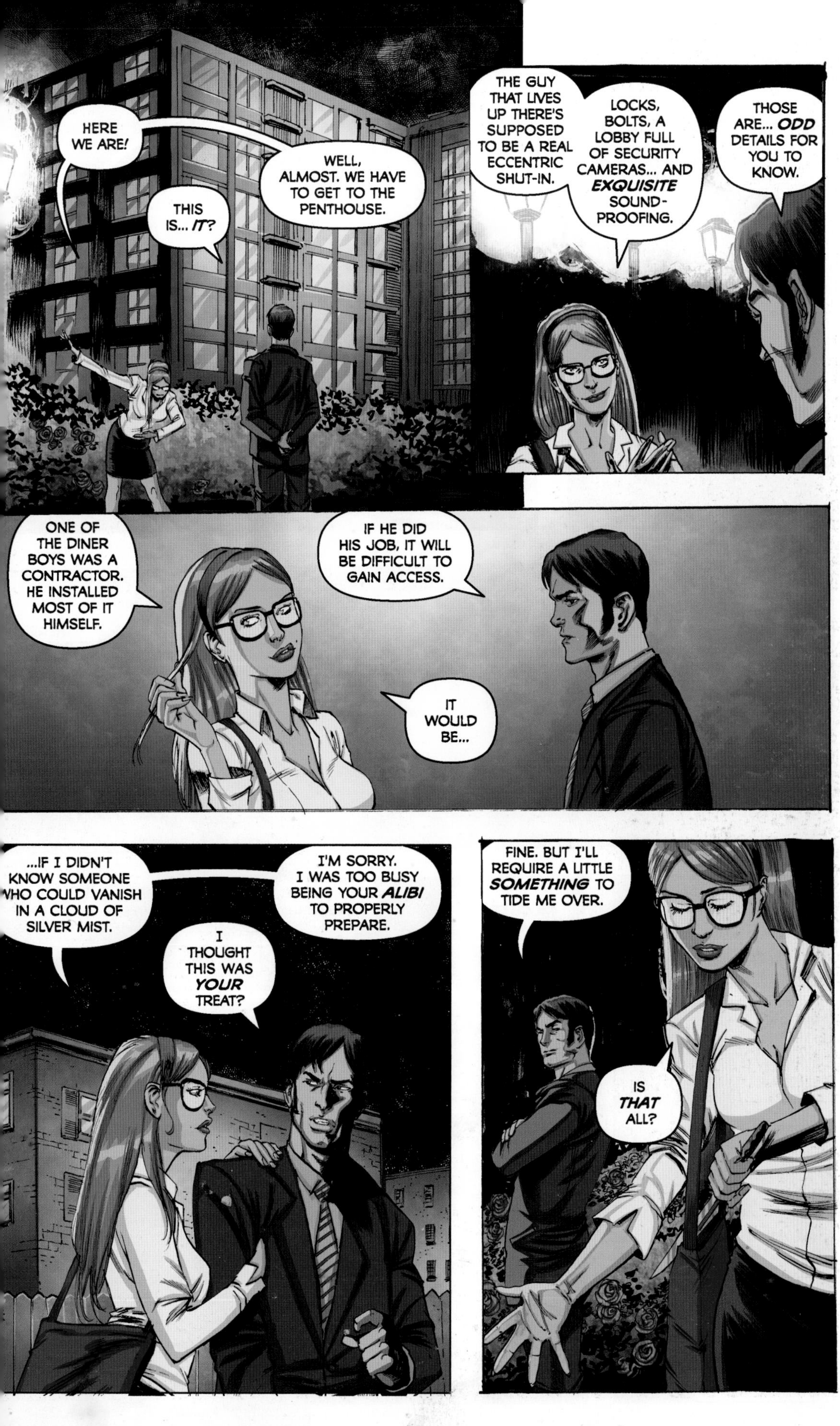
HERE WE ARE!
WELL, ALMOST. WE HAVE TO GET TO THE PENTHOUSE.
THIS IS... *IT*?
THE GUY THAT LIVES UP THERE'S SUPPOSED TO BE A REAL ECCENTRIC SHUT-IN.
LOCKS, BOLTS, A LOBBY FULL OF SECURITY CAMERAS... AND ***EXQUISITE*** SOUND-PROOFING.
THOSE ARE... ***ODD*** DETAILS FOR YOU TO KNOW.
ONE OF THE DINER BOYS WAS A CONTRACTOR. HE INSTALLED MOST OF IT HIMSELF.
IF HE DID HIS JOB, IT WILL BE DIFFICULT TO GAIN ACCESS.
IT WOULD BE...
...IF I DIDN'T KNOW SOMEONE WHO COULD VANISH IN A CLOUD OF SILVER MIST.
I'M SORRY. I WAS TOO BUSY BEING YOUR ***ALIBI*** TO PROPERLY PREPARE.
I THOUGHT THIS WAS ***YOUR*** TREAT?
FINE. BUT I'LL REQUIRE A LITTLE ***SOMETHING*** TO TIDE ME OVER.
IS ***THAT*** ALL?

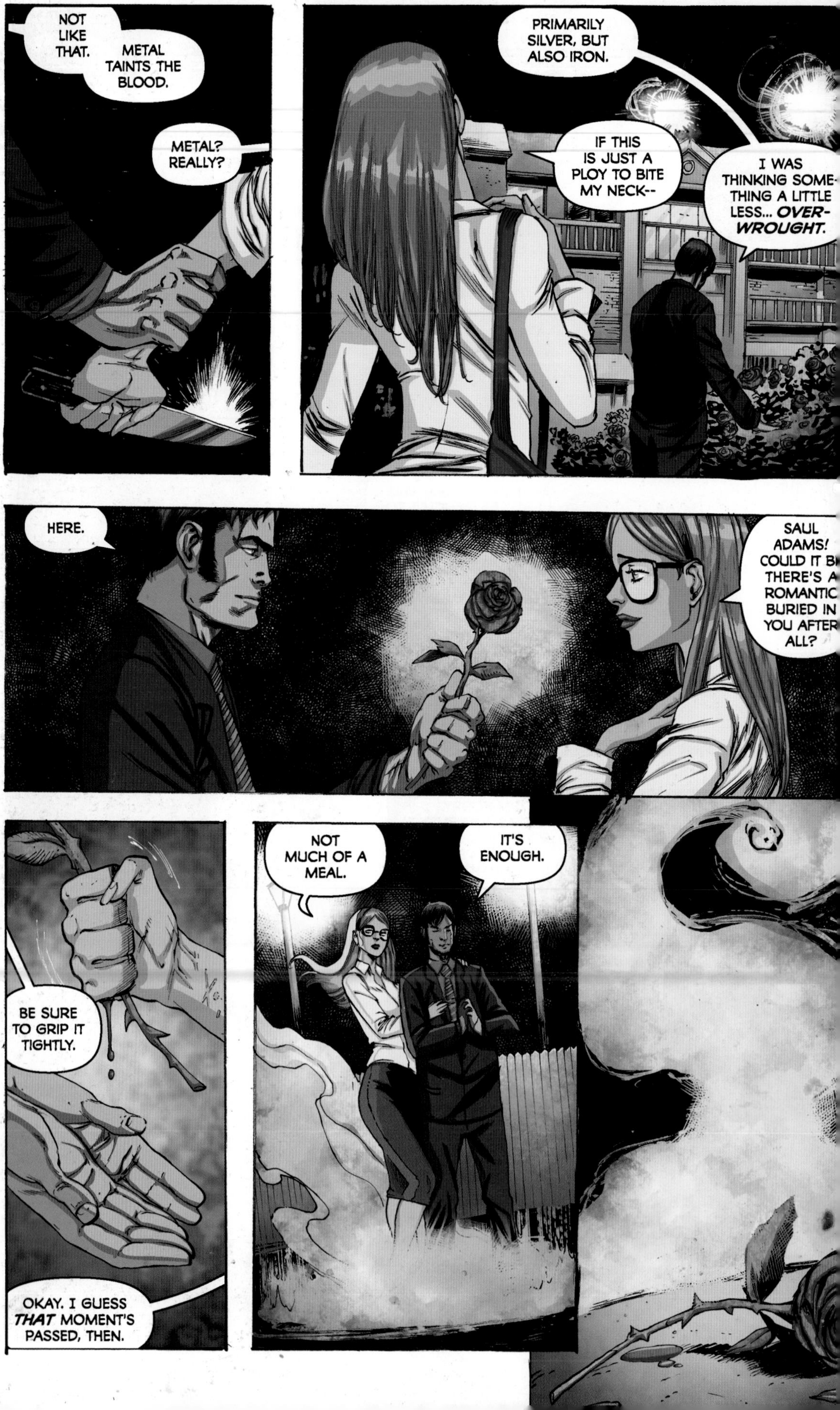
NOT LIKE THAT.
METAL TAINTS THE BLOOD.
METAL? REALLY?
PRIMARILY SILVER, BUT ALSO IRON.
IF THIS IS JUST A PLOY TO BITE MY NECK--
I WAS THINKING SOMETHING A LITTLE LESS... *OVERWROUGHT.*
HERE.
SAUL ADAMS! COULD IT B THERE'S A ROMANTIC BURIED IN YOU AFTER ALL?
BE SURE TO GRIP IT TIGHTLY.
OKAY. I GUESS *THAT* MOMENT'S PASSED, THEN.
NOT MUCH OF A MEAL.
IT'S ENOUGH.

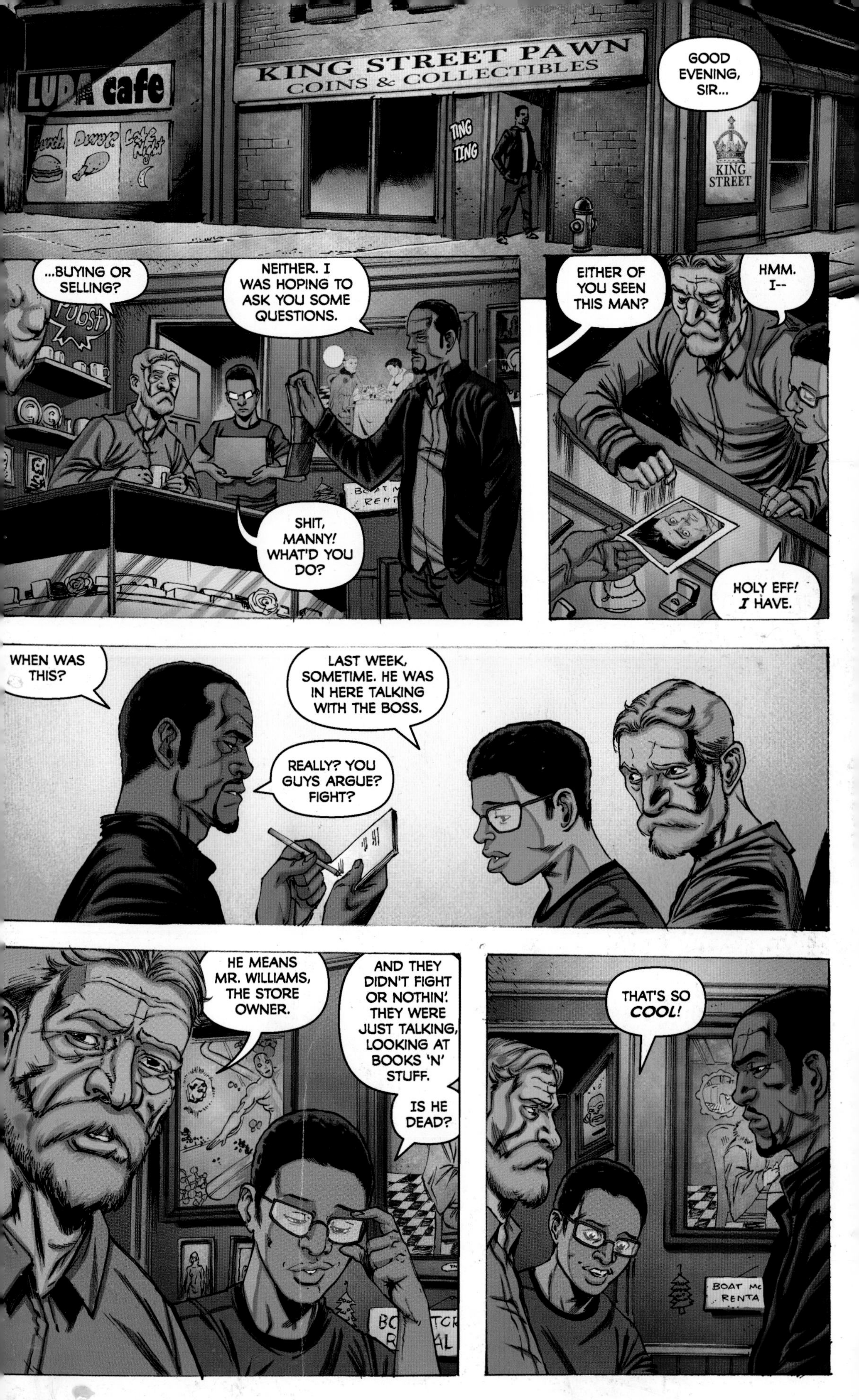
KING STREET PAWN
COINS & COLLECTIBLES
LUDA cafe
TING TING
GOOD EVENING, SIR...
KING STREET
...BUYING OR SELLING?
NEITHER. I WAS HOPING TO ASK YOU SOME QUESTIONS.
SHIT, MANNY! WHAT'D YOU DO?
EITHER OF YOU SEEN THIS MAN?
HMM. I--
HOLY EFF! I HAVE.
WHEN WAS THIS?
LAST WEEK, SOMETIME. HE WAS IN HERE TALKING WITH THE BOSS.
REALLY? YOU GUYS ARGUE? FIGHT?
HE MEANS MR. WILLIAMS, THE STORE OWNER.
AND THEY DIDN'T FIGHT OR NOTHIN'. THEY WERE JUST TALKING, LOOKING AT BOOKS 'N' STUFF.
IS HE DEAD?
THAT'S SO COOL!

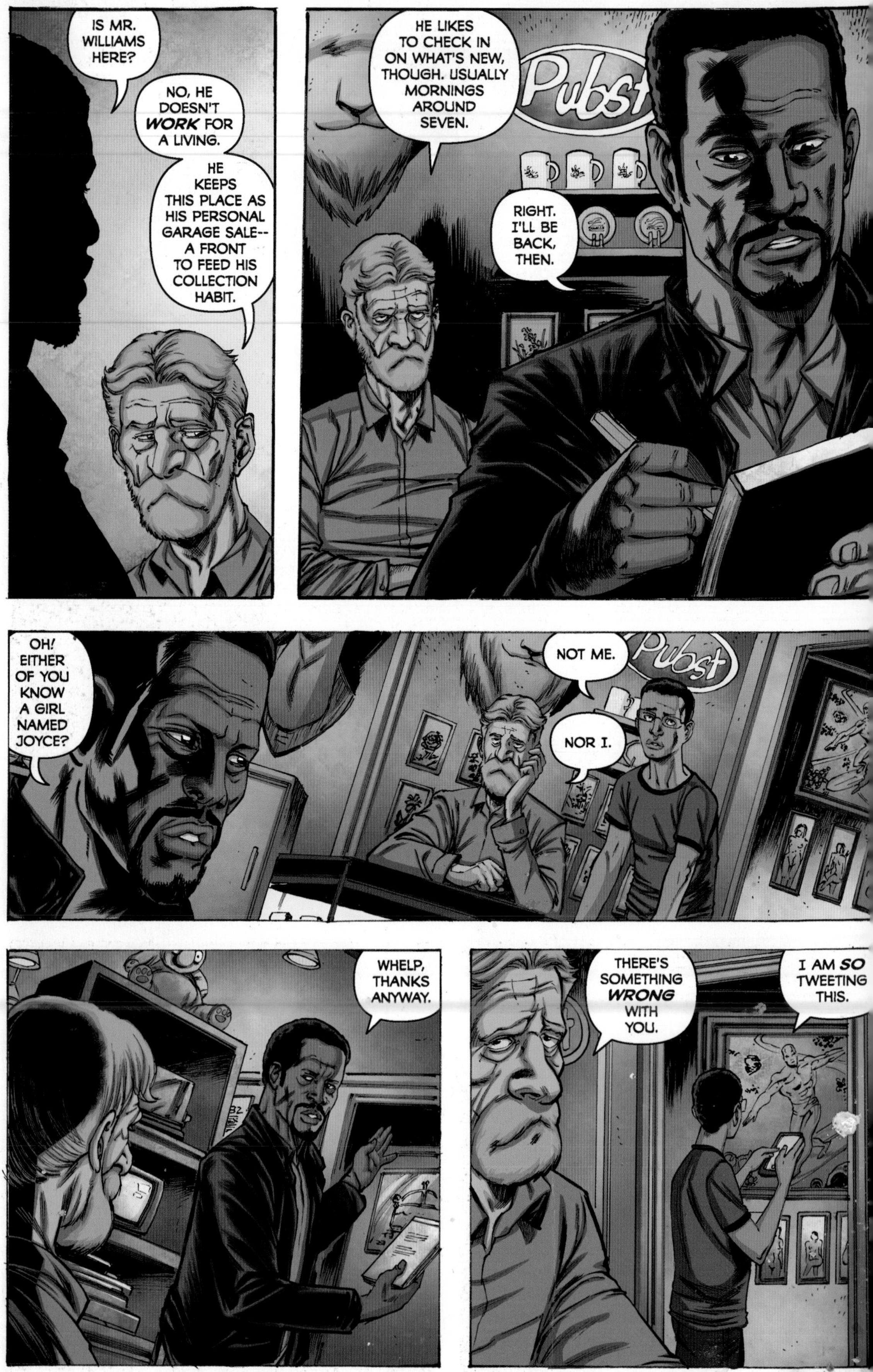
IS MR. WILLIAMS HERE?
NO, HE DOESN'T *WORK* FOR A LIVING.
HE KEEPS THIS PLACE AS HIS PERSONAL GARAGE SALE-- A FRONT TO FEED HIS COLLECTION HABIT.
HE LIKES TO CHECK IN ON WHAT'S NEW, THOUGH. USUALLY MORNINGS AROUND SEVEN.
Pubst
RIGHT. I'LL BE BACK, THEN.
OH! EITHER OF YOU KNOW A GIRL NAMED JOYCE?
Pubst
NOT ME.
NOR I.
WHELP, THANKS ANYWAY.
THERE'S SOMETHING *WRONG* WITH YOU.
I AM *SO* TWEETING THIS.

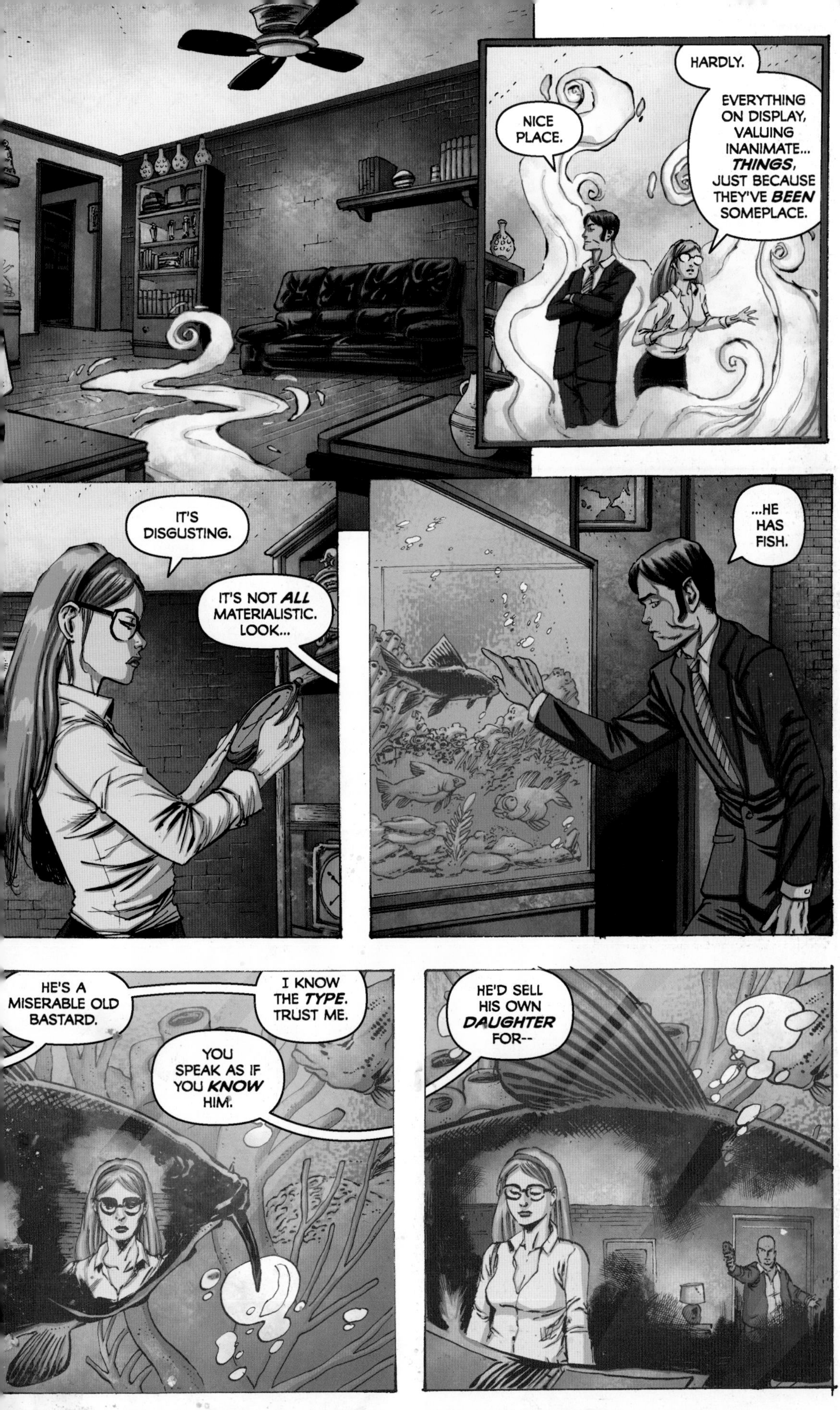
NICE PLACE.
HARDLY.
EVERYTHING ON DISPLAY, VALUING INANIMATE... *THINGS*, JUST BECAUSE THEY'VE *BEEN* SOMEPLACE.
IT'S DISGUSTING.
IT'S NOT *ALL* MATERIALISTIC. LOOK...
...HE HAS FISH.
HE'S A MISERABLE OLD BASTARD.
I KNOW THE *TYPE*. TRUST ME.
YOU SPEAK AS IF YOU *KNOW* HIM.
HE'D SELL HIS OWN *DAUGHTER* FOR--

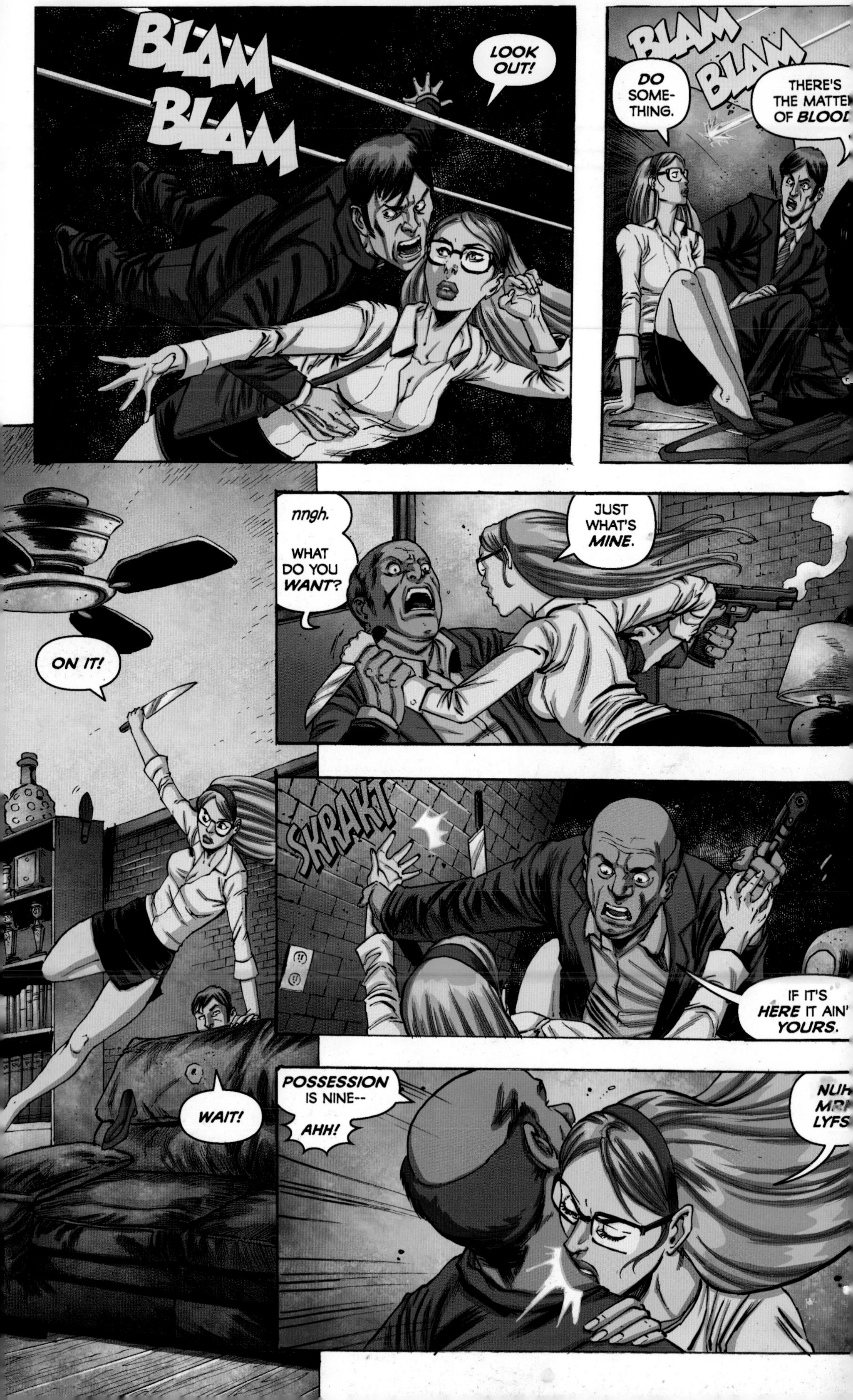
BLAM
BLAM
LOOK OUT!
BLAM
BLAM
DO SOME-THING.
THERE'S THE MATTE OF BLOOD
nngh.
WHAT DO YOU WANT?
JUST WHAT'S MINE.
ON IT!
SKRAKT
IF IT'S HERE IT AIN' YOURS.
WAIT!
POSSESSION IS NINE--
AHH!

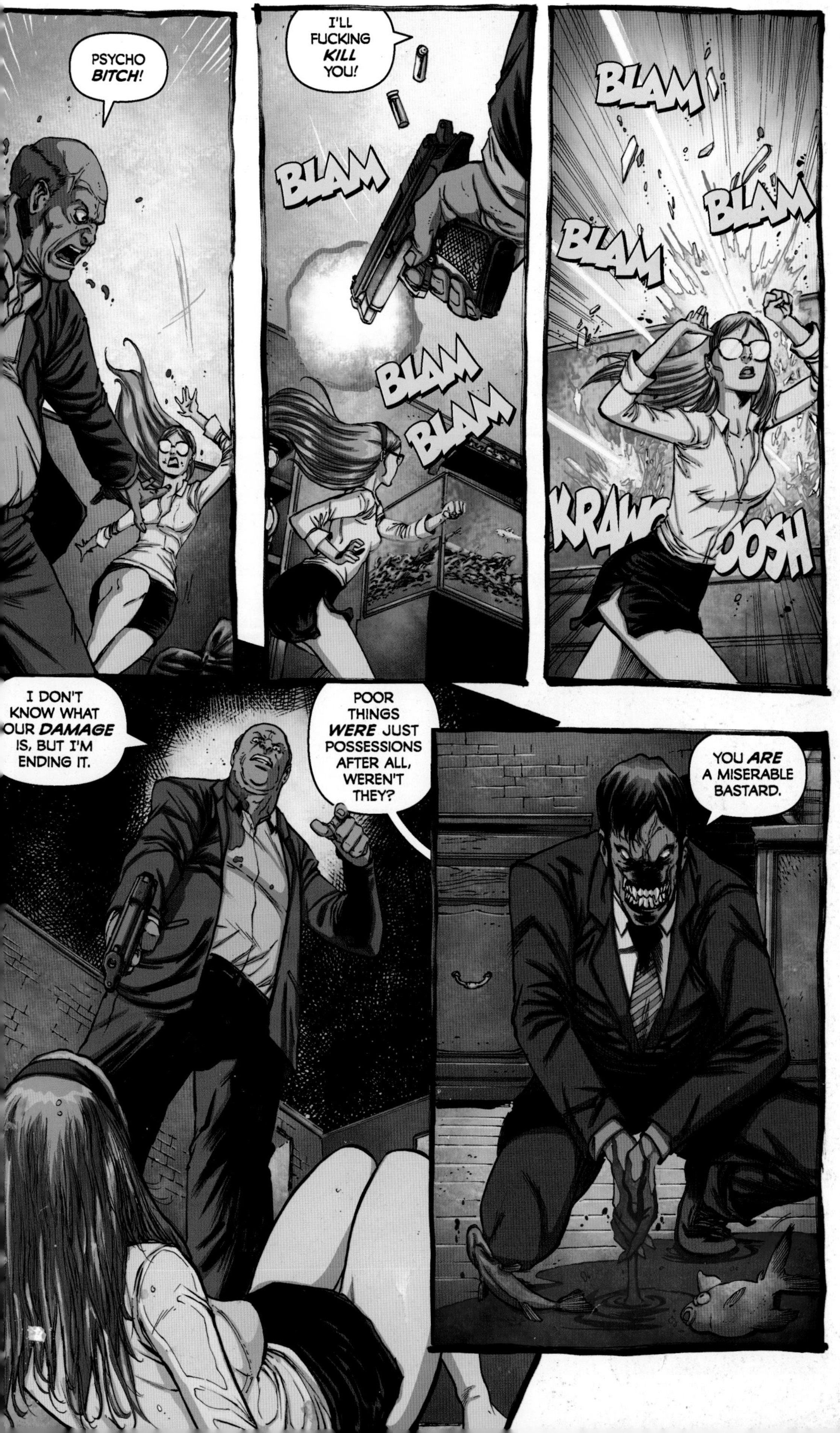
PSYCHO BITCH!
I'LL FUCKING KILL YOU!
BLAM
BLAM
BLAM
BLAM
BLAM
BLAM
KRAW
OOSH
I DON'T KNOW WHAT OUR DAMAGE IS, BUT I'M ENDING IT.
POOR THINGS WERE JUST POSSESSIONS AFTER ALL, WEREN'T THEY?
YOU ARE A MISERABLE BASTARD.

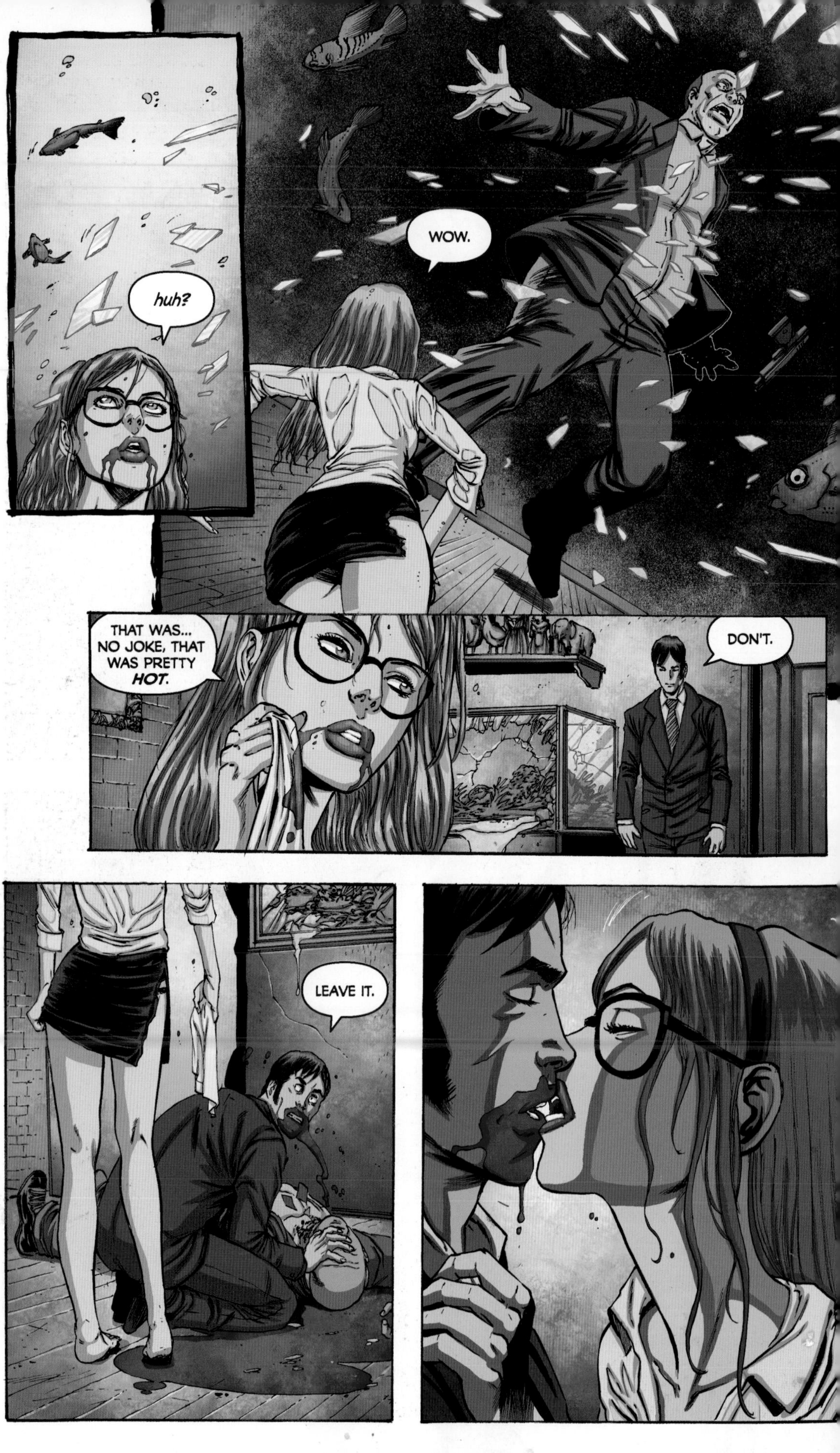
huh?
WOW.
THAT WAS... NO JOKE, THAT WAS PRETTY *HOT*.
DON'T.
LEAVE IT.

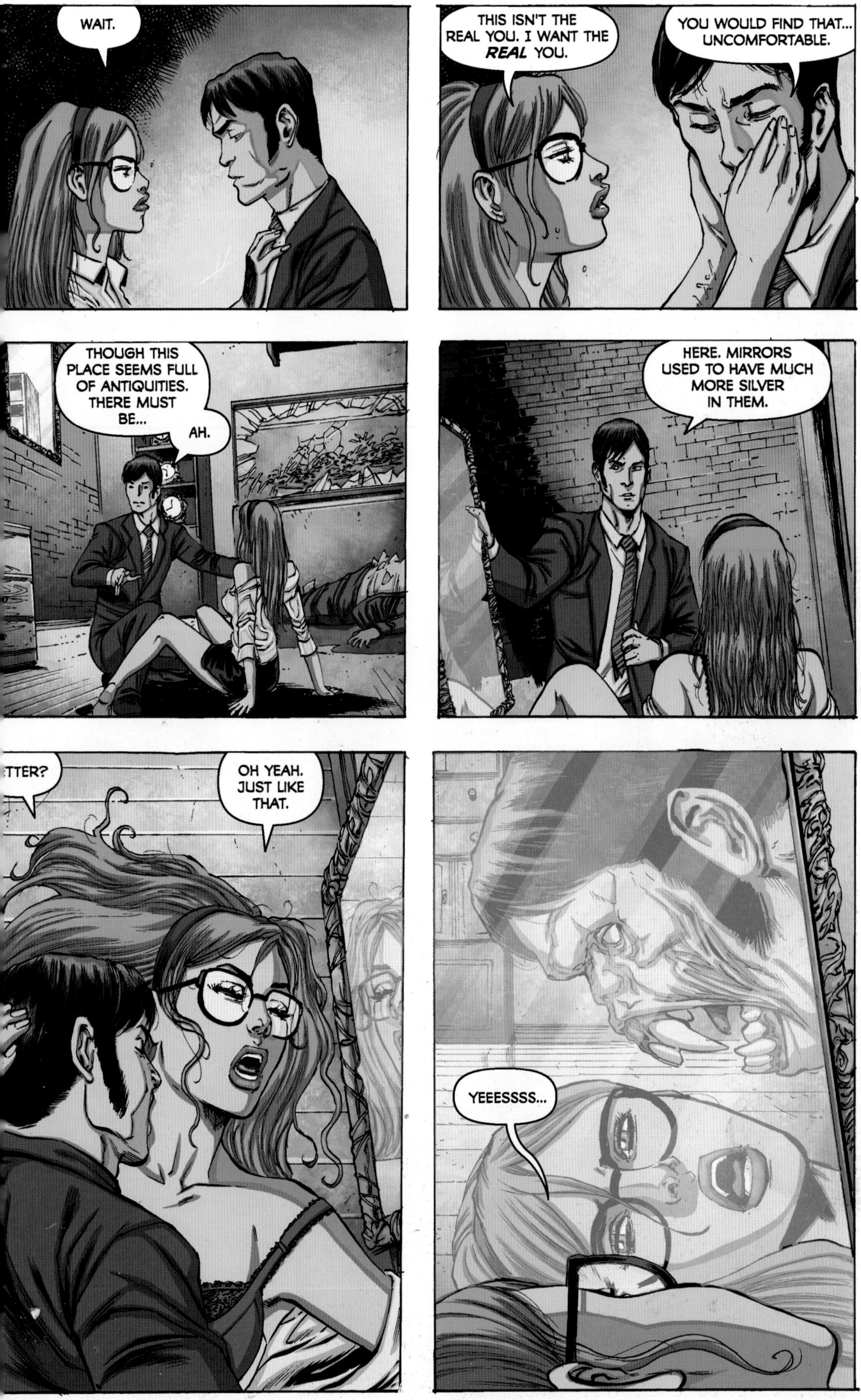
WAIT.
THIS ISN'T THE REAL YOU. I WANT THE *REAL* YOU.
YOU WOULD FIND THAT... UNCOMFORTABLE.
THOUGH THIS PLACE SEEMS FULL OF ANTIQUITIES. THERE MUST BE...
AH.
HERE. MIRRORS USED TO HAVE MUCH MORE SILVER IN THEM.
TTER?
OH YEAH. JUST LIKE THAT.
YEEESSSS...

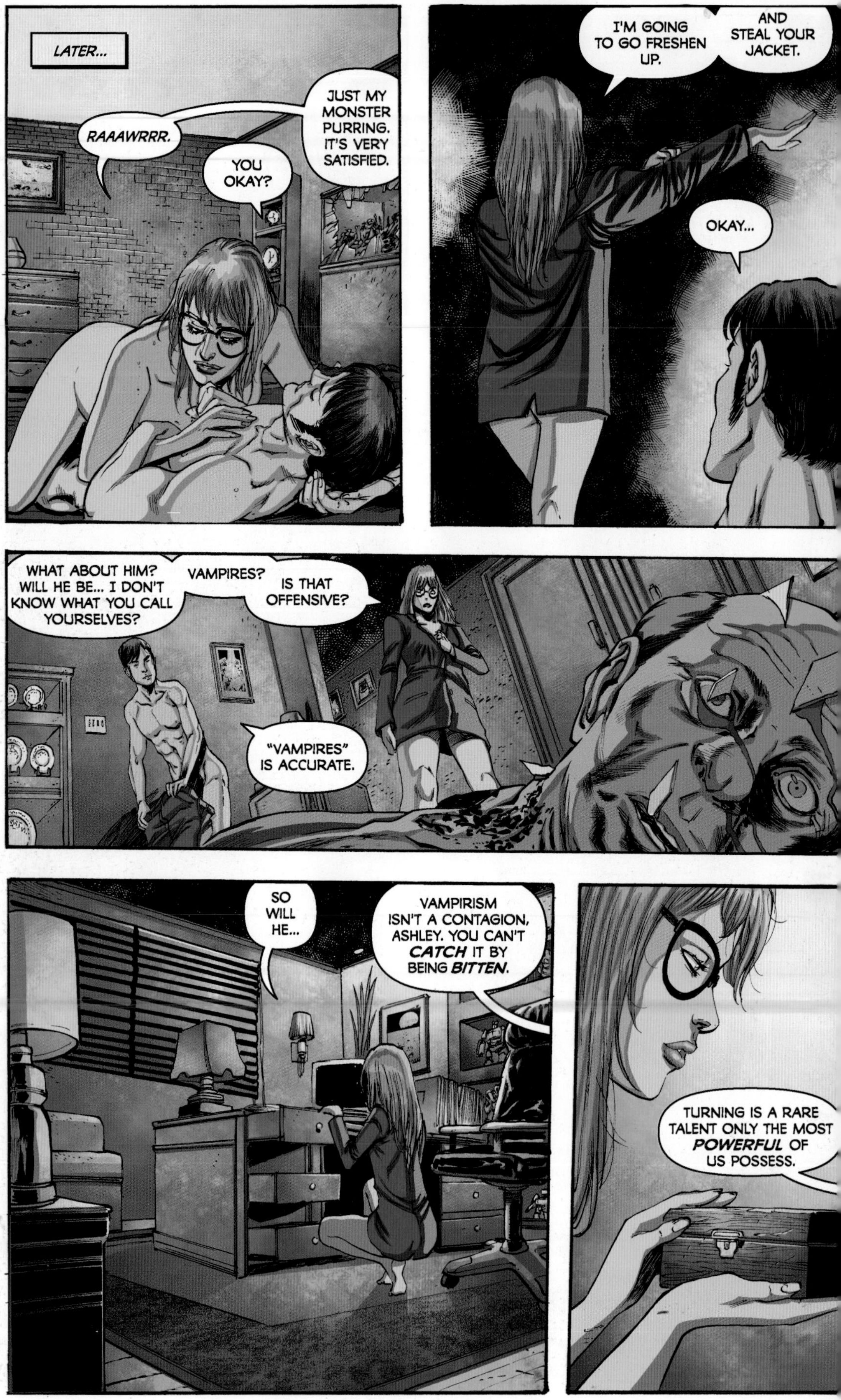
LATER...
RAAAWRRR.
YOU OKAY?
JUST MY MONSTER PURRING. IT'S VERY SATISFIED.
I'M GOING TO GO FRESHEN UP.
AND STEAL YOUR JACKET.
OKAY...
WHAT ABOUT HIM? WILL HE BE... I DON'T KNOW WHAT YOU CALL YOURSELVES?
VAMPIRES?
IS THAT OFFENSIVE?
"VAMPIRES" IS ACCURATE.
SO WILL HE...
VAMPIRISM ISN'T A CONTAGION, ASHLEY. YOU CAN'T *CATCH* IT BY BEING *BITTEN*.
TURNING IS A RARE TALENT ONLY THE MOST *POWERFUL* OF US POSSESS.

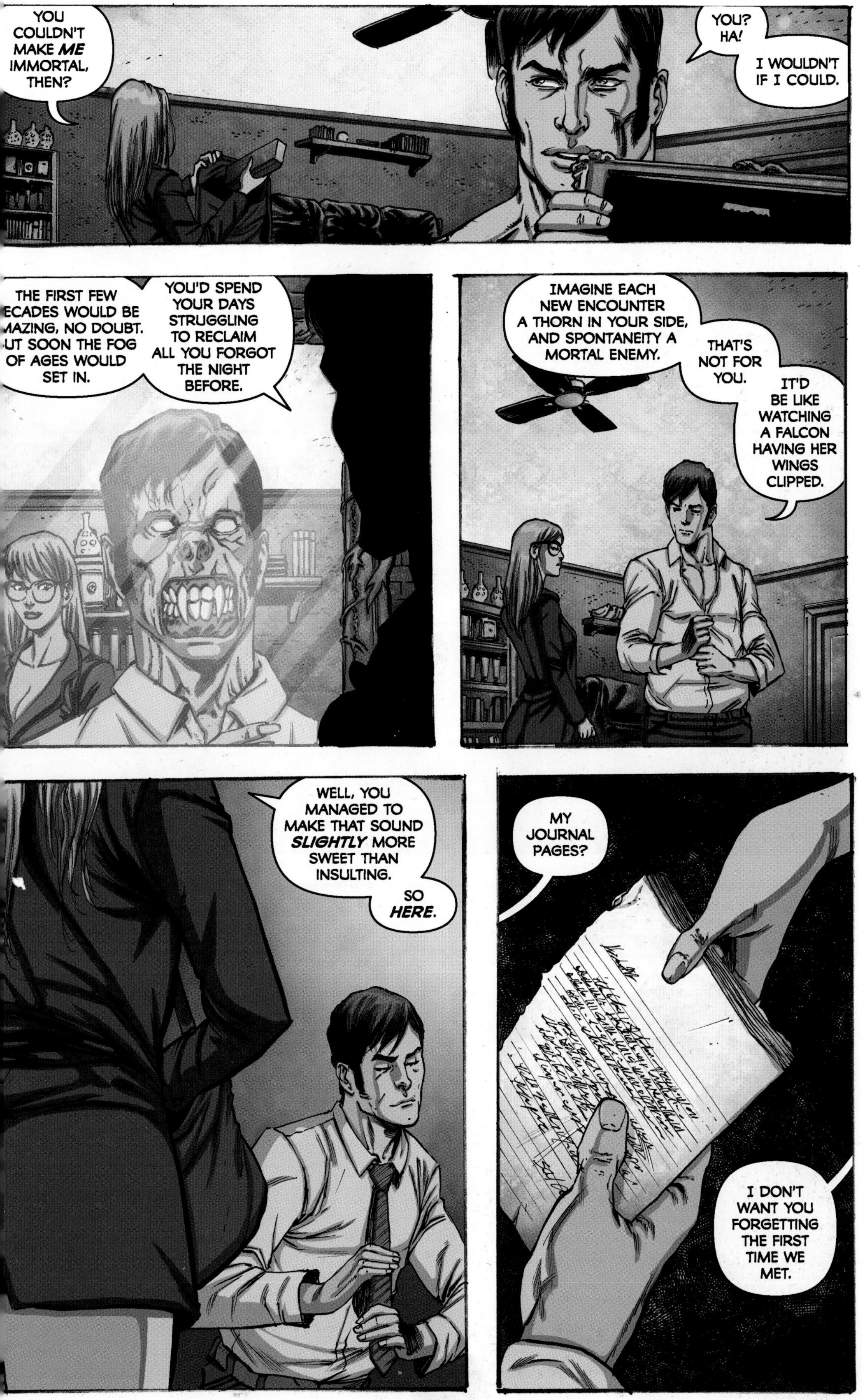
YOU COULDN'T MAKE *ME* IMMORTAL, THEN?
YOU? HA!
I WOULDN'T IF I COULD.
THE FIRST FEW ECADES WOULD BE MAZING, NO DOUBT. UT SOON THE FOG OF AGES WOULD SET IN.
YOU'D SPEND YOUR DAYS STRUGGLING TO RECLAIM ALL YOU FORGOT THE NIGHT BEFORE.
IMAGINE EACH NEW ENCOUNTER A THORN IN YOUR SIDE, AND SPONTANEITY A MORTAL ENEMY.
THAT'S NOT FOR YOU.
IT'D BE LIKE WATCHING A FALCON HAVING HER WINGS CLIPPED.
WELL, YOU MANAGED TO MAKE THAT SOUND *SLIGHTLY* MORE SWEET THAN INSULTING.
SO *HERE*.
MY JOURNAL PAGES?
I DON'T WANT YOU FORGETTING THE FIRST TIME WE MET.

THANK YOU.

AT THE MOMENT I CAN THINK OF LITTLE ELSE.

BUT THE TIME WILL COME...

IT ALWAYS DOES.

I'M GOING TO WRITE THAT DOWN.

WHY?

BECAUSE IT'S *TRUE*.

YOU WRITE TO *PRESERVE* YOUR IMMORTALITY.

I WRITE TO *CREATE* MINE.

THERE!

IT'S ALMOST DAWN. WE SHOULD LEAVE.

THIS WAS FUN. WE SHOULD DO IT AGAIN, SOMETIME.

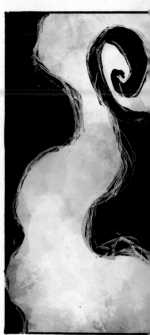

YOU GOT HERE QUICK.

I WAS ALREADY ON MY WAY TO MEET THE OWNER OF THAT PAWN-SHOP, MR. WILLIAMS...

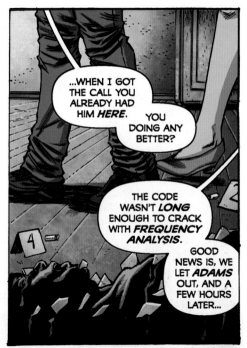

...WHEN I GOT THE CALL YOU ALREADY HAD HIM *HERE*.

YOU DOING ANY BETTER?

THE CODE WASN'T *LONG* ENOUGH TO CRACK WITH *FREQUENCY ANALYSIS*.

GOOD NEWS IS, WE LET *ADAMS* OUT, AND A FEW HOURS LATER...

...WE GET *MORE CODE*.

HE'S SETTLING INTO A PATTERN.

PATTERNS WE CAN PREDICT. *PATTERNS* WILL LEAD US RIGHT TO ADAMS'S DOOR.

THIS IS *GOOD* NEWS?

QUINN, WE DON'T *KNOW* THIS WAS ADAMS.

HELL, WE'RE NOT EVEN *SURE* THIS WAS *SANGUINE*.

YOU GROW A SENSE OF *HUMOR* OVERNIGHT?

LOOK AT THAT WALL!

PICTURES OF THE LAST CRIME SCENE WERE ALL OVER THE PAPERS.

THIS COULD BE A COPYCAT.

OR SOME *OTHER* CRIMINAL TRYING TO THROW US OFF THE SCENT.

LIKE A *THIEF*, MAYBE?

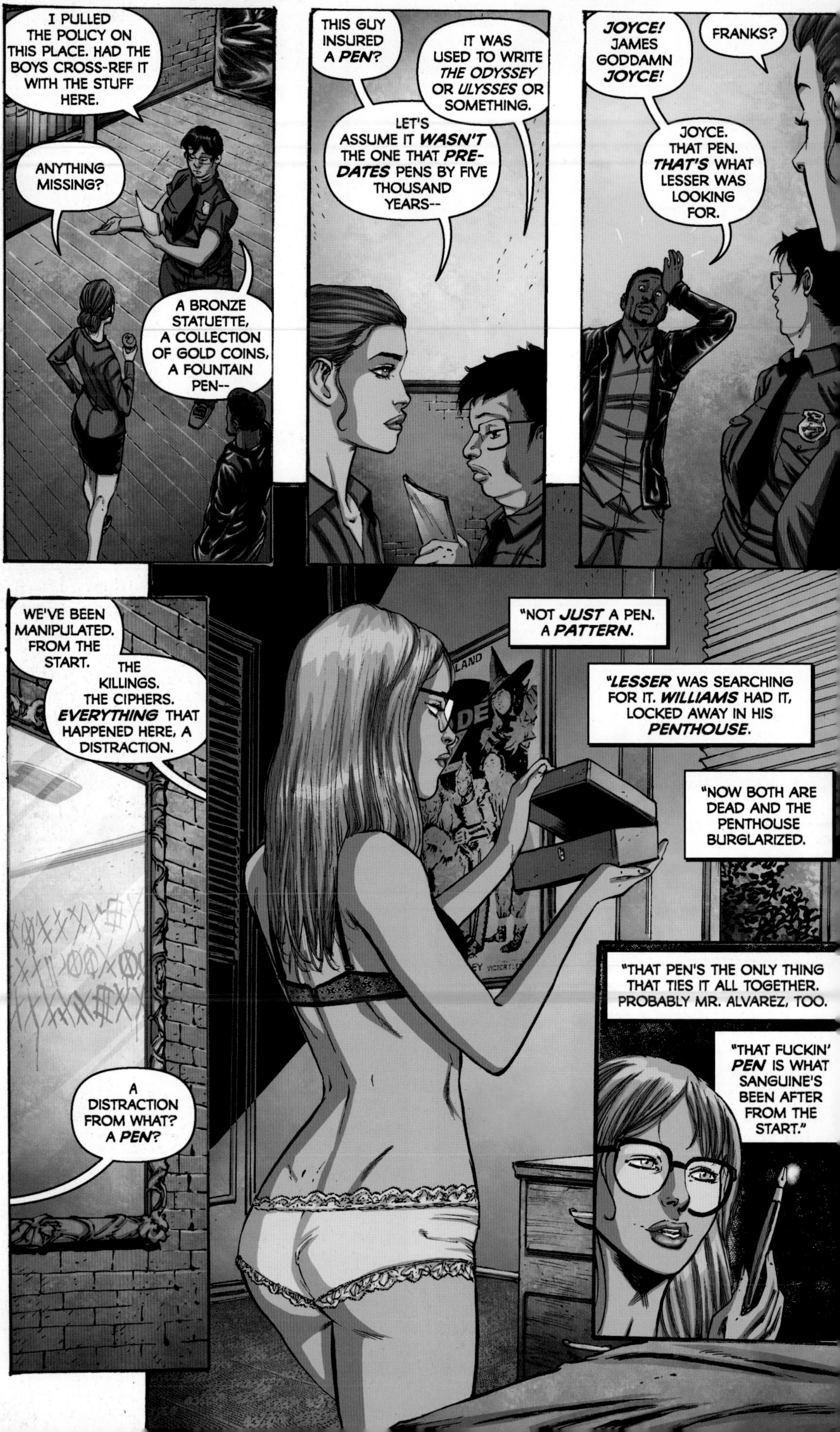
I PULLED THE POLICY ON THIS PLACE. HAD THE BOYS CROSS-REF IT WITH THE STUFF HERE.
ANYTHING MISSING?
A BRONZE STATUETTE, A COLLECTION OF GOLD COINS, A FOUNTAIN PEN--
THIS GUY INSURED A *PEN*?
IT WAS USED TO WRITE *THE ODYSSEY* OR *ULYSSES* OR SOMETHING.
LET'S ASSUME IT ***WASN'T*** THE ONE THAT ***PRE-DATES*** PENS BY FIVE THOUSAND YEARS--
JOYCE! JAMES GODDAMN ***JOYCE!***
FRANKS?
JOYCE. THAT PEN. ***THAT'S*** WHAT LESSER WAS LOOKING FOR.
WE'VE BEEN MANIPULATED. FROM THE START.
THE KILLINGS. THE CIPHERS. ***EVERYTHING*** THAT HAPPENED HERE, A DISTRACTION.
A DISTRACTION FROM WHAT? A ***PEN***?
"NOT ***JUST*** A PEN. A ***PATTERN***.
"***LESSER*** WAS SEARCHING FOR IT. ***WILLIAMS*** HAD IT, LOCKED AWAY IN HIS ***PENTHOUSE***.
"NOW BOTH ARE DEAD AND THE PENTHOUSE BURGLARIZED.
"THAT PEN'S THE ONLY THING THAT TIES IT ALL TOGETHER. PROBABLY MR. ALVAREZ, TOO.
"THAT FUCKIN' ***PEN*** IS WHAT SANGUINE'S BEEN AFTER FROM THE START."

CHAPTER THREE

A LONELY WORD

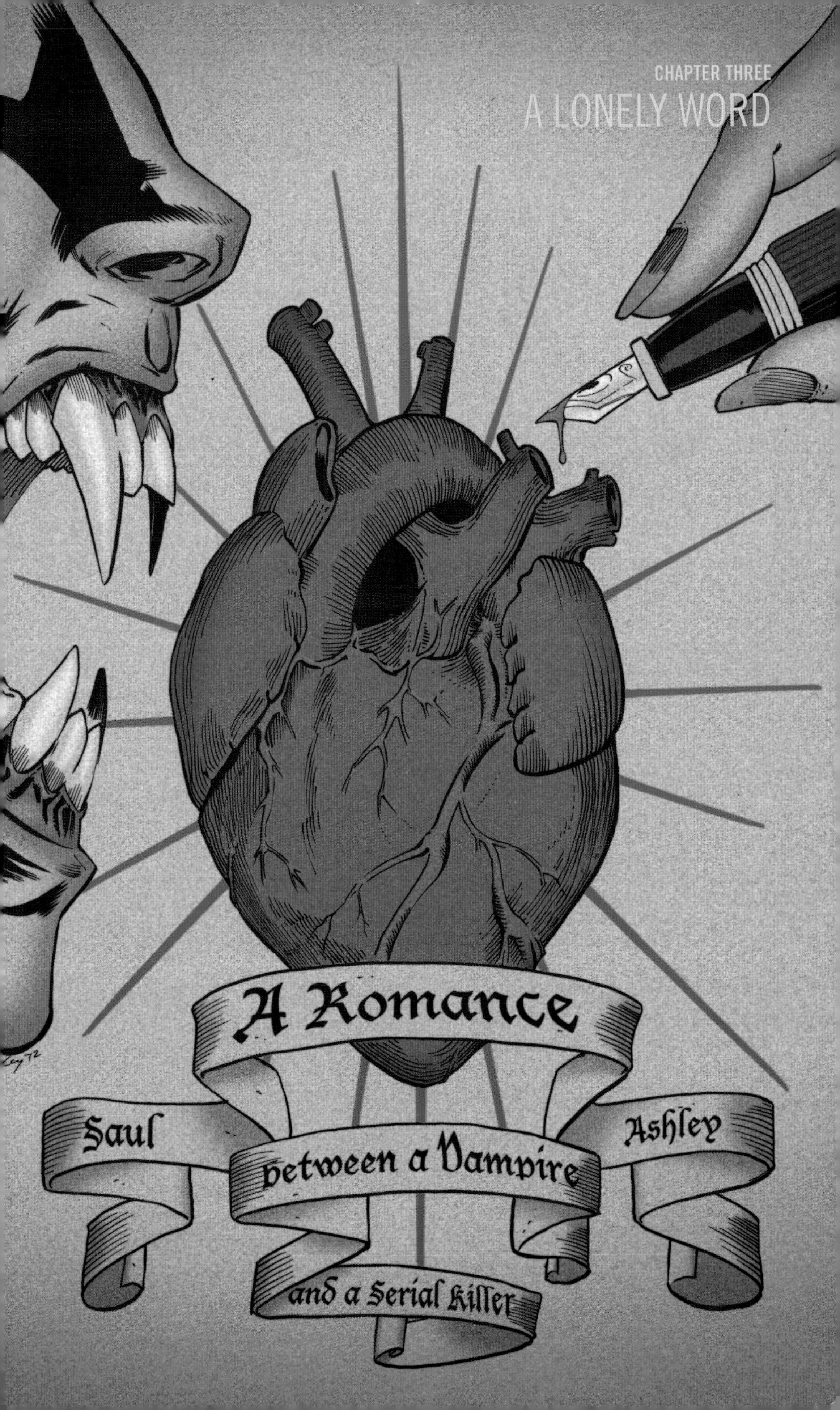
A Romance
Saul
between a Vampire
Ashley
and a Serial Killer

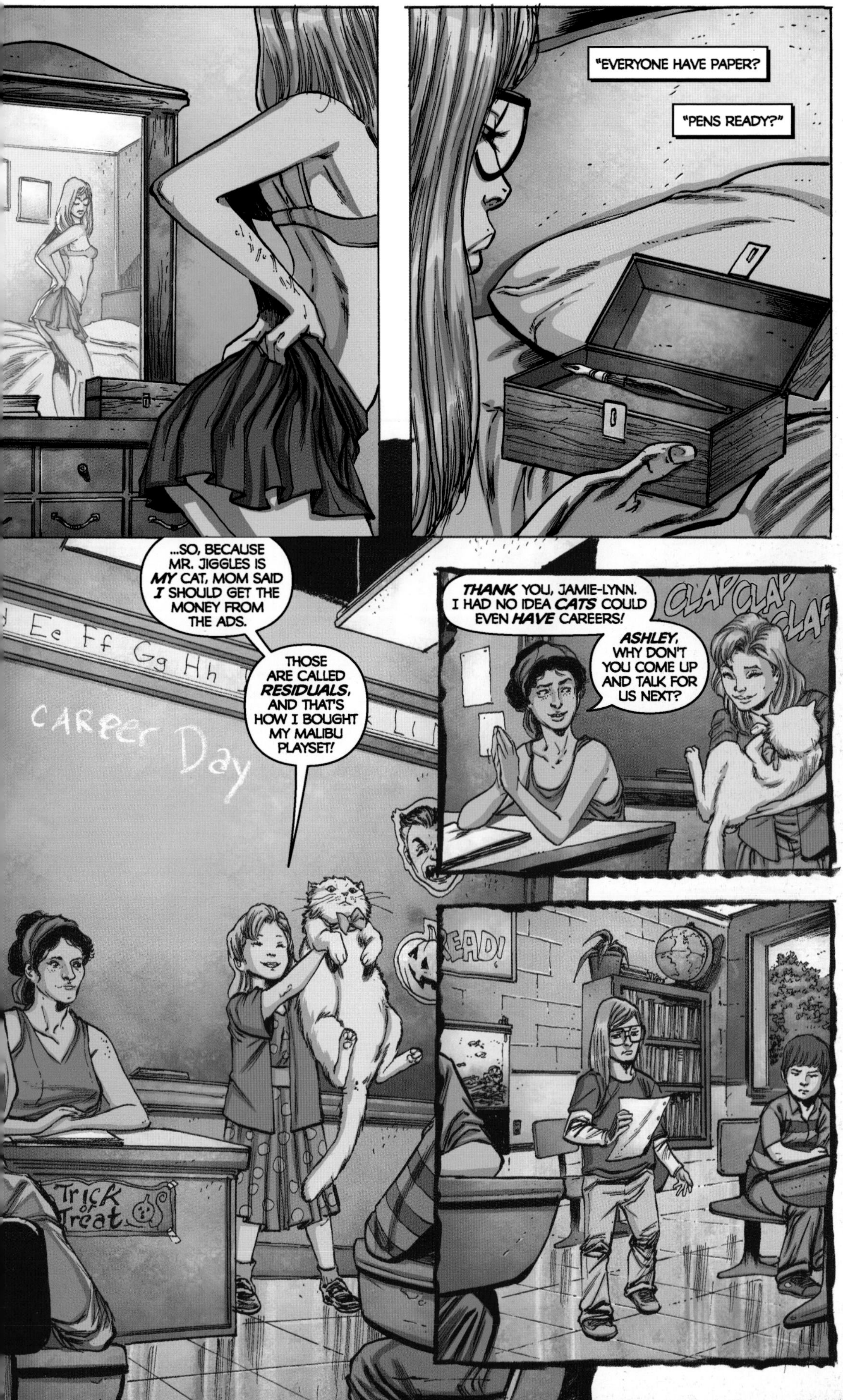
"EVERYONE HAVE PAPER?
"PENS READY?"
...SO, BECAUSE MR. JIGGLES IS MY CAT, MOM SAID I SHOULD GET THE MONEY FROM THE ADS.
THOSE ARE CALLED RESIDUALS, AND THAT'S HOW I BOUGHT MY MALIBU PLAYSET!
Ee Ff Gg Hh
CAReer Day
Trick or Treat
THANK YOU, JAMIE-LYNN. I HAD NO IDEA CATS COULD EVEN HAVE CAREERS!
CLAP CLAP CLAP
ASHLEY, WHY DON'T YOU COME UP AND TALK FOR US NEXT?
READ!

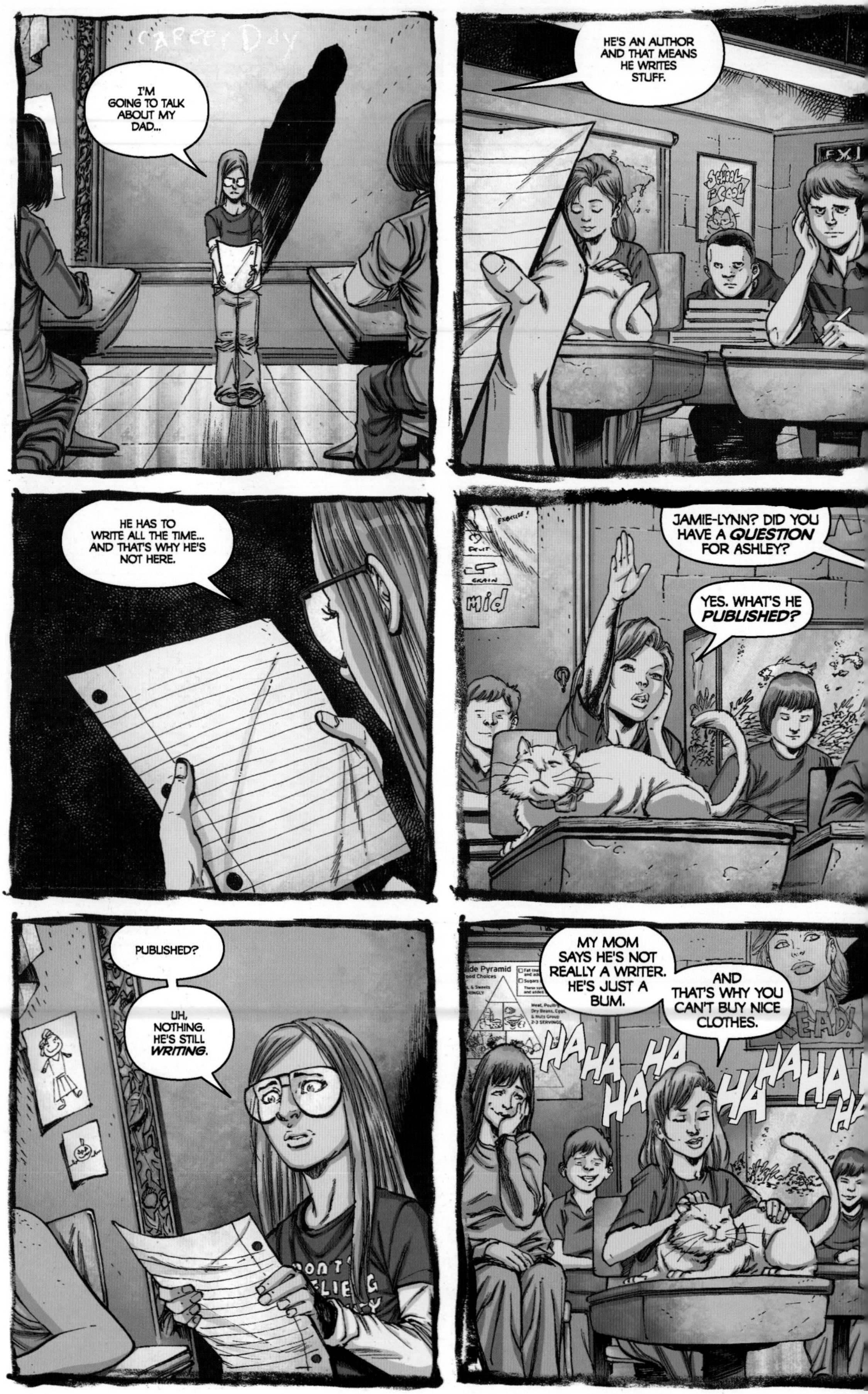
CAREER DAY
I'M GOING TO TALK ABOUT MY DAD...
HE'S AN AUTHOR AND THAT MEANS HE WRITES STUFF.
HE HAS TO WRITE ALL THE TIME... AND THAT'S WHY HE'S NOT HERE.
JAMIE-LYNN? DID YOU HAVE A *QUESTION* FOR ASHLEY?
YES. WHAT'S HE *PUBLISHED?*
PUBLISHED?
UH, NOTHING. HE'S STILL *WRITING*.
MY MOM SAYS HE'S NOT REALLY A WRITER. HE'S JUST A BUM.
AND THAT'S WHY YOU CAN'T BUY NICE CLOTHES.
HAHA HA HA HAHA HAHA
READ!

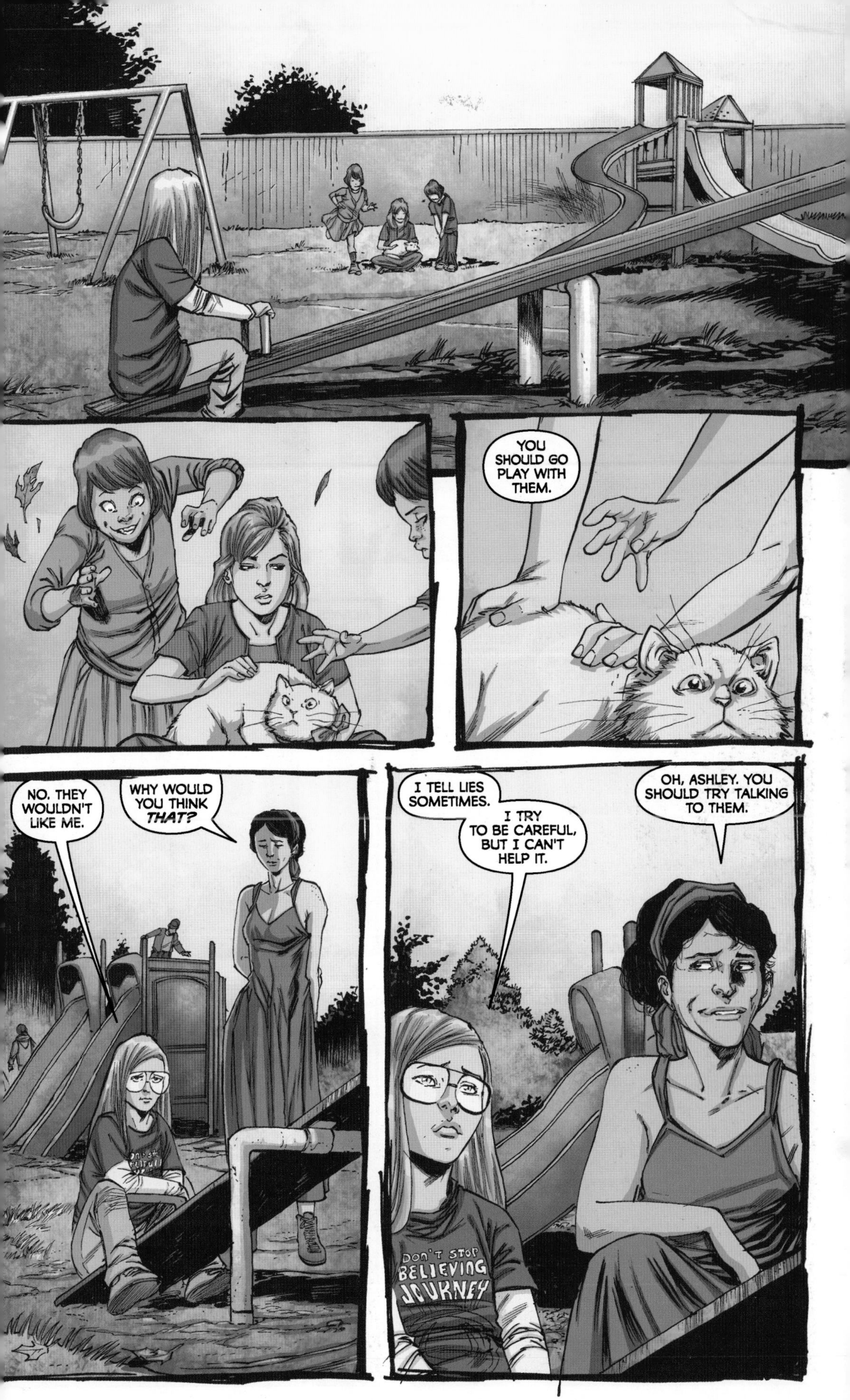
YOU SHOULD GO PLAY WITH THEM.
NO. THEY WOULDN'T LIKE ME.
WHY WOULD YOU THINK *THAT?*
I TELL LIES SOMETIMES.
I TRY TO BE CAREFUL, BUT I CAN'T HELP IT.
OH, ASHLEY. YOU SHOULD TRY TALKING TO THEM.
DON'T STOP BELIEVING JOURNEY

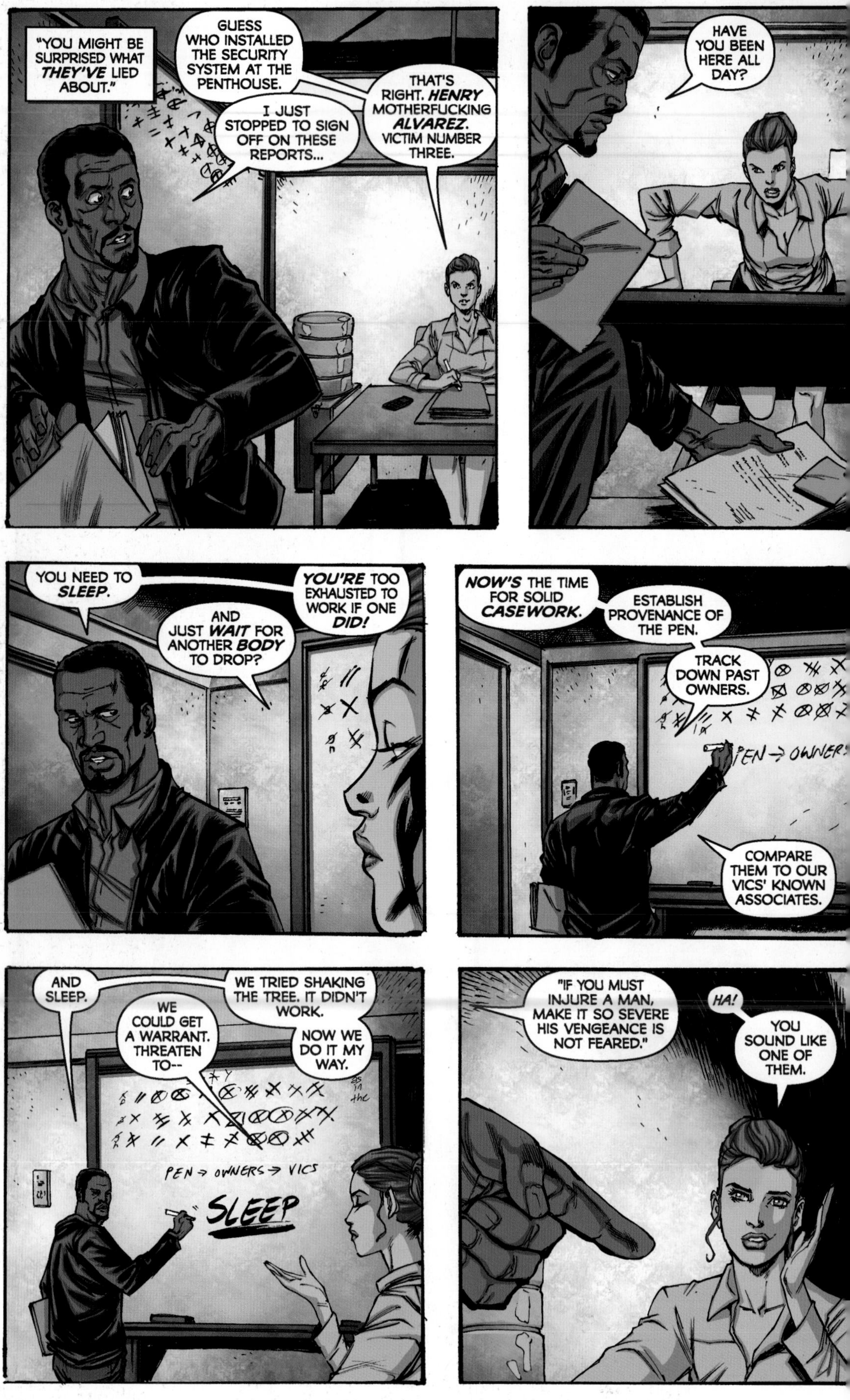

"YOU MIGHT BE SURPRISED WHAT *THEY'VE* LIED ABOUT."
GUESS WHO INSTALLED THE SECURITY SYSTEM AT THE PENTHOUSE.
I JUST STOPPED TO SIGN OFF ON THESE REPORTS...
THAT'S RIGHT. *HENRY* MOTHERFUCKING *ALVAREZ*. VICTIM NUMBER THREE.
HAVE YOU BEEN HERE ALL DAY?
YOU NEED TO *SLEEP*.
AND JUST *WAIT* FOR ANOTHER *BODY* TO DROP?
YOU'RE TOO EXHAUSTED TO WORK IF ONE *DID!*
NOW'S THE TIME FOR SOLID *CASEWORK*.
ESTABLISH PROVENANCE OF THE PEN.
TRACK DOWN PAST OWNERS.
PEN → OWNERS
COMPARE THEM TO OUR VICS' KNOWN ASSOCIATES.
AND SLEEP.
WE COULD GET A WARRANT. THREATEN TO--
WE TRIED SHAKING THE TREE. IT DIDN'T WORK.
NOW WE DO IT MY WAY.
PEN → OWNERS → VICS
SLEEP
"IF YOU MUST INJURE A MAN, MAKE IT SO SEVERE HIS VENGEANCE IS NOT FEARED."
HA!
YOU SOUND LIKE ONE OF THEM.

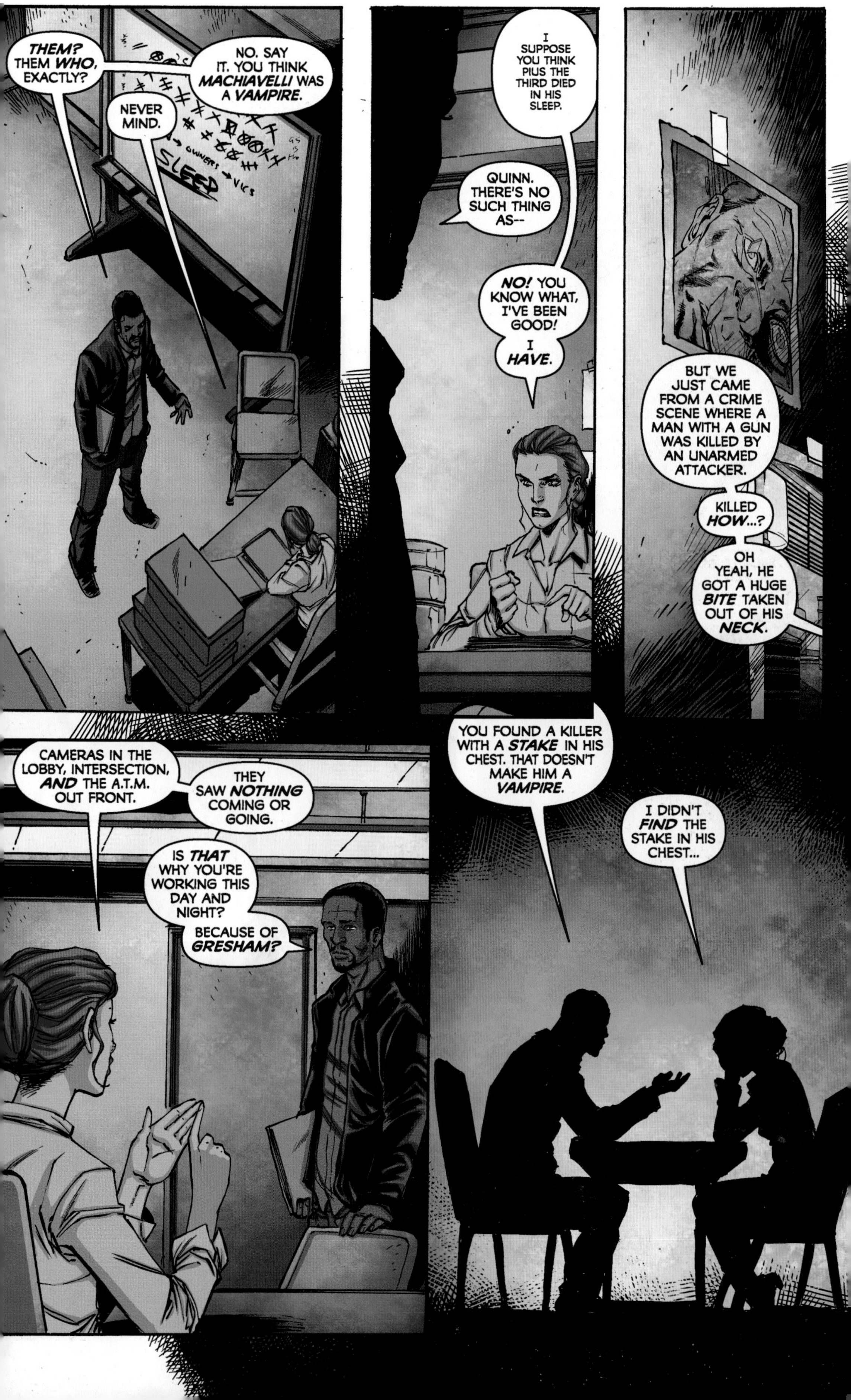
THEM? THEM WHO, EXACTLY?
NO. SAY IT. YOU THINK MACHIAVELLI WAS A VAMPIRE.
NEVER MIND.
SLEEP
I SUPPOSE YOU THINK PIUS THE THIRD DIED IN HIS SLEEP.
QUINN. THERE'S NO SUCH THING AS--
NO! YOU KNOW WHAT, I'VE BEEN GOOD!
I HAVE.
BUT WE JUST CAME FROM A CRIME SCENE WHERE A MAN WITH A GUN WAS KILLED BY AN UNARMED ATTACKER.
KILLED HOW...?
OH YEAH, HE GOT A HUGE BITE TAKEN OUT OF HIS NECK.
CAMERAS IN THE LOBBY, INTERSECTION, AND THE A.T.M. OUT FRONT.
THEY SAW NOTHING COMING OR GOING.
IS THAT WHY YOU'RE WORKING THIS DAY AND NIGHT?
BECAUSE OF GRESHAM?
YOU FOUND A KILLER WITH A STAKE IN HIS CHEST. THAT DOESN'T MAKE HIM A VAMPIRE.
I DIDN'T FIND THE STAKE IN HIS CHEST...

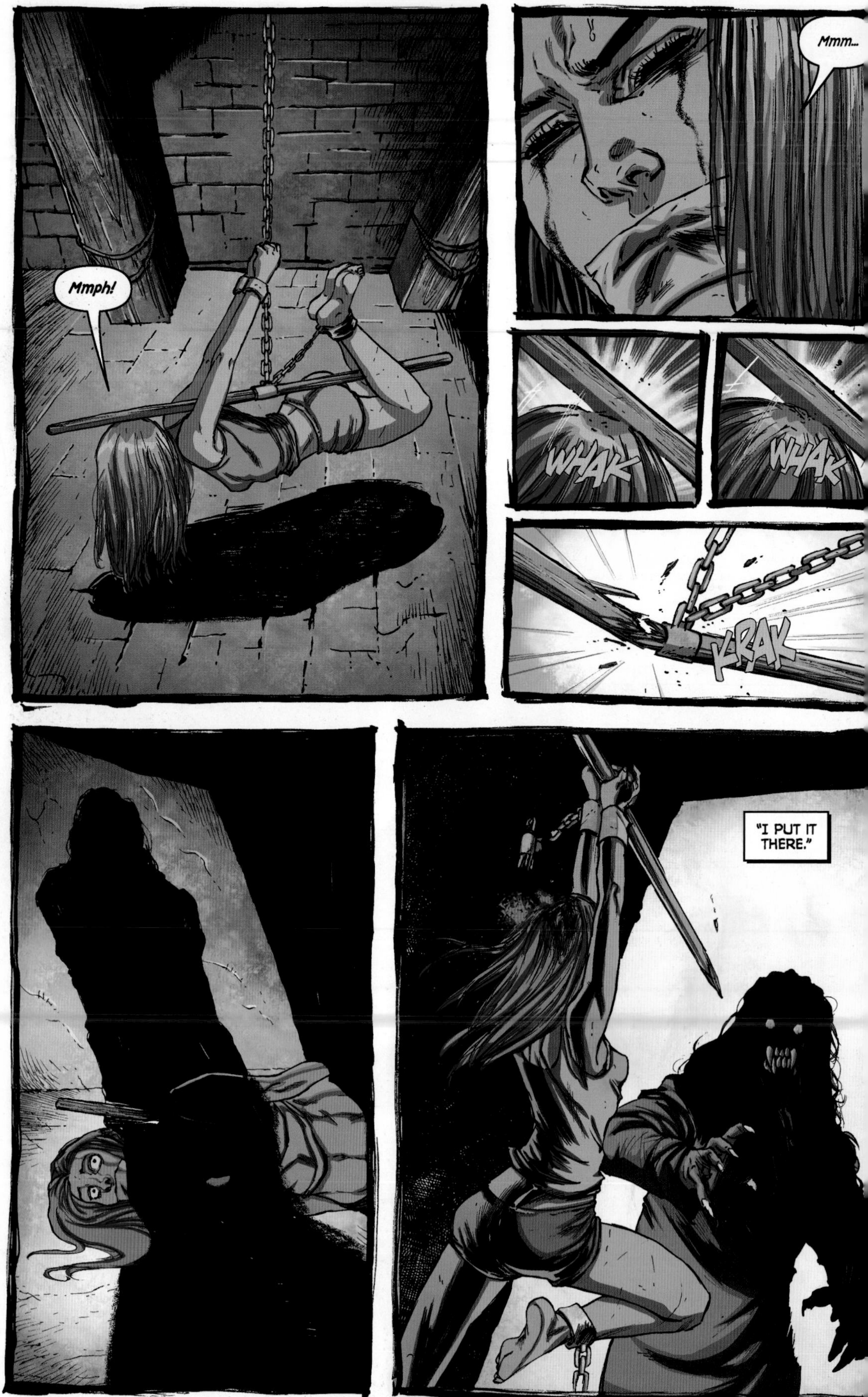

Mmph!
Mmm...
WHAK
WHAK
KRAK
"I PUT IT THERE."

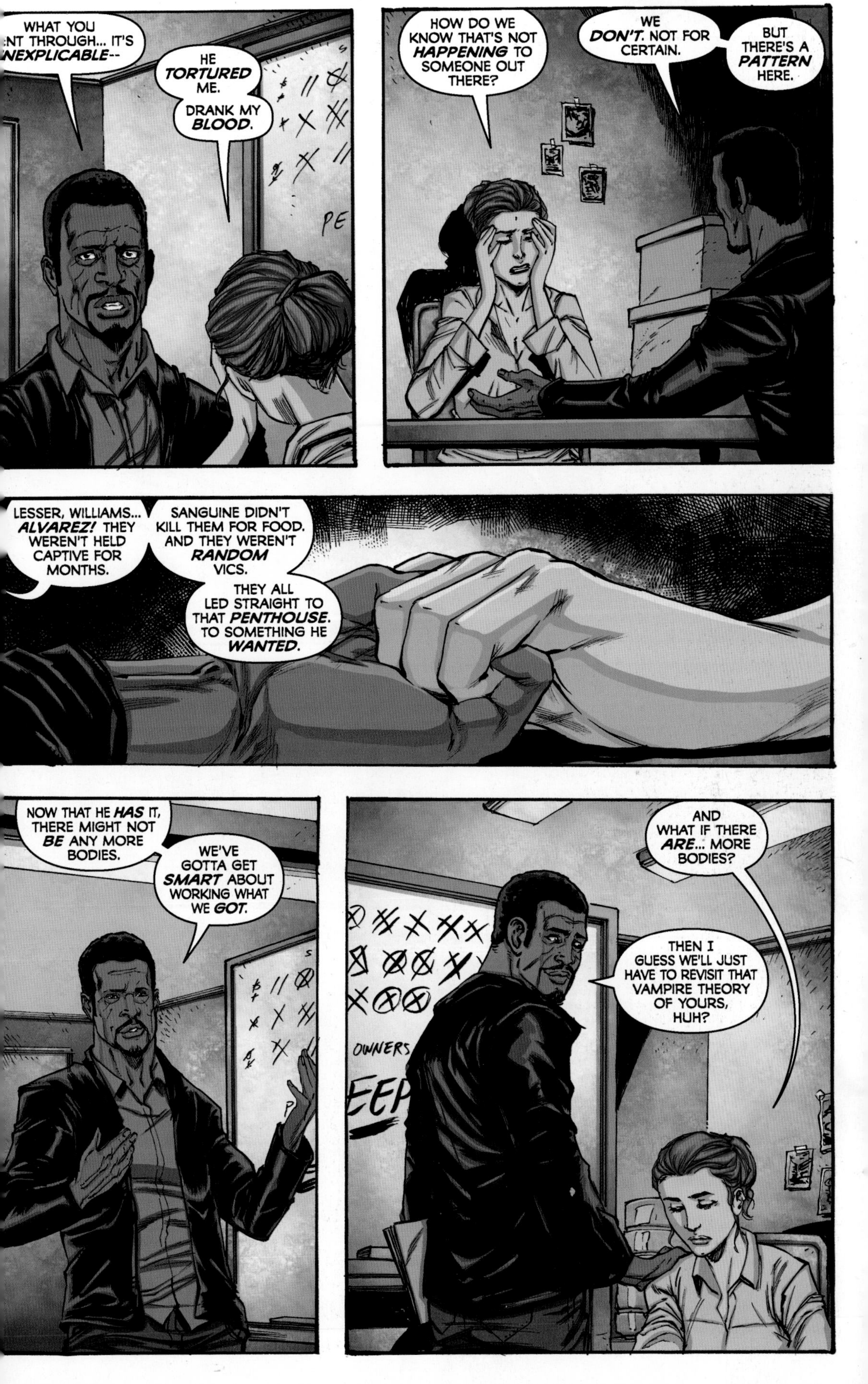
WHAT YOU
-NT THROUGH... IT'S
-NEXPLICABLE--
HE TORTURED ME.
DRANK MY BLOOD.
HOW DO WE KNOW THAT'S NOT HAPPENING TO SOMEONE OUT THERE?
WE DON'T. NOT FOR CERTAIN.
BUT THERE'S A PATTERN HERE.
LESSER, WILLIAMS... ALVAREZ! THEY WEREN'T HELD CAPTIVE FOR MONTHS.
SANGUINE DIDN'T KILL THEM FOR FOOD. AND THEY WEREN'T RANDOM VICS.
THEY ALL LED STRAIGHT TO THAT PENTHOUSE. TO SOMETHING HE WANTED.
NOW THAT HE HAS IT, THERE MIGHT NOT BE ANY MORE BODIES.
WE'VE GOTTA GET SMART ABOUT WORKING WHAT WE GOT.
AND WHAT IF THERE ARE... MORE BODIES?
THEN I GUESS WE'LL JUST HAVE TO REVISIT THAT VAMPIRE THEORY OF YOURS, HUH?
OWNERS

REMEMBER...

MY NAME IS SAUL ADAMS...

I AM A REMORSELESS PREDATOR, AN IMMORTAL HUNTER OF THE--

PLOP

JULIUS?

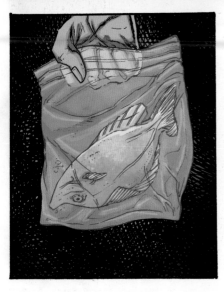

I DON'T KNOW THE VIRTUE OF A YELLOW TANG.

BUT I KNOW, ON OCCASION, YOU MADE ME HAPPY.

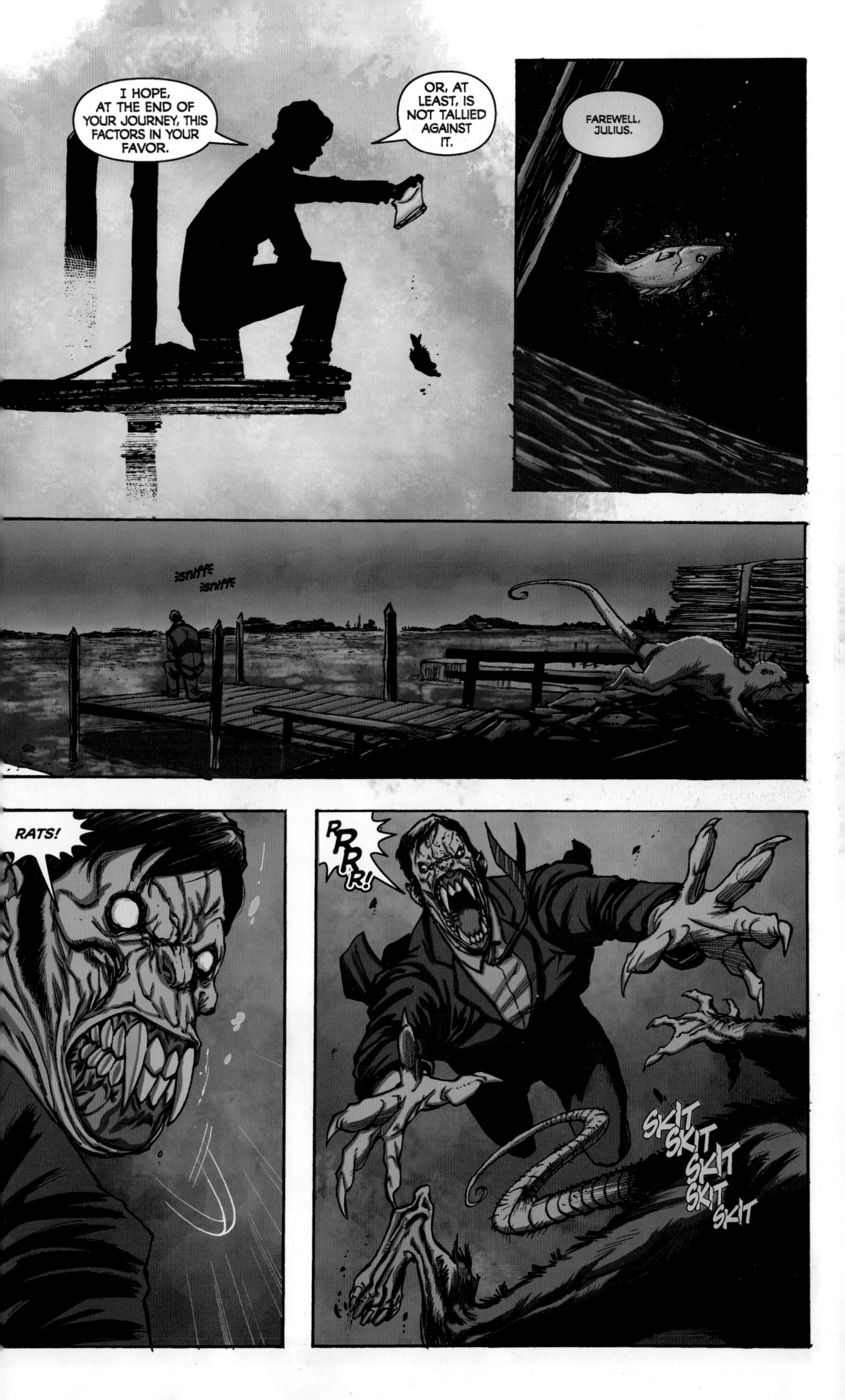
I HOPE, AT THE END OF YOUR JOURNEY, THIS FACTORS IN YOUR FAVOR.
OR, AT LEAST, IS NOT TALLIED AGAINST IT.
FAREWELL, JULIUS.
SNIFF
SNIFF
RATS!
RRRR!
SKIT SKIT SKIT SKIT SKIT

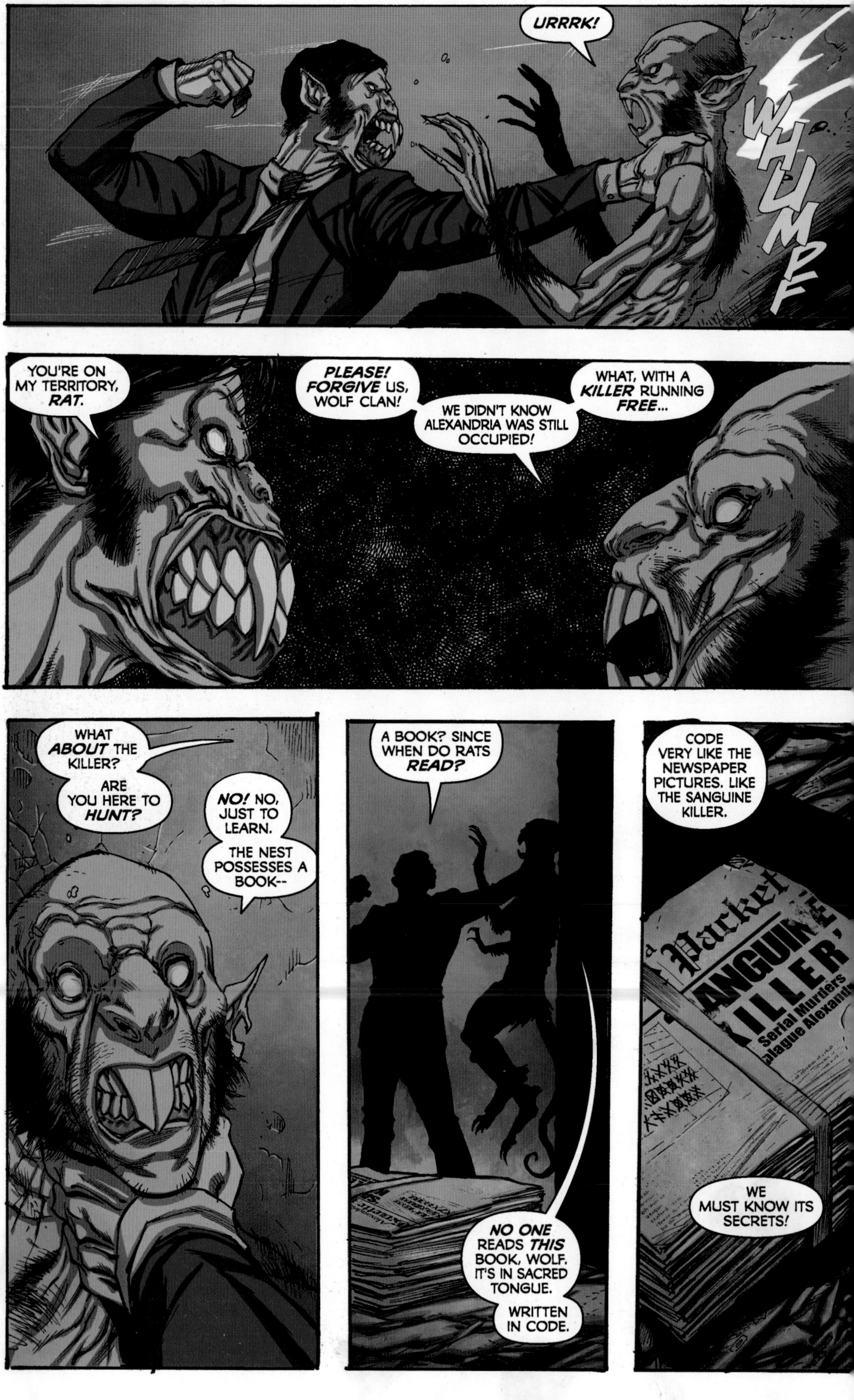
URRRK!
WHUMPF
YOU'RE ON MY TERRITORY, RAT.
PLEASE! FORGIVE US, WOLF CLAN!
WE DIDN'T KNOW ALEXANDRIA WAS STILL OCCUPIED!
WHAT, WITH A KILLER RUNNING FREE...
WHAT ABOUT THE KILLER?
ARE YOU HERE TO HUNT?
NO! NO, JUST TO LEARN.
THE NEST POSSESSES A BOOK--
A BOOK? SINCE WHEN DO RATS READ?
NO ONE READS THIS BOOK, WOLF. IT'S IN SACRED TONGUE.
WRITTEN IN CODE.
CODE VERY LIKE THE NEWSPAPER PICTURES. LIKE THE SANGUINE KILLER.
WE MUST KNOW ITS SECRETS!

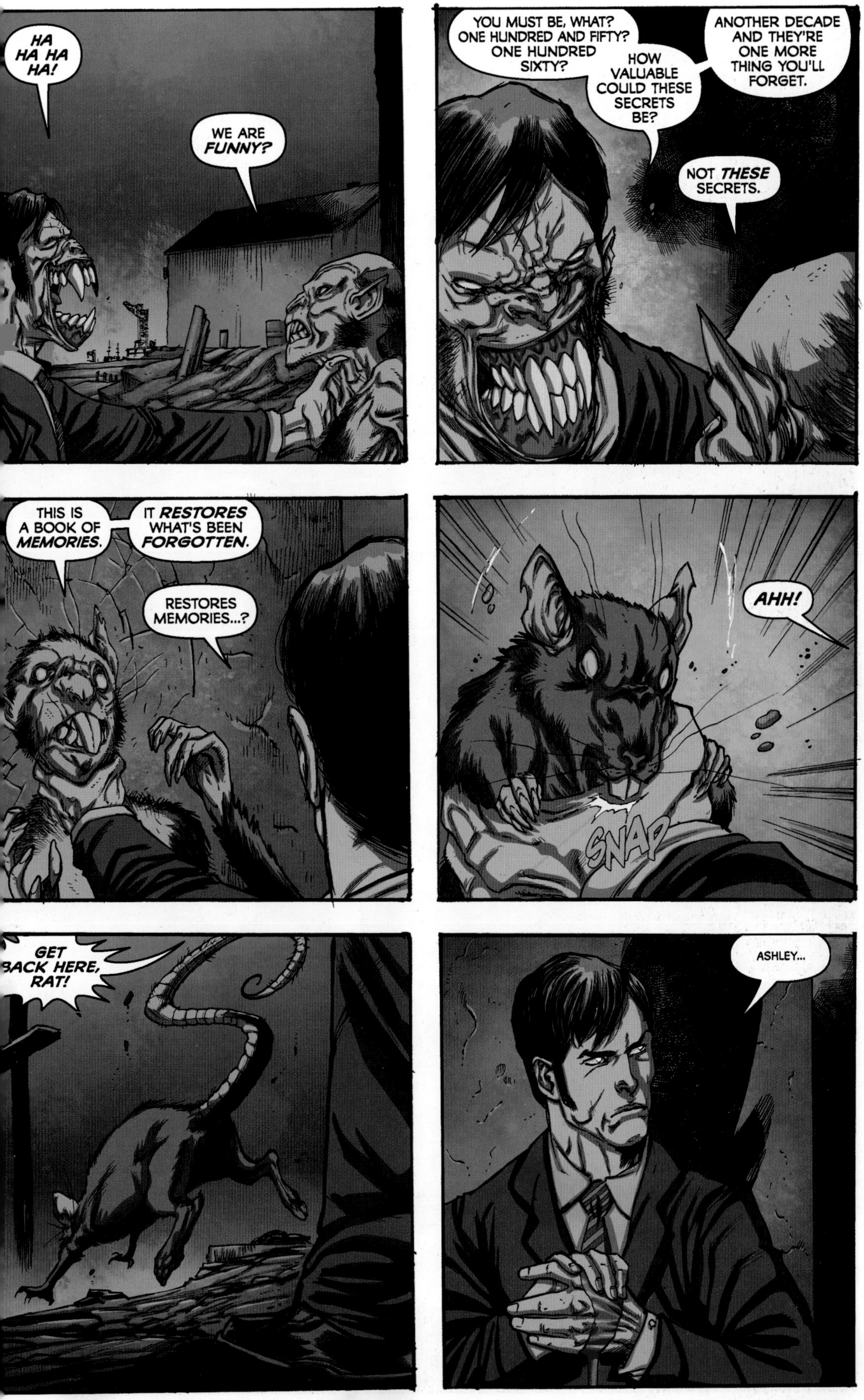
HA HA HA HA!
WE ARE FUNNY?
YOU MUST BE, WHAT? ONE HUNDRED AND FIFTY? ONE HUNDRED SIXTY?
HOW VALUABLE COULD THESE SECRETS BE?
ANOTHER DECADE AND THEY'RE ONE MORE THING YOU'LL FORGET.
NOT THESE SECRETS.
THIS IS A BOOK OF MEMORIES.
IT RESTORES WHAT'S BEEN FORGOTTEN.
RESTORES MEMORIES...?
AHH!
SNAP
GET BACK HERE, RAT!
ASHLEY...

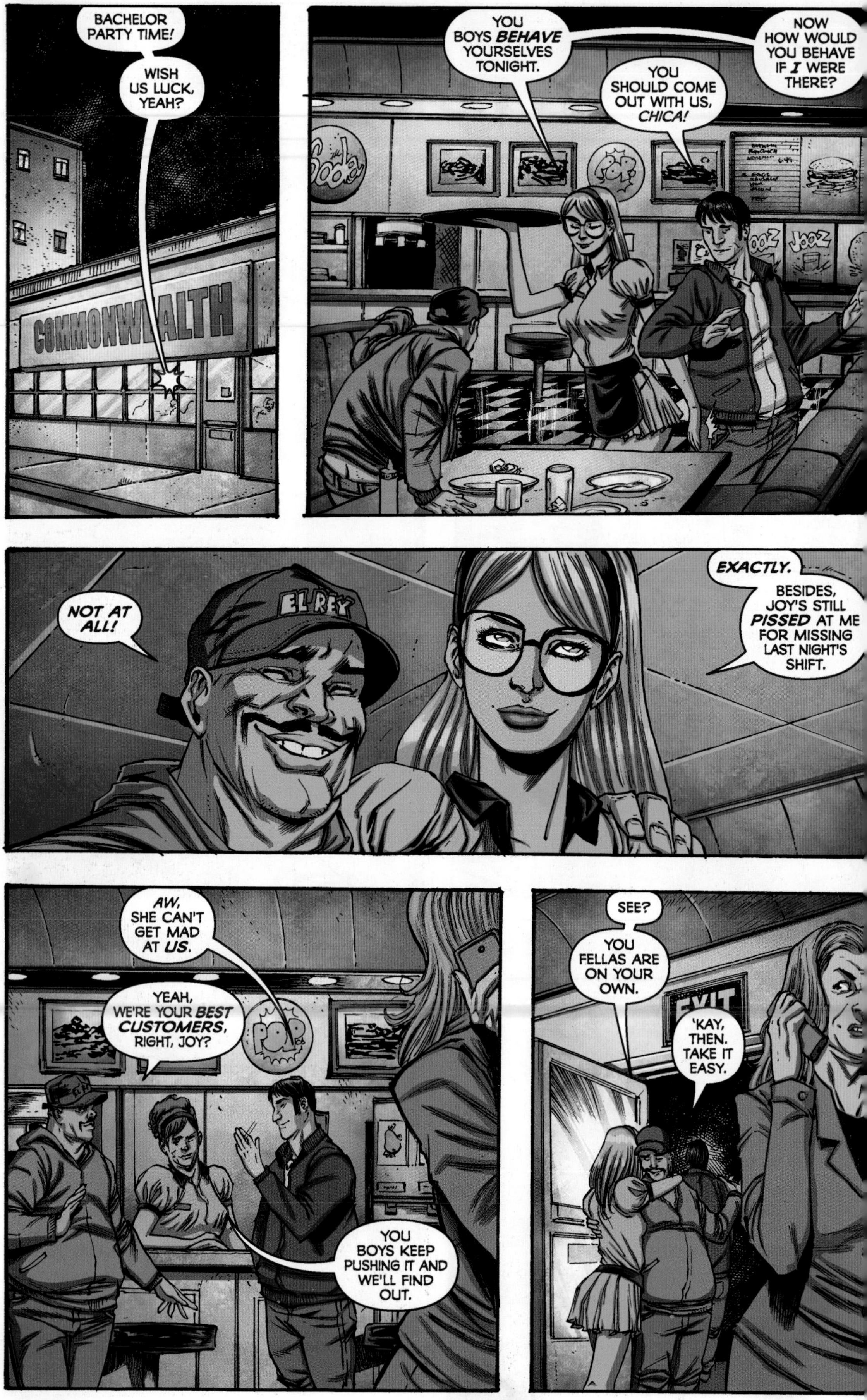

BACHELOR PARTY TIME!
WISH US LUCK, YEAH?
COMMONWEALTH
YOU BOYS BEHAVE YOURSELVES TONIGHT.
NOW HOW WOULD YOU BEHAVE IF I WERE THERE?
YOU SHOULD COME OUT WITH US, CHICA!
EL REY
NOT AT ALL!
EXACTLY.
BESIDES, JOY'S STILL PISSED AT ME FOR MISSING LAST NIGHT'S SHIFT.
AW, SHE CAN'T GET MAD AT US.
YEAH, WE'RE YOUR BEST CUSTOMERS, RIGHT, JOY?
YOU BOYS KEEP PUSHING IT AND WE'LL FIND OUT.
SEE?
YOU FELLAS ARE ON YOUR OWN.
EXIT
'KAY, THEN. TAKE IT EASY.

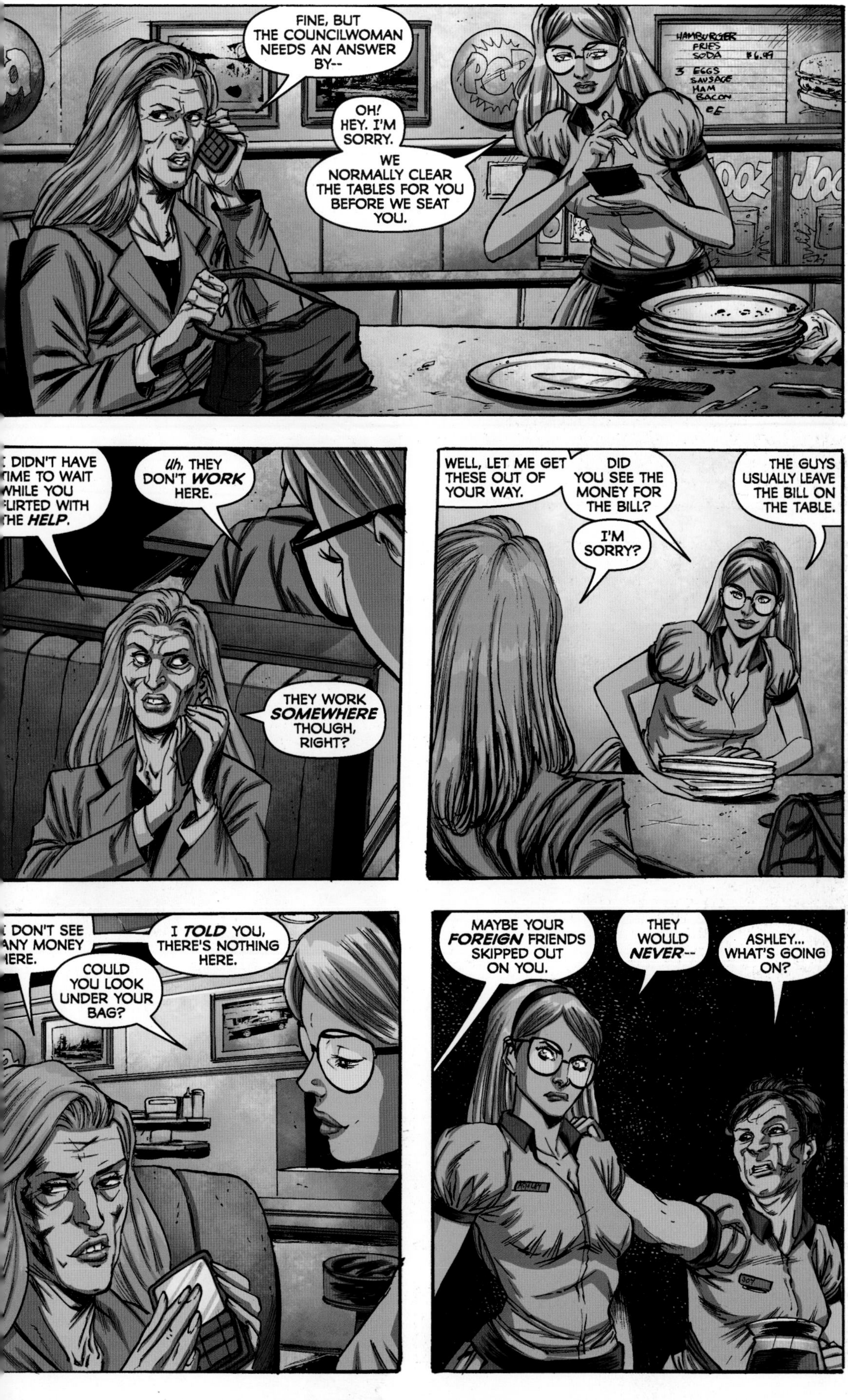
FINE, BUT THE COUNCILWOMAN NEEDS AN ANSWER BY--
OH! HEY. I'M SORRY.
WE NORMALLY CLEAR THE TABLES FOR YOU BEFORE WE SEAT YOU.
HAMBURGER FRIES SODA $6.99
3 EGGS SAUSAGE HAM BACON
POP
: DIDN'T HAVE IME TO WAIT VHILE YOU LIRTED WITH HE *HELP*.
Uh, THEY DON'T ***WORK*** HERE.
THEY WORK ***SOMEWHERE*** THOUGH, RIGHT?
WELL, LET ME GET THESE OUT OF YOUR WAY.
DID YOU SEE THE MONEY FOR THE BILL?
I'M SORRY?
THE GUYS USUALLY LEAVE THE BILL ON THE TABLE.
: DON'T SEE ANY MONEY HERE.
I ***TOLD*** YOU, THERE'S NOTHING HERE.
COULD YOU LOOK UNDER YOUR BAG?
MAYBE YOUR ***FOREIGN*** FRIENDS SKIPPED OUT ON YOU.
THEY WOULD ***NEVER***--
ASHLEY... WHAT'S GOING ON?

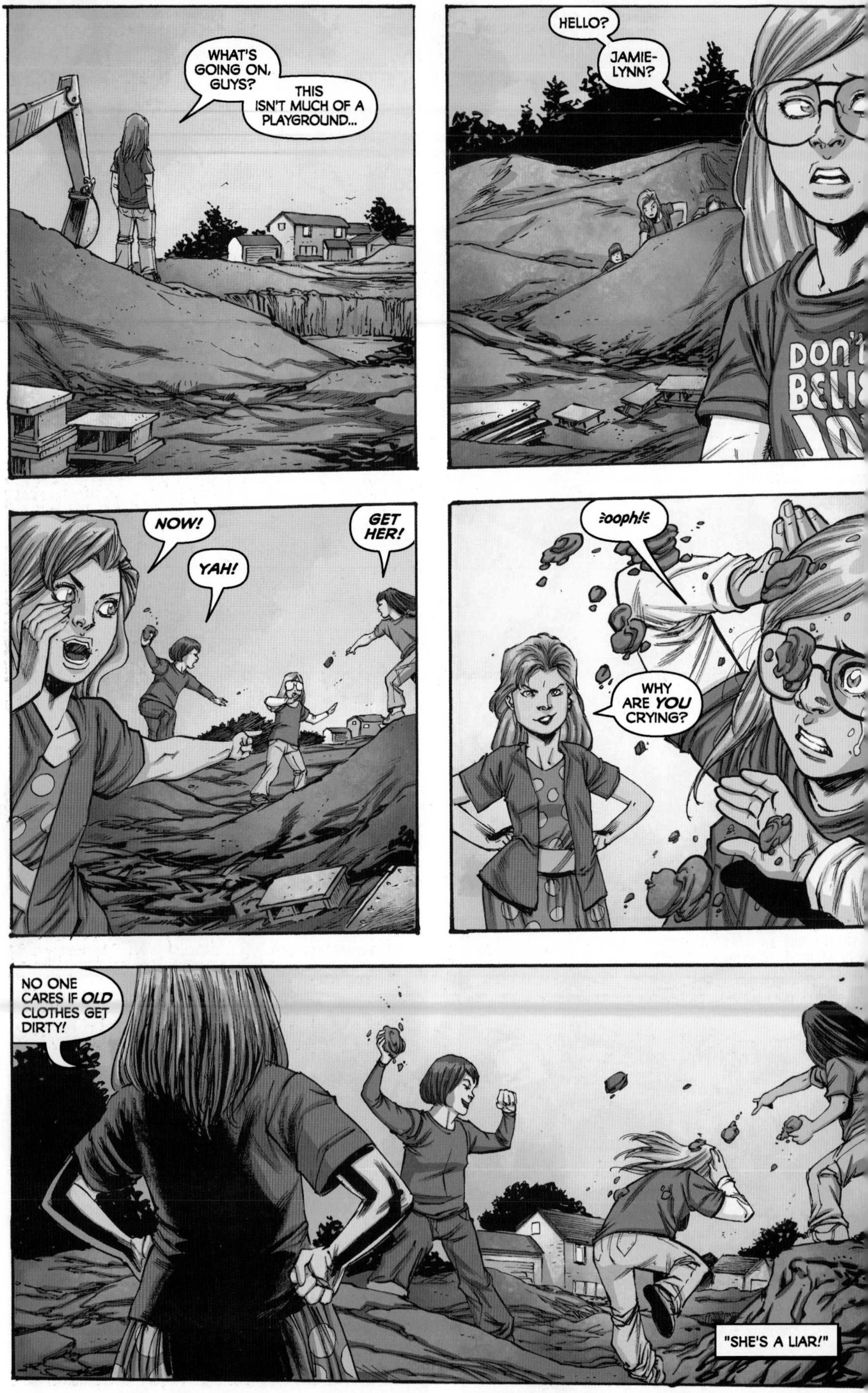
WHAT'S GOING ON, GUYS?
THIS ISN'T MUCH OF A PLAYGROUND...
HELLO?
JAMIE-LYNN?
NOW!
YAH!
GET HER!
ooph!
WHY ARE *YOU* CRYING?
NO ONE CARES IF *OLD* CLOTHES GET DIRTY!
"SHE'S A LIAR!"

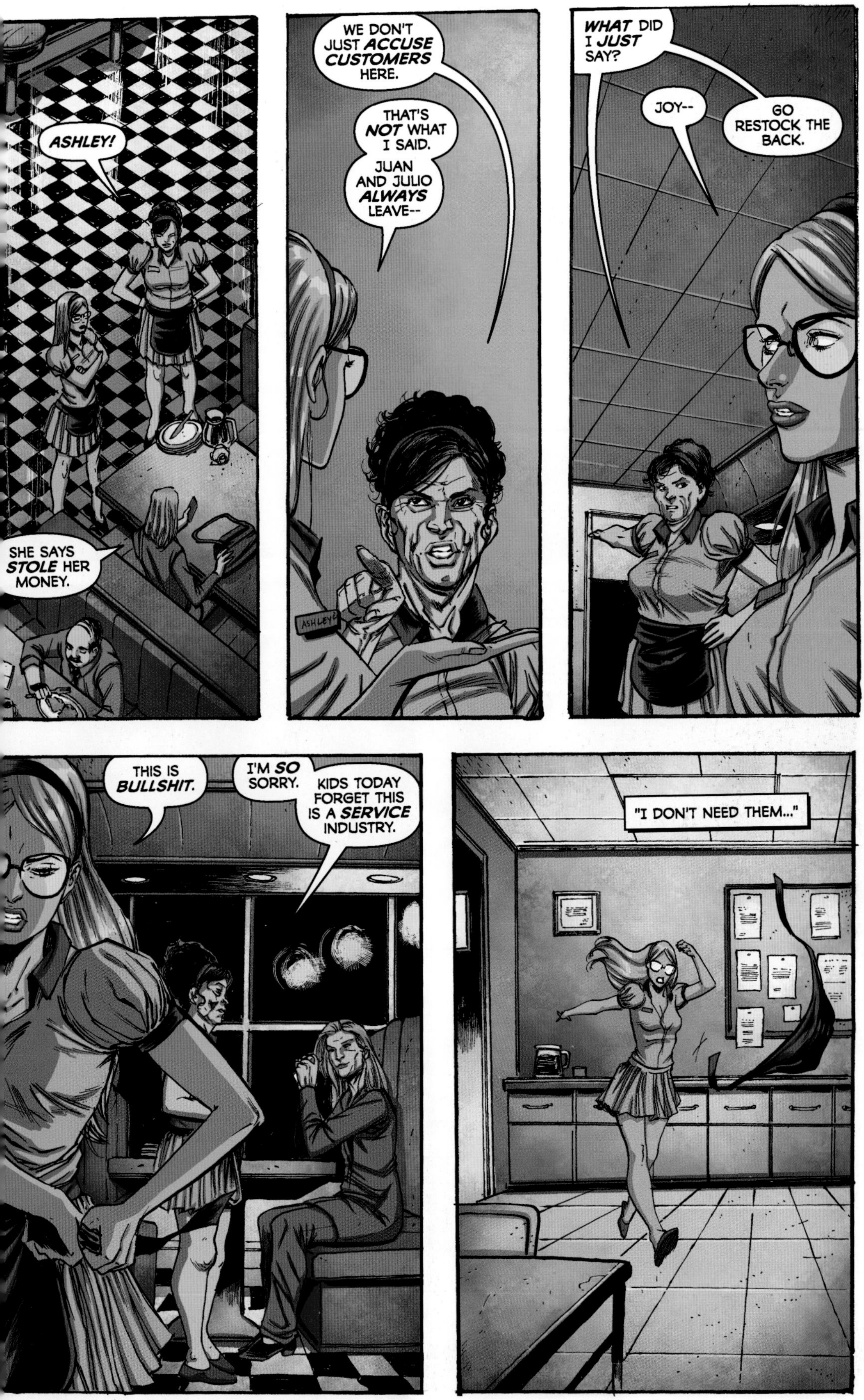
ASHLEY!
SHE SAYS STOLE HER MONEY.
WE DON'T JUST ACCUSE CUSTOMERS HERE.
THAT'S NOT WHAT I SAID.
JUAN AND JULIO ALWAYS LEAVE--
ASHLEY
WHAT DID I JUST SAY?
JOY--
GO RESTOCK THE BACK.
THIS IS BULLSHIT.
I'M SO SORRY.
KIDS TODAY FORGET THIS IS A SERVICE INDUSTRY.
"I DON'T NEED THEM..."

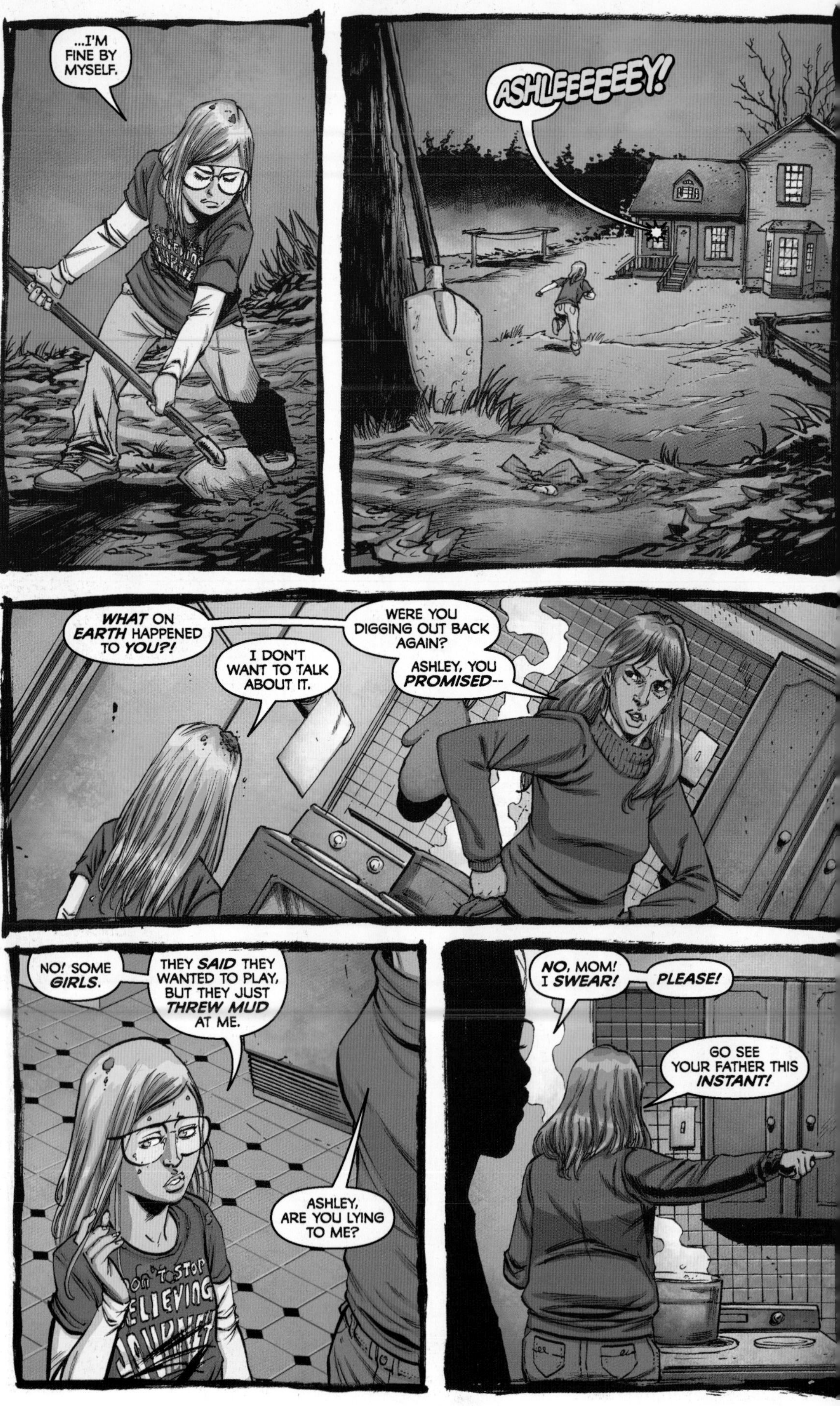
...I'M FINE BY MYSELF.
ASHLEEEEEEY!
WHAT ON EARTH HAPPENED TO YOU?!
I DON'T WANT TO TALK ABOUT IT.
WERE YOU DIGGING OUT BACK AGAIN?
ASHLEY, YOU PROMISED--
NO! SOME GIRLS.
THEY SAID THEY WANTED TO PLAY, BUT THEY JUST THREW MUD AT ME.
ASHLEY, ARE YOU LYING TO ME?
NO, MOM! I SWEAR!
PLEASE!
GO SEE YOUR FATHER THIS INSTANT!

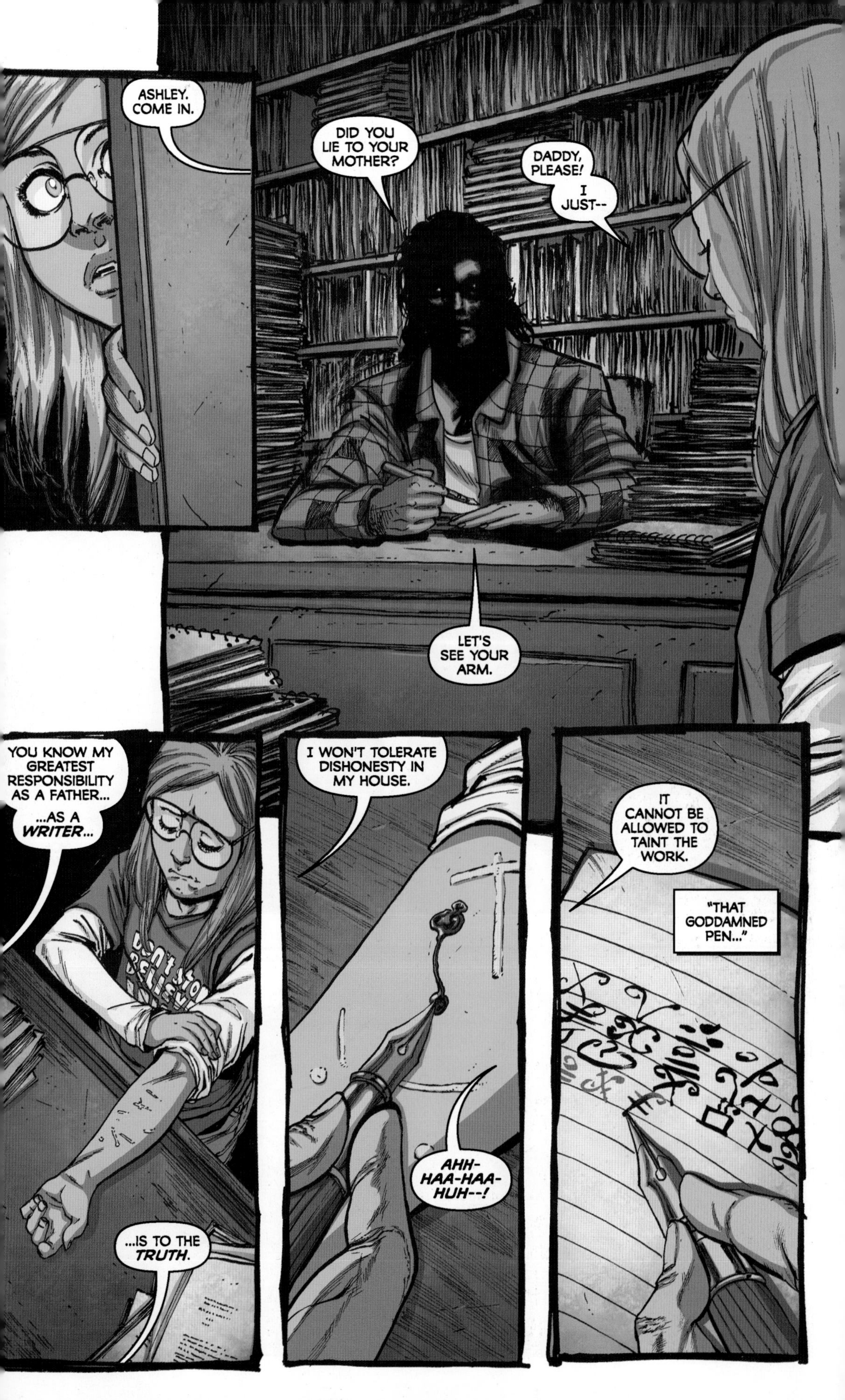

ASHLEY. COME IN.
DID YOU LIE TO YOUR MOTHER?
DADDY, PLEASE!
I JUST--
LET'S SEE YOUR ARM.
YOU KNOW MY GREATEST RESPONSIBILITY AS A FATHER...
...AS A *WRITER*...
...IS TO THE *TRUTH*.
I WON'T TOLERATE DISHONESTY IN MY HOUSE.
AHH-HAA-HAA-HUH--!
IT CANNOT BE ALLOWED TO TAINT THE WORK.
"THAT GODDAMNED PEN..."

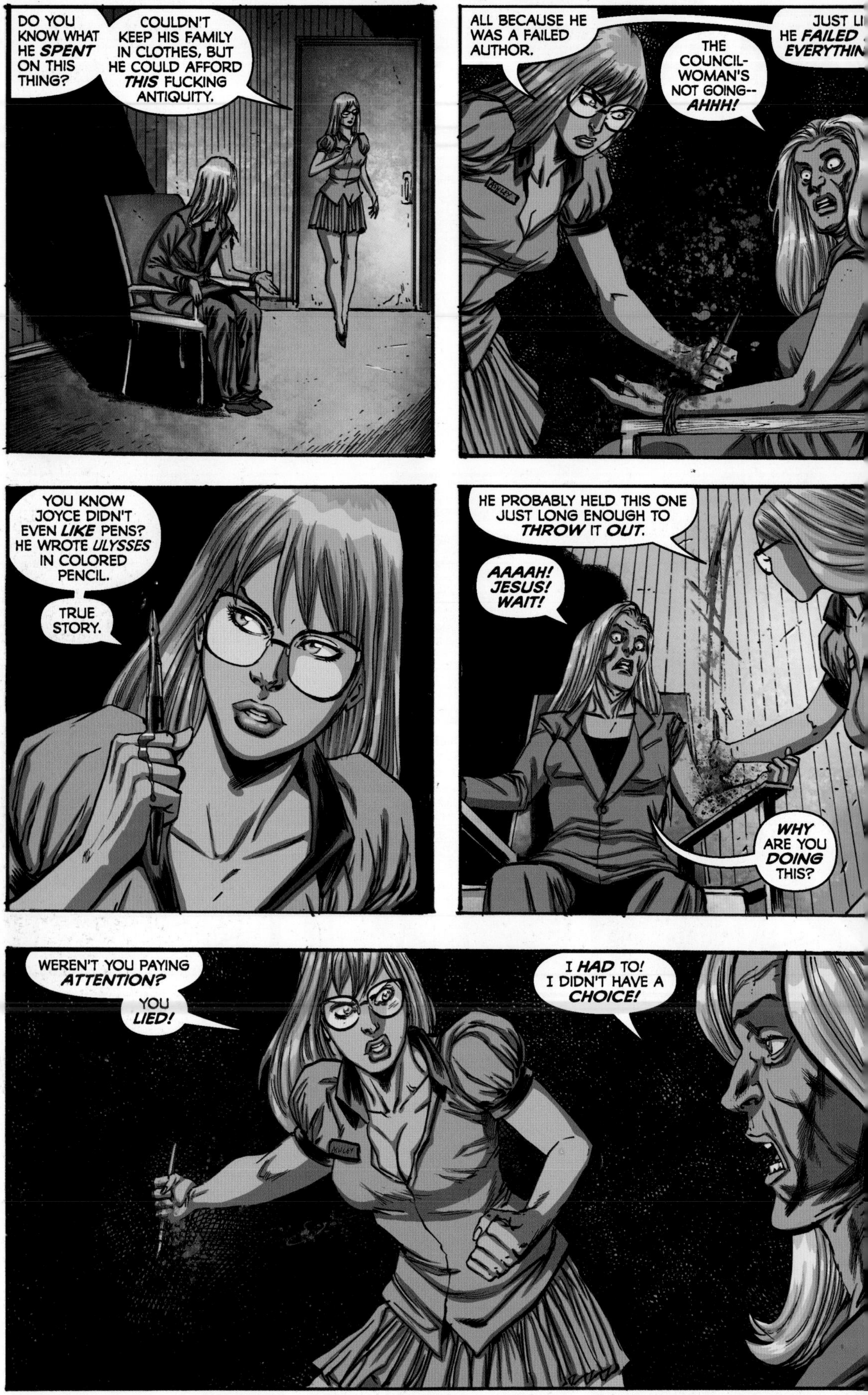
DO YOU KNOW WHAT HE *SPENT* ON THIS THING?
COULDN'T KEEP HIS FAMILY IN CLOTHES, BUT HE COULD AFFORD *THIS* FUCKING ANTIQUITY.
ALL BECAUSE HE WAS A FAILED AUTHOR.
JUST LI HE *FAILED* *EVERYTHIN*
THE COUNCIL-WOMAN'S NOT GOING-- *AHHH!*
YOU KNOW JOYCE DIDN'T EVEN *LIKE* PENS? HE WROTE *ULYSSES* IN COLORED PENCIL.
TRUE STORY.
HE PROBABLY HELD THIS ONE JUST LONG ENOUGH TO *THROW* IT *OUT*.
AAAAH! JESUS! WAIT!
WHY ARE YOU *DOING* THIS?
WEREN'T YOU PAYING *ATTENTION?*
YOU *LIED!*
I *HAD* TO! I DIDN'T HAVE A *CHOICE!*

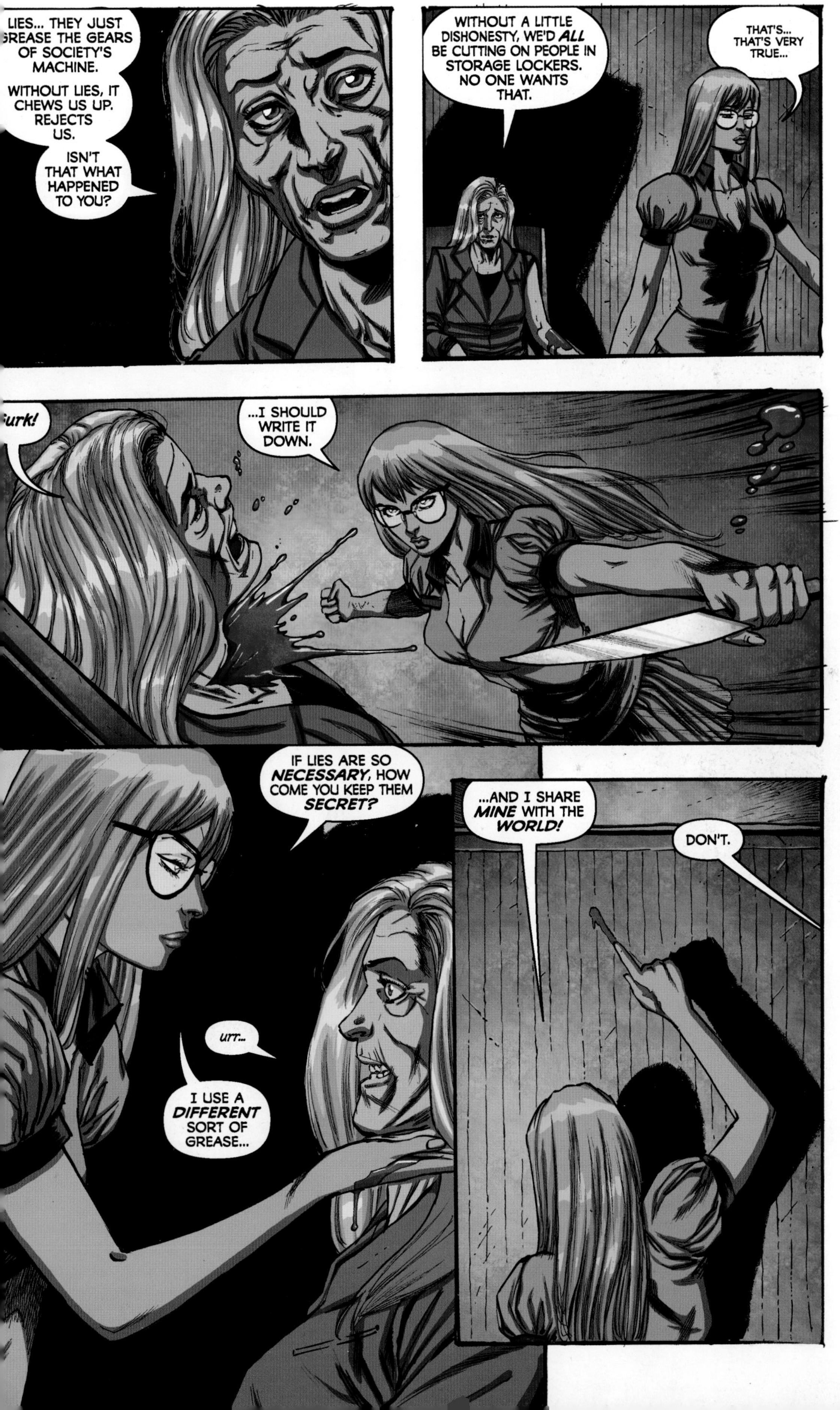
LIES... THEY JUST GREASE THE GEARS OF SOCIETY'S MACHINE.
WITHOUT LIES, IT CHEWS US UP. REJECTS US.
ISN'T THAT WHAT HAPPENED TO YOU?
WITHOUT A LITTLE DISHONESTY, WE'D ALL BE CUTTING ON PEOPLE IN STORAGE LOCKERS. NO ONE WANTS THAT.
THAT'S... THAT'S VERY TRUE...
urk!
...I SHOULD WRITE IT DOWN.
IF LIES ARE SO NECESSARY, HOW COME YOU KEEP THEM SECRET?
urr...
I USE A DIFFERENT SORT OF GREASE...
...AND I SHARE MINE WITH THE WORLD!
DON'T.

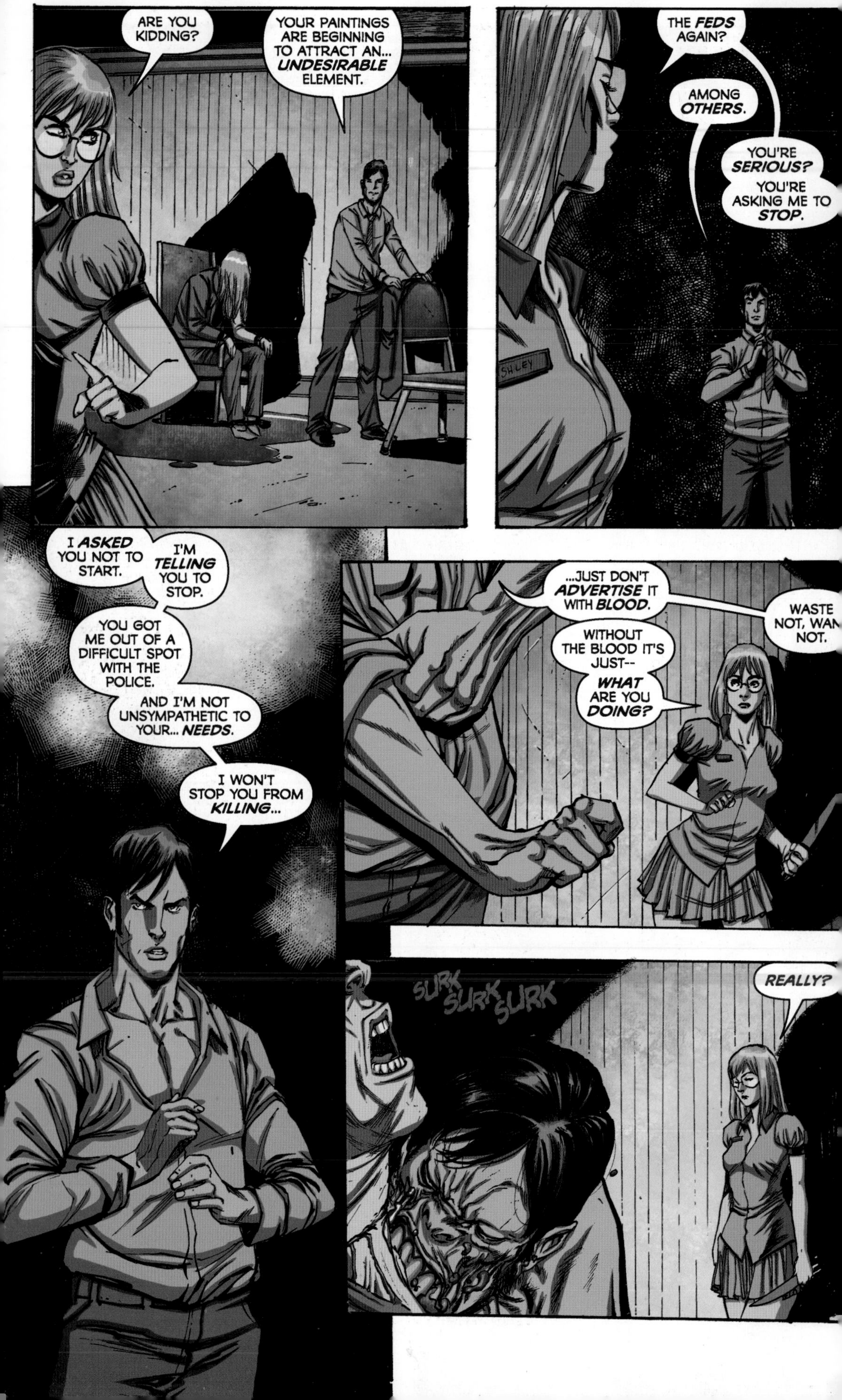
ARE YOU KIDDING?
YOUR PAINTINGS ARE BEGINNING TO ATTRACT AN... UNDESIRABLE ELEMENT.
THE FEDS AGAIN?
AMONG OTHERS.
YOU'RE SERIOUS?
YOU'RE ASKING ME TO STOP.
I ASKED YOU NOT TO START.
I'M TELLING YOU TO STOP.
YOU GOT ME OUT OF A DIFFICULT SPOT WITH THE POLICE.
AND I'M NOT UNSYMPATHETIC TO YOUR... NEEDS.
I WON'T STOP YOU FROM KILLING...
...JUST DON'T ADVERTISE IT WITH BLOOD.
WASTE NOT, WAN NOT.
WITHOUT THE BLOOD IT'S JUST--
WHAT ARE YOU DOING?
SURK SURK SURK
REALLY?

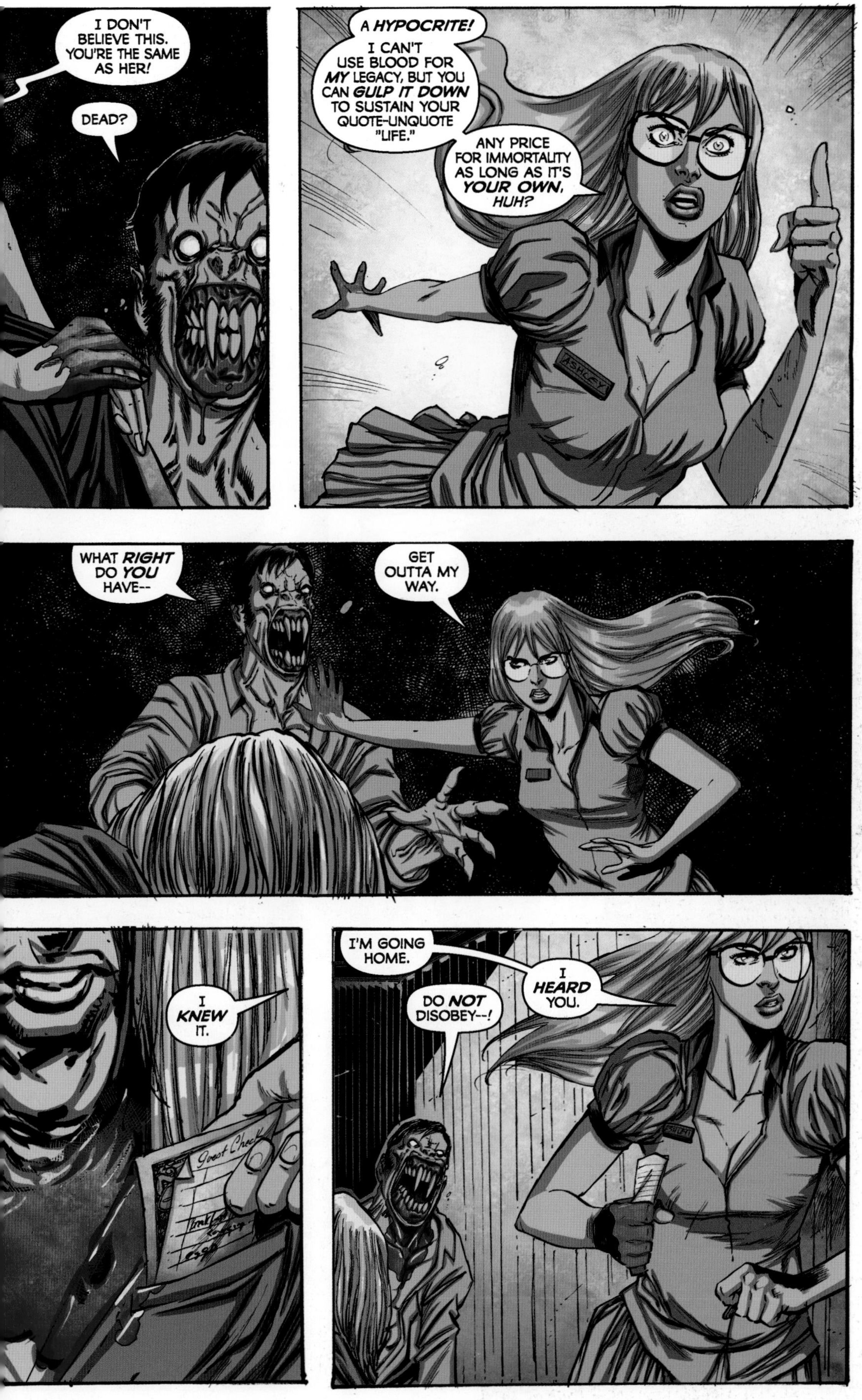

I DON'T BELIEVE THIS. YOU'RE THE SAME AS HER!
DEAD?
A HYPOCRITE!
I CAN'T USE BLOOD FOR MY LEGACY, BUT YOU CAN GULP IT DOWN TO SUSTAIN YOUR QUOTE-UNQUOTE "LIFE."
ANY PRICE FOR IMMORTALITY AS LONG AS IT'S YOUR OWN, HUH?
ASHLEY
WHAT RIGHT DO YOU HAVE--
GET OUTTA MY WAY.
I KNEW IT.
Guest Check
I'M GOING HOME.
DO NOT DISOBEY--!
I HEARD YOU.

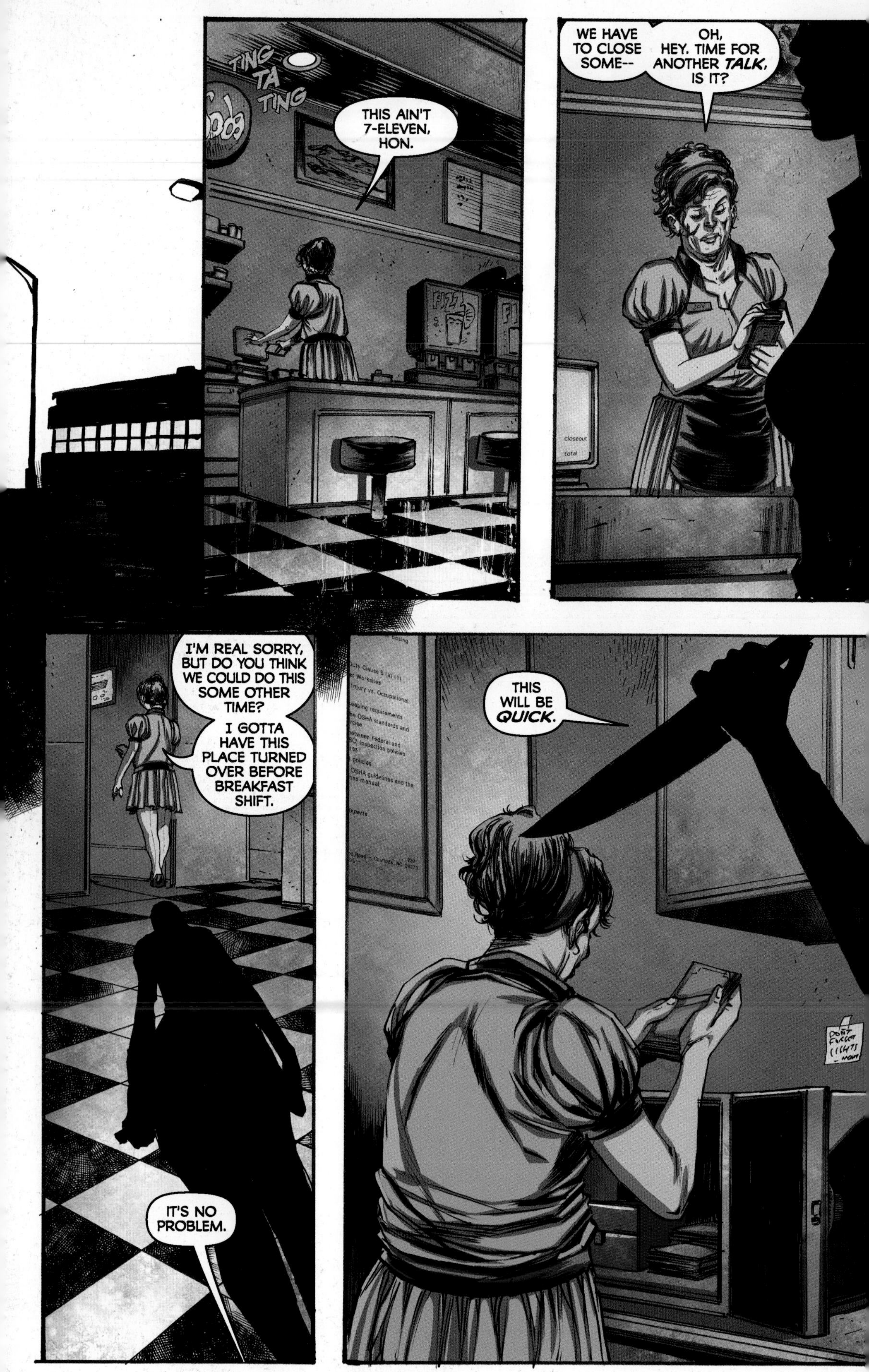
TING
TA
TING
THIS AIN'T 7-ELEVEN, HON.
WE HAVE TO CLOSE SOME--
OH, HEY. TIME FOR ANOTHER *TALK*, IS IT?
I'M REAL SORRY, BUT DO YOU THINK WE COULD DO THIS SOME OTHER TIME?
I GOTTA HAVE THIS PLACE TURNED OVER BEFORE BREAKFAST SHIFT.
IT'S NO PROBLEM.
THIS WILL BE *QUICK*.

CHAPTER FOUR
BASKERVILLE

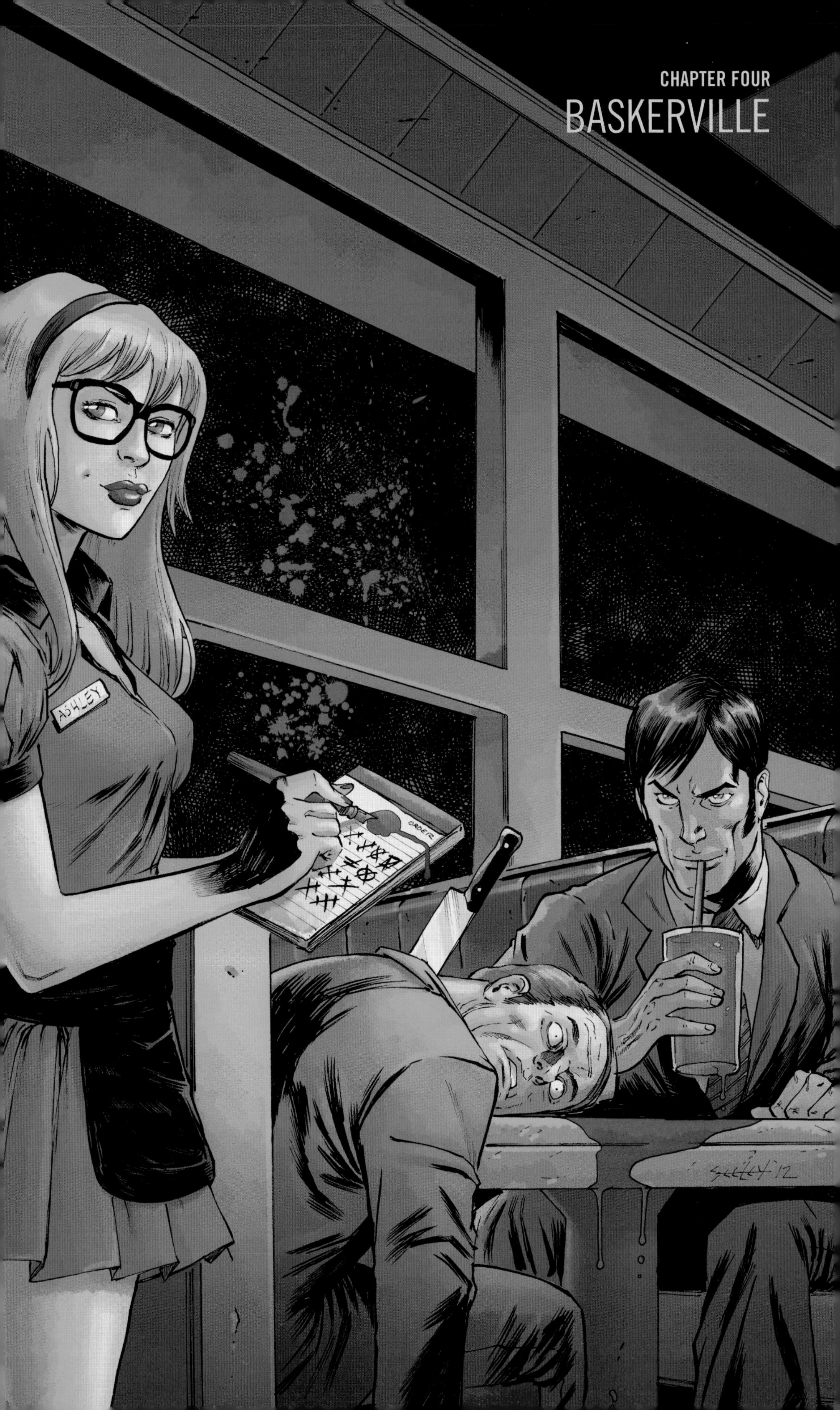
ASHLEY
ORDER
SEELEY '12

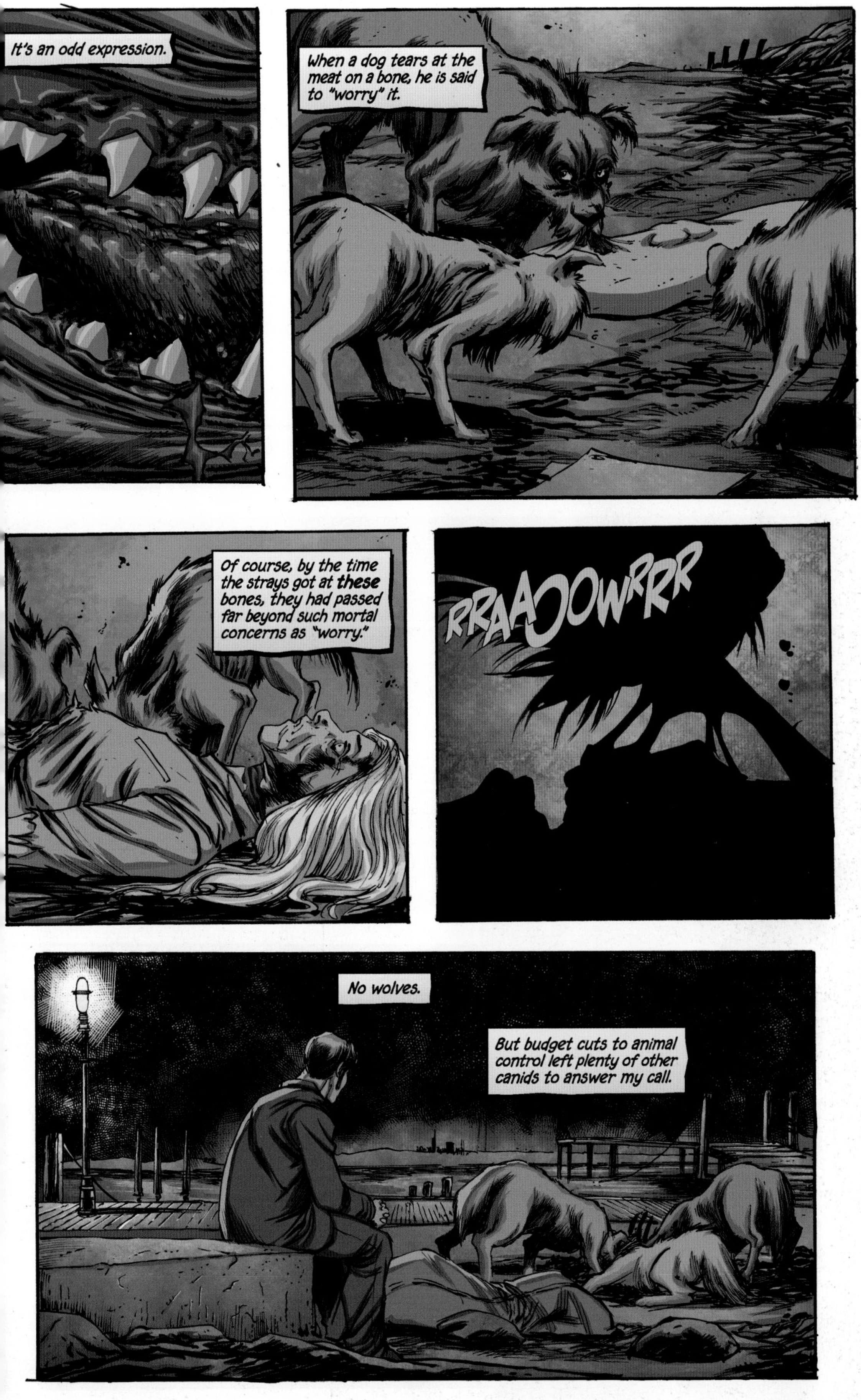
It's an odd expression.
When a dog tears at the meat on a bone, he is said to "worry" it.
Of course, by the time the strays got at **these** bones, they had passed far beyond such mortal concerns as "worry."
RRAAOOWRRR
No wolves.
But budget cuts to animal control left plenty of other canids to answer my call.

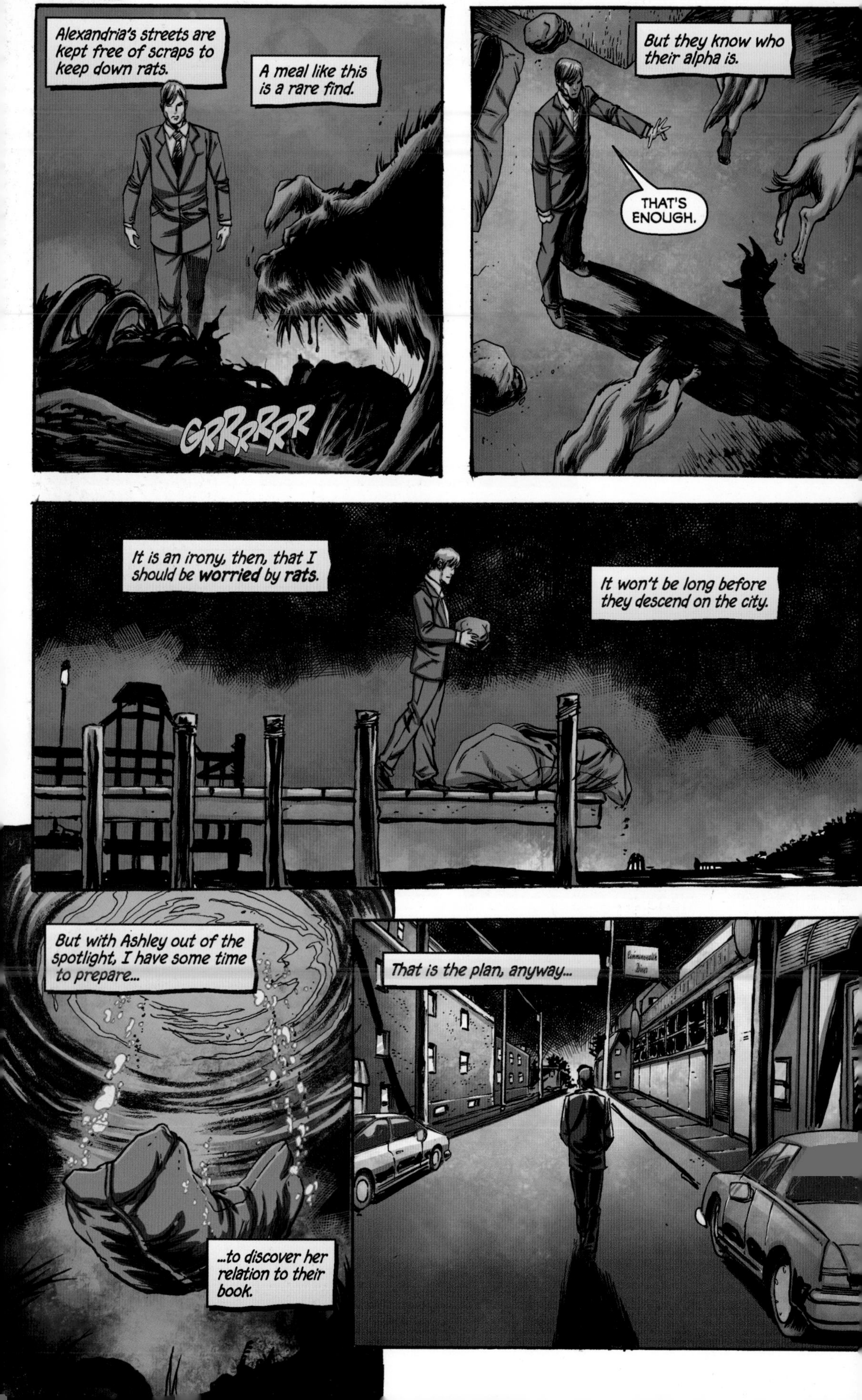
Alexandria's streets are kept free of scraps to keep down rats.
A meal like this is a rare find.
GRRRRRR
But they know who their alpha is.
THAT'S ENOUGH.
It is an irony, then, that I should be worried by rats.
It won't be long before they descend on the city.
But with Ashley out of the spotlight, I have some time to prepare...
...to discover her relation to their book.
That is the plan, anyway...

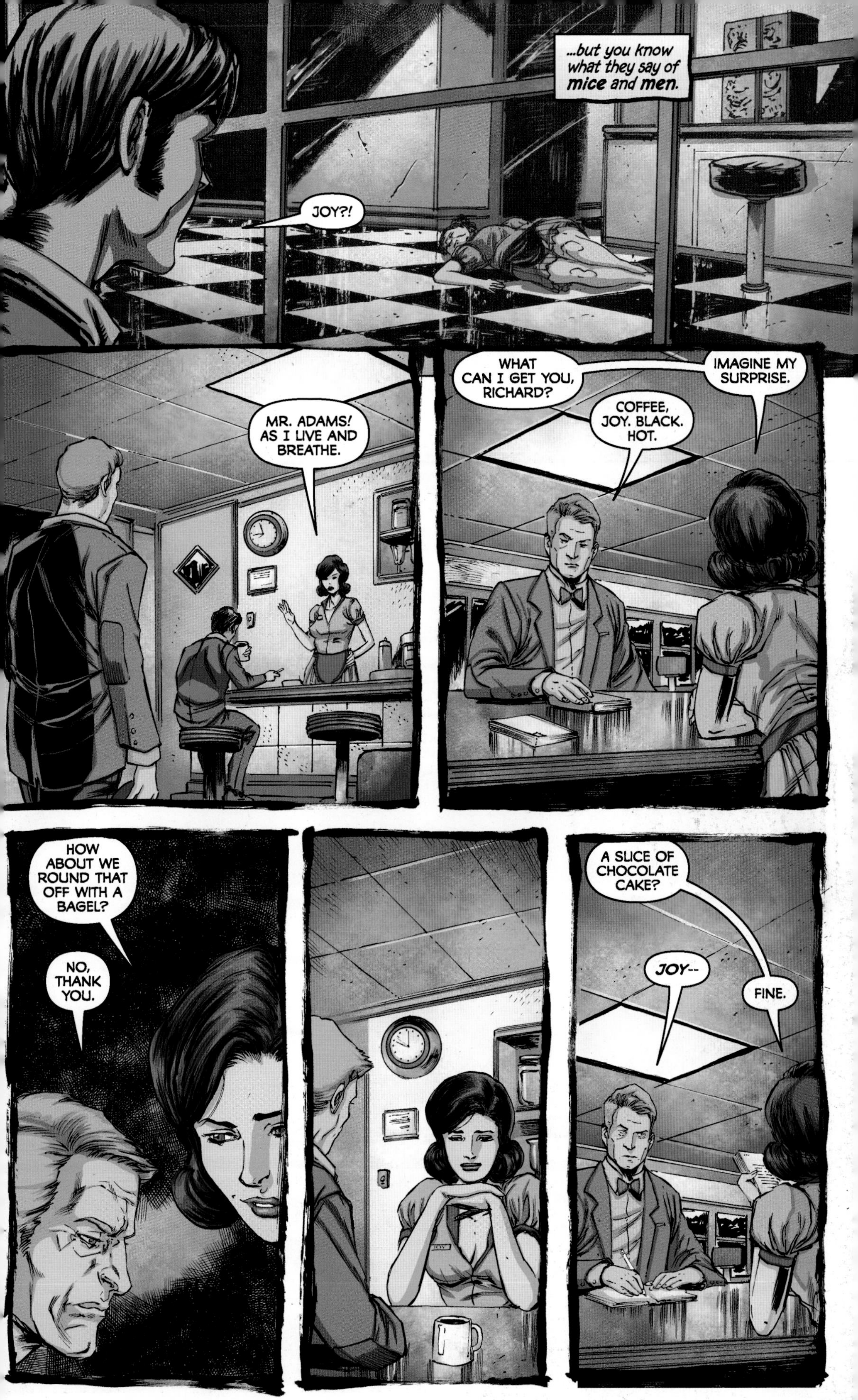
...but you know what they say of *mice* and *men*.
JOY?!
MR. ADAMS! AS I LIVE AND BREATHE.
WHAT CAN I GET YOU, RICHARD?
IMAGINE MY SURPRISE.
COFFEE, JOY. BLACK. HOT.
HOW ABOUT WE ROUND THAT OFF WITH A BAGEL?
NO, THANK YOU.
A SLICE OF CHOCOLATE CAKE?
JOY--
FINE.

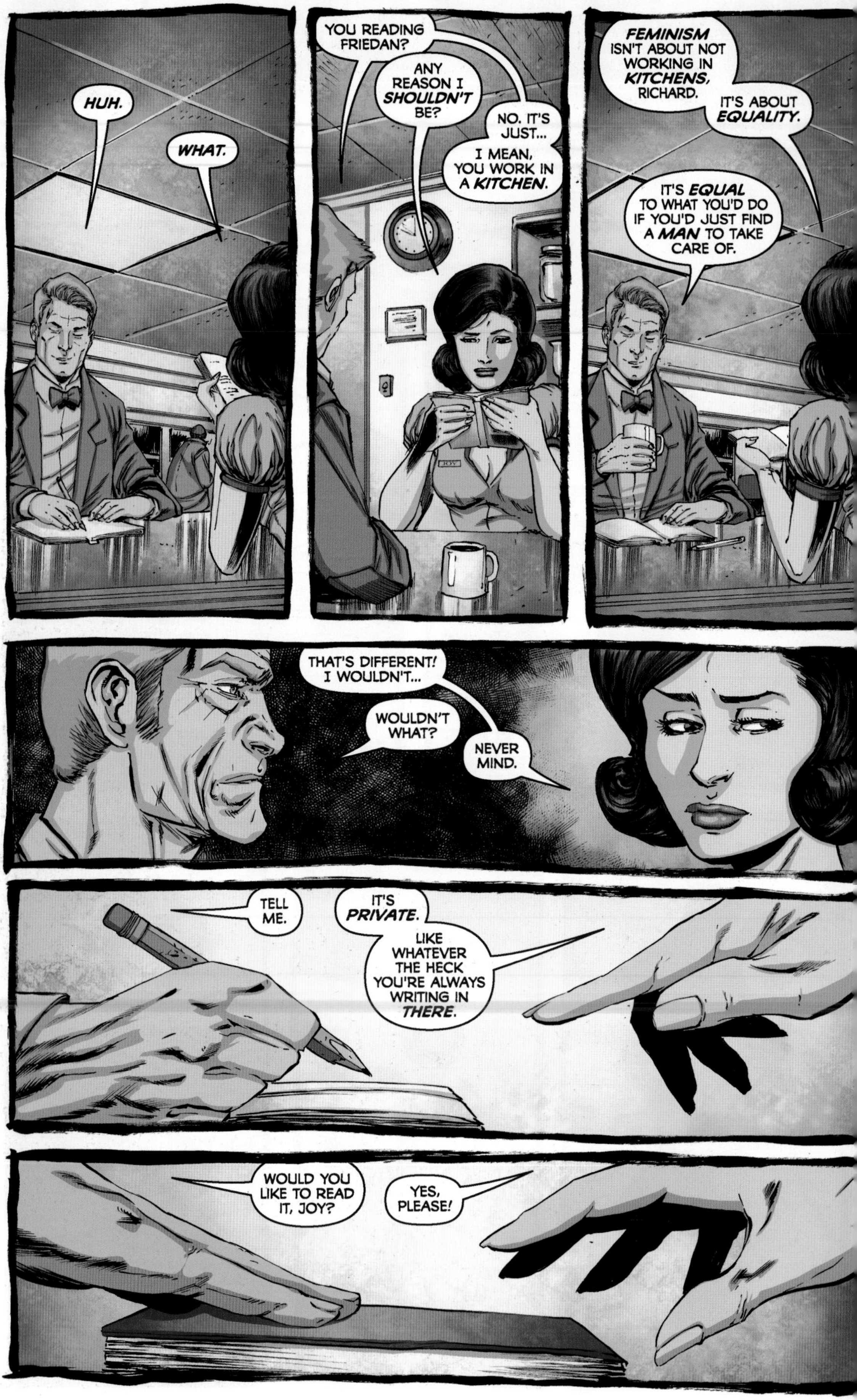
HUH.
WHAT.
YOU READING FRIEDAN?
ANY REASON I *SHOULDN'T* BE?
NO. IT'S JUST...
I MEAN, YOU WORK IN A *KITCHEN*.
FEMINISM ISN'T ABOUT NOT WORKING IN *KITCHENS,* RICHARD.
IT'S ABOUT *EQUALITY*.
IT'S *EQUAL* TO WHAT YOU'D DO IF YOU'D JUST FIND A *MAN* TO TAKE CARE OF.
THAT'S DIFFERENT! I WOULDN'T...
WOULDN'T WHAT?
NEVER MIND.
TELL ME.
IT'S *PRIVATE*.
LIKE WHATEVER THE HECK YOU'RE ALWAYS WRITING IN *THERE*.
WOULD YOU LIKE TO READ IT, JOY?
YES, PLEASE!

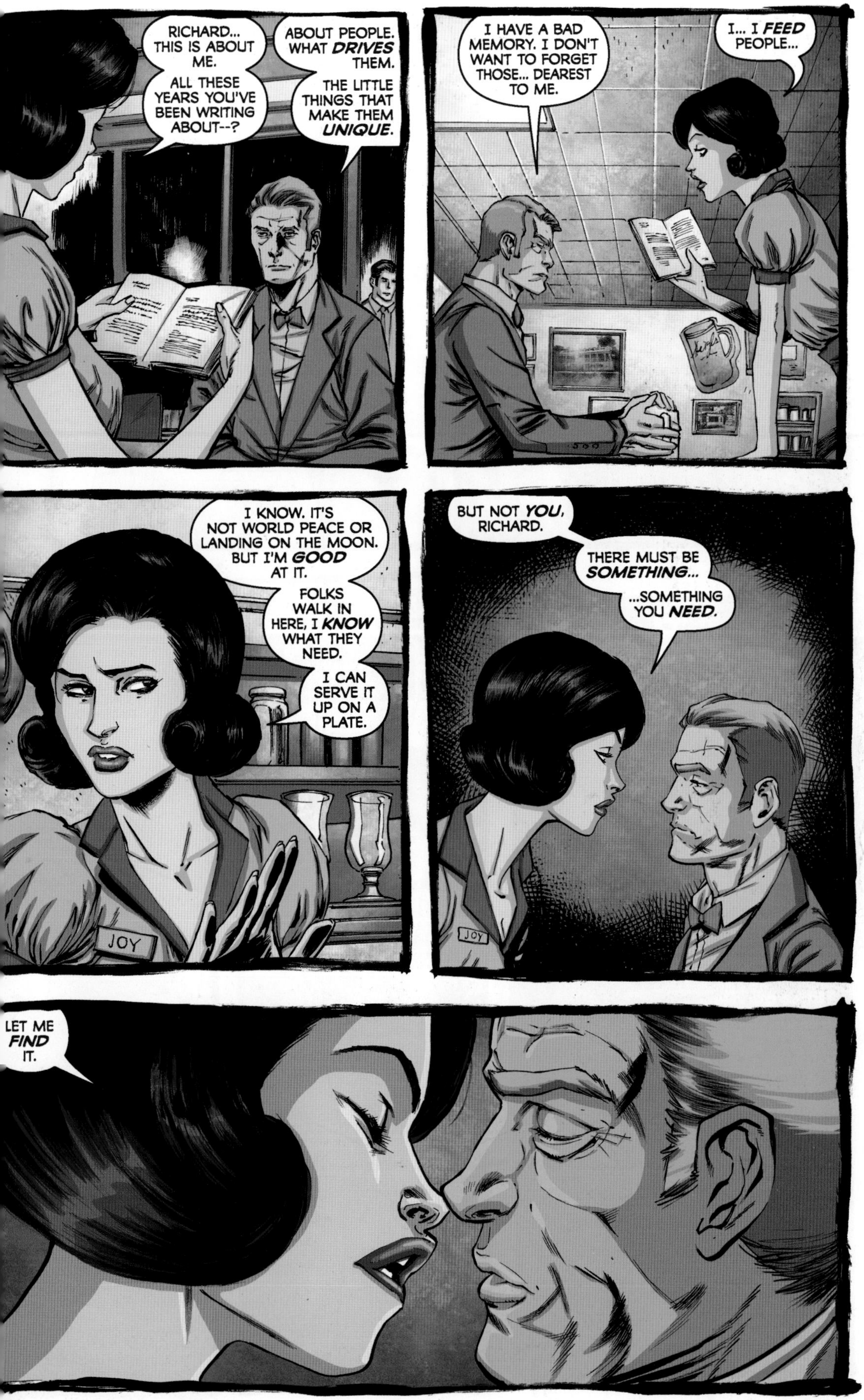
RICHARD... THIS IS ABOUT ME.
ALL THESE YEARS YOU'VE BEEN WRITING ABOUT--?
ABOUT PEOPLE. WHAT DRIVES THEM.
THE LITTLE THINGS THAT MAKE THEM UNIQUE.
I HAVE A BAD MEMORY. I DON'T WANT TO FORGET THOSE... DEAREST TO ME.
I... I FEED PEOPLE...
I KNOW. IT'S NOT WORLD PEACE OR LANDING ON THE MOON. BUT I'M GOOD AT IT.
FOLKS WALK IN HERE, I KNOW WHAT THEY NEED.
I CAN SERVE IT UP ON A PLATE.
JOY
BUT NOT YOU, RICHARD.
THERE MUST BE SOMETHING...
...SOMETHING YOU NEED.
JOY
LET ME FIND IT.

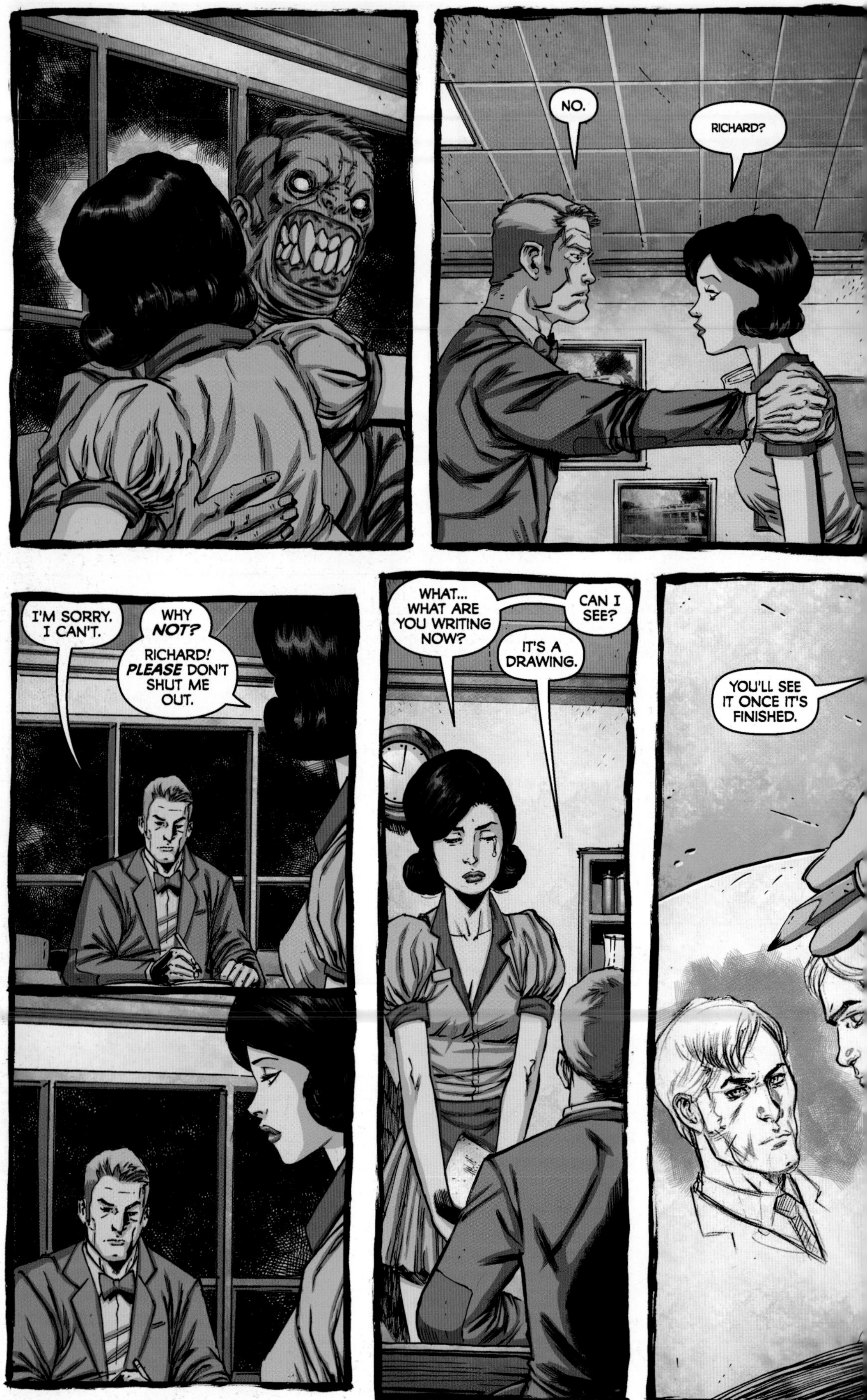
NO.
RICHARD?
I'M SORRY. I CAN'T.
WHY *NOT?*
RICHARD! *PLEASE* DON'T SHUT ME OUT.
WHAT... WHAT ARE YOU WRITING NOW?
CAN I SEE?
IT'S A DRAWING.
YOU'LL SEE IT ONCE IT'S FINISHED.

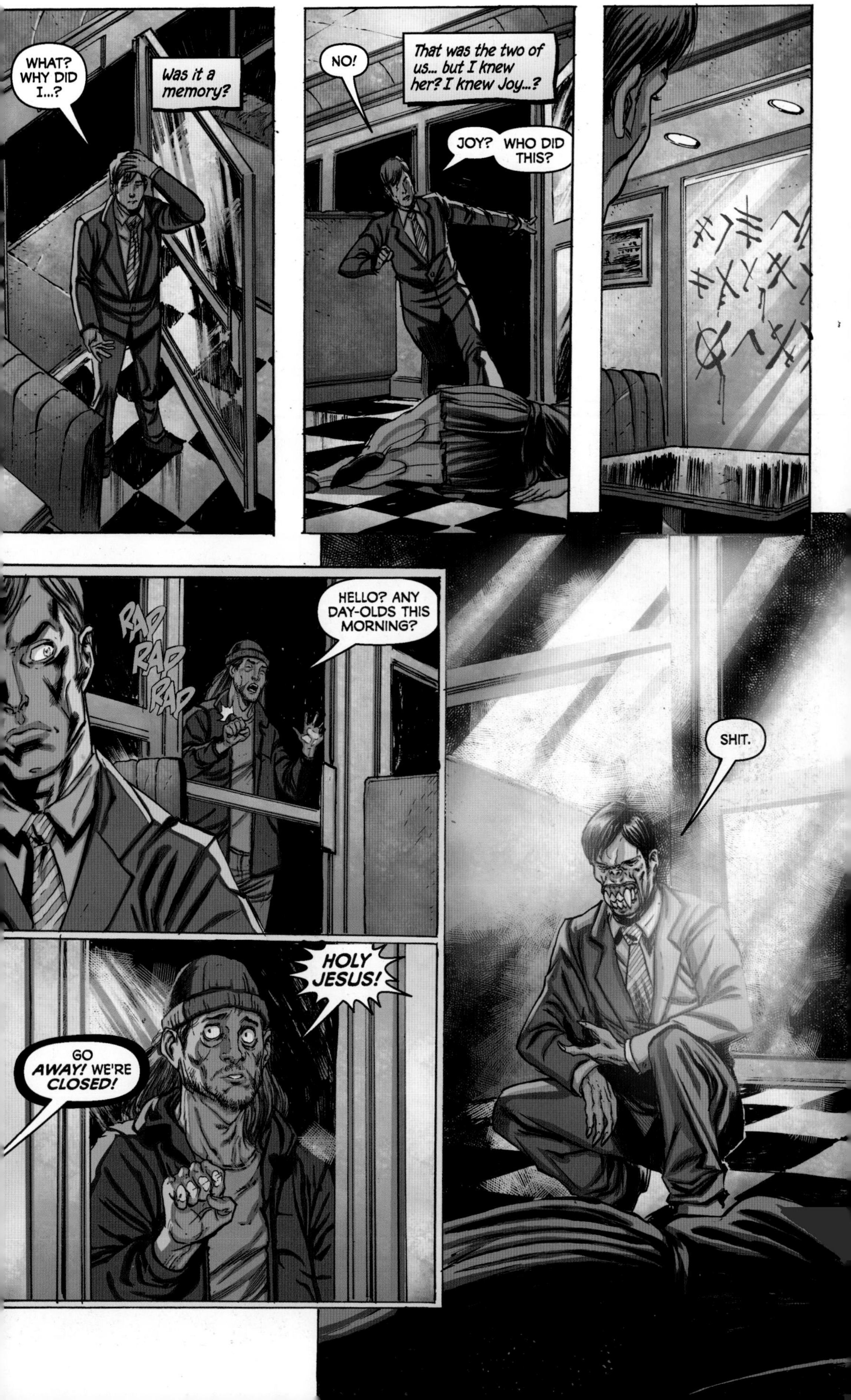
WHAT? WHY DID I...?
Was it a memory?
NO!
That was the two of us... but I knew her? I knew Joy...?
JOY?
WHO DID THIS?
HELLO? ANY DAY-OLDS THIS MORNING?
RAP RAP RAP
HOLY JESUS!
GO AWAY! WE'RE CLOSED!
SHIT.

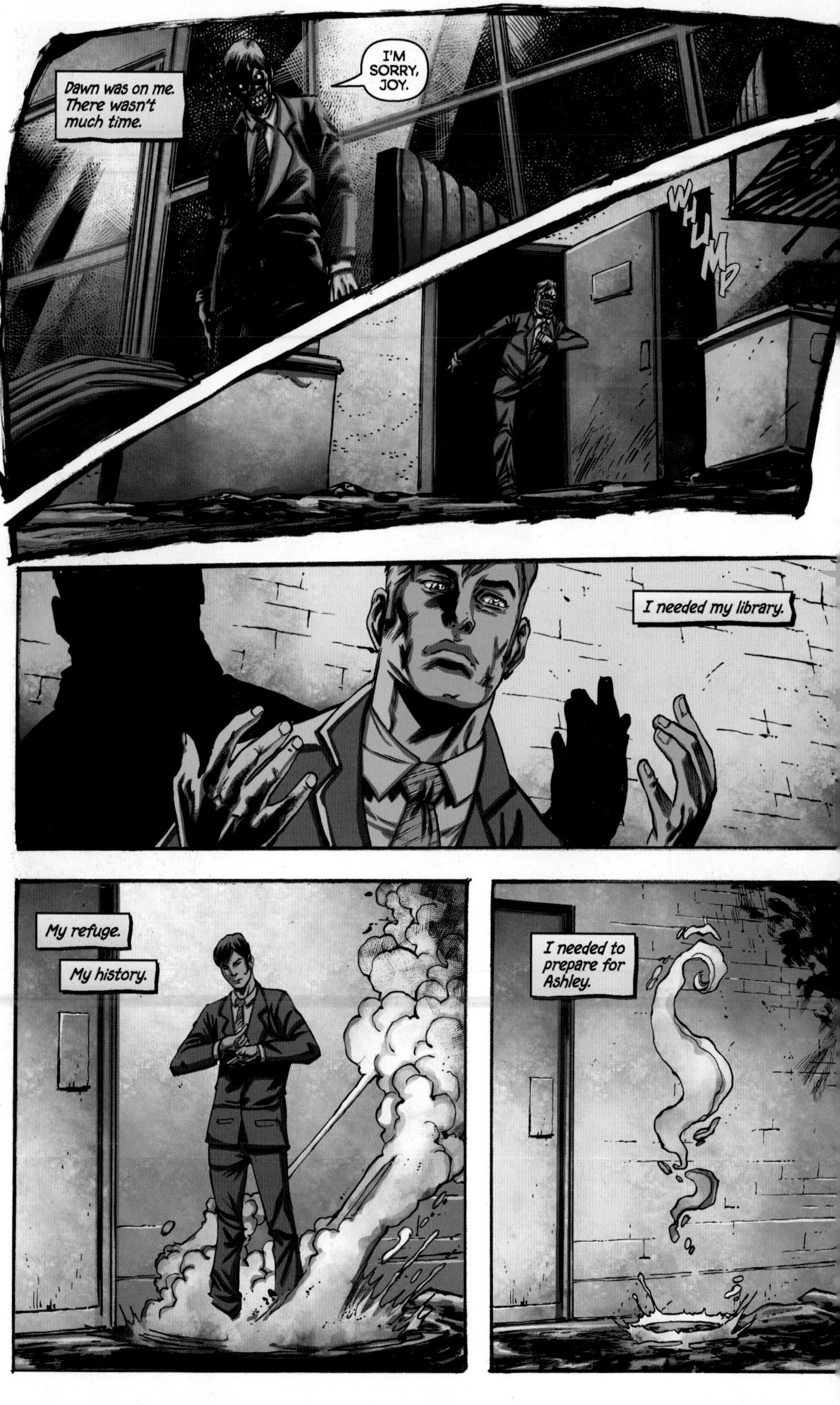
Dawn was on me. There wasn't much time.
I'M SORRY, JOY.
WHUMP
I needed my library.
My refuge.
My history.
I needed to prepare for Ashley.

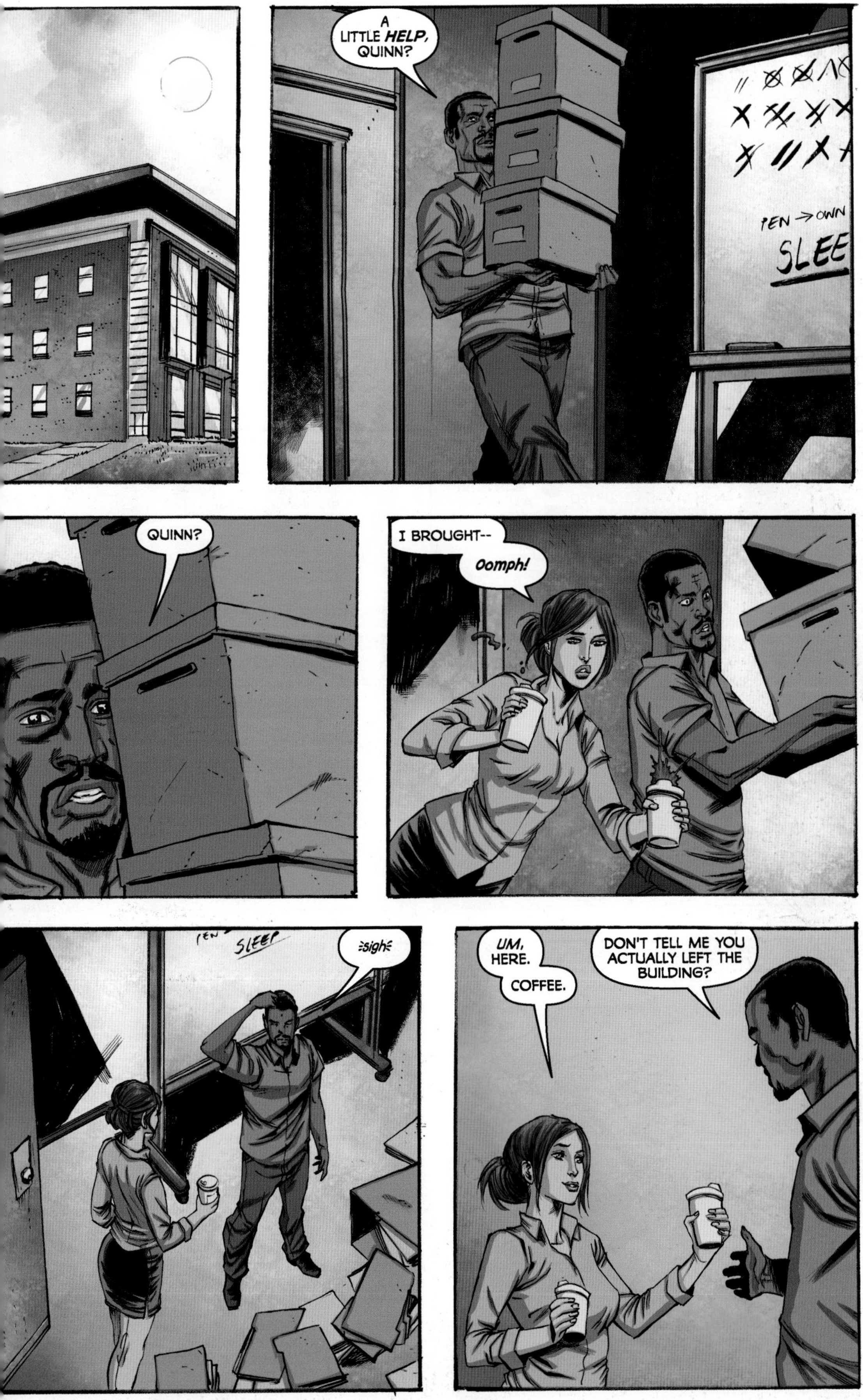
A LITTLE HELP, QUINN?
PEN → OWN
SLEE
QUINN?
I BROUGHT--
Oomph!
SLEEP
sigh
UM, HERE.
COFFEE.
DON'T TELL ME YOU ACTUALLY LEFT THE BUILDING?

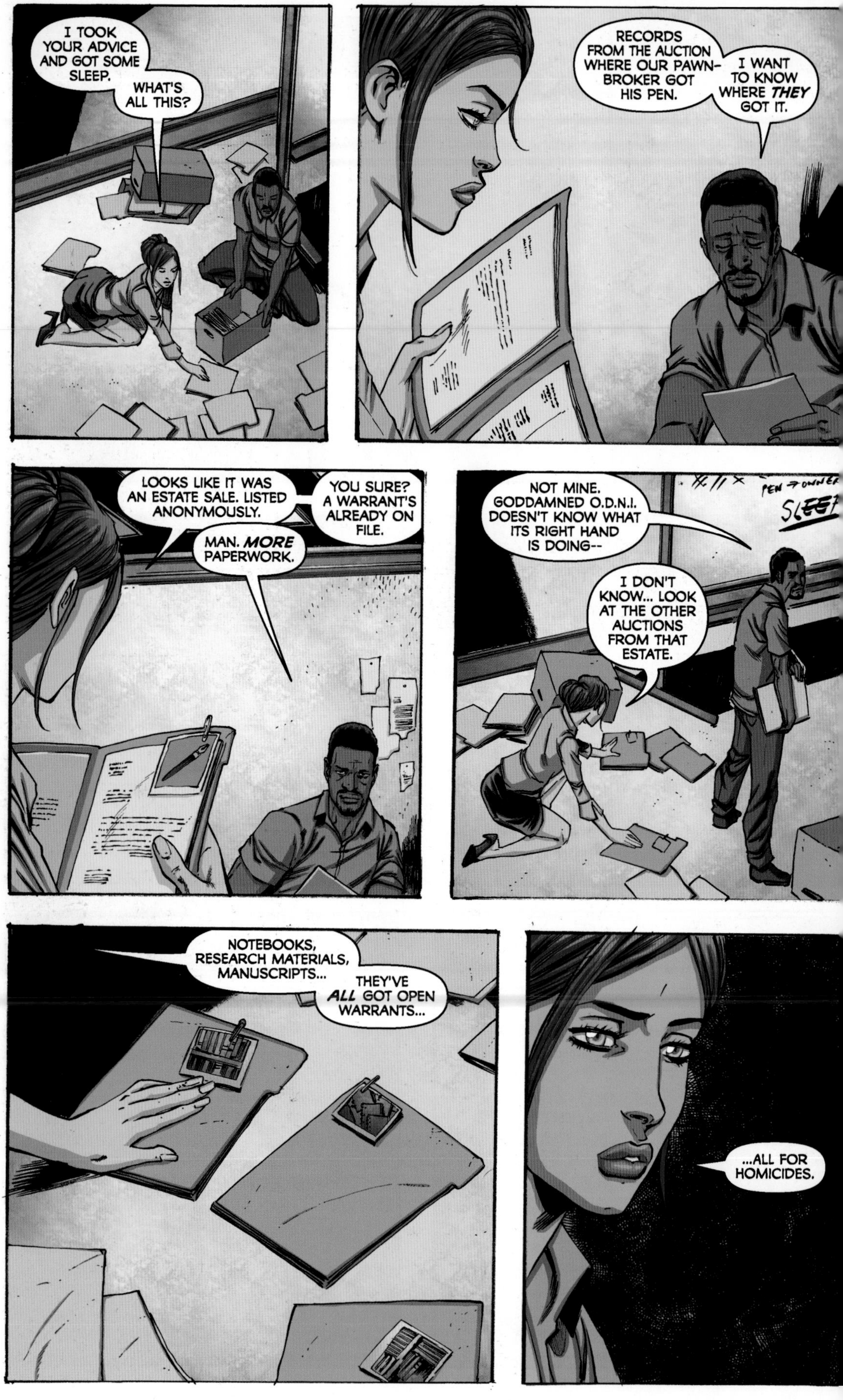
I TOOK YOUR ADVICE AND GOT SOME SLEEP.
WHAT'S ALL THIS?
RECORDS FROM THE AUCTION WHERE OUR PAWN-BROKER GOT HIS PEN.
I WANT TO KNOW WHERE *THEY* GOT IT.
LOOKS LIKE IT WAS AN ESTATE SALE. LISTED ANONYMOUSLY.
YOU SURE? A WARRANT'S ALREADY ON FILE.
MAN. *MORE* PAPERWORK.
NOT MINE. GODDAMNED O.D.N.I. DOESN'T KNOW WHAT ITS RIGHT HAND IS DOING--
I DON'T KNOW... LOOK AT THE OTHER AUCTIONS FROM THAT ESTATE.
NOTEBOOKS, RESEARCH MATERIALS, MANUSCRIPTS...
THEY'VE *ALL* GOT OPEN WARRANTS...
...ALL FOR HOMICIDES.

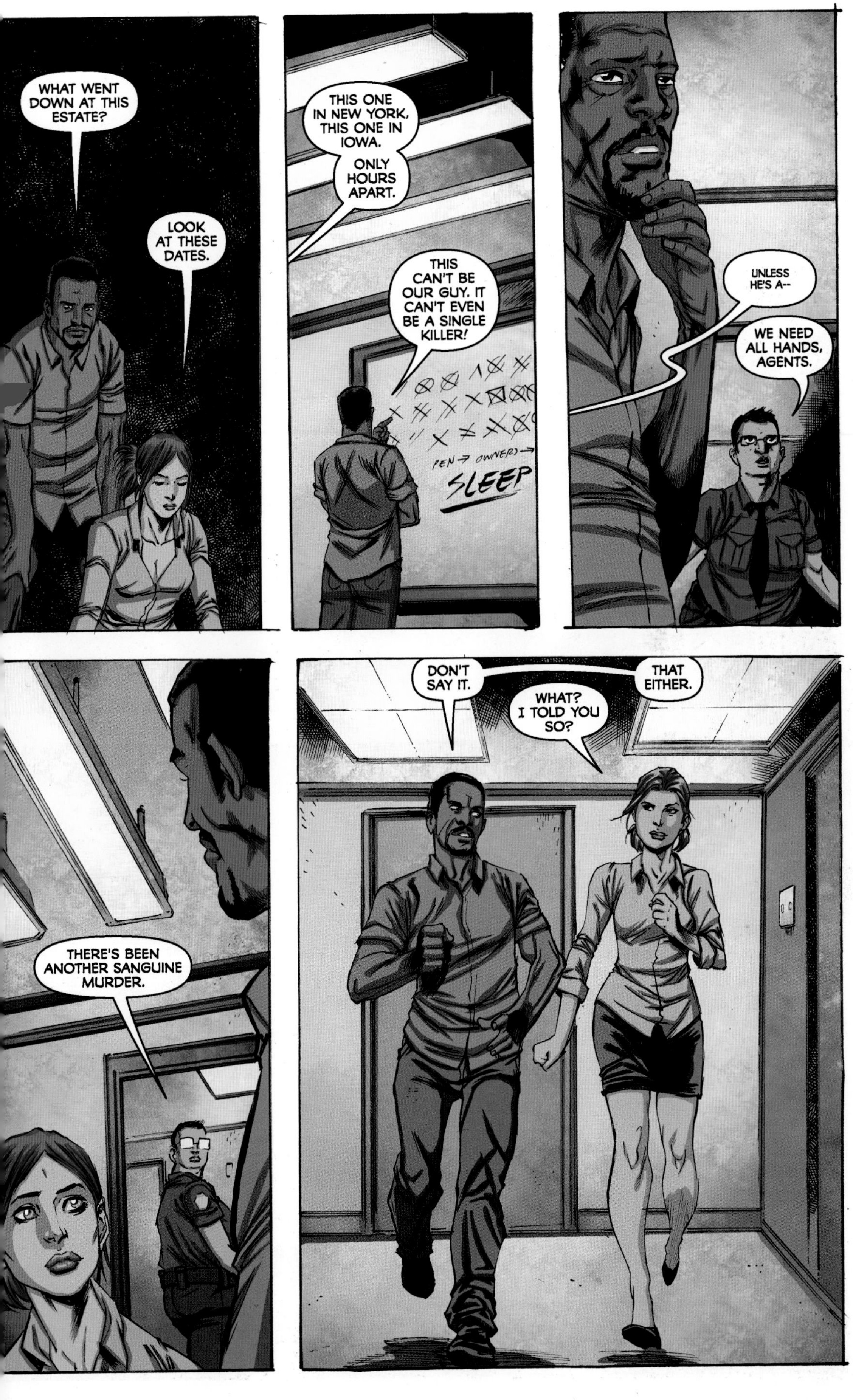
WHAT WENT DOWN AT THIS ESTATE?
LOOK AT THESE DATES.
THIS ONE IN NEW YORK, THIS ONE IN IOWA.
ONLY HOURS APART.
THIS CAN'T BE OUR GUY. IT CAN'T EVEN BE A SINGLE KILLER!
PEN → OWNER →
SLEEP
UNLESS HE'S A--
WE NEED ALL HANDS, AGENTS.
THERE'S BEEN ANOTHER SANGUINE MURDER.
DON'T SAY IT.
WHAT? I TOLD YOU SO?
THAT EITHER.

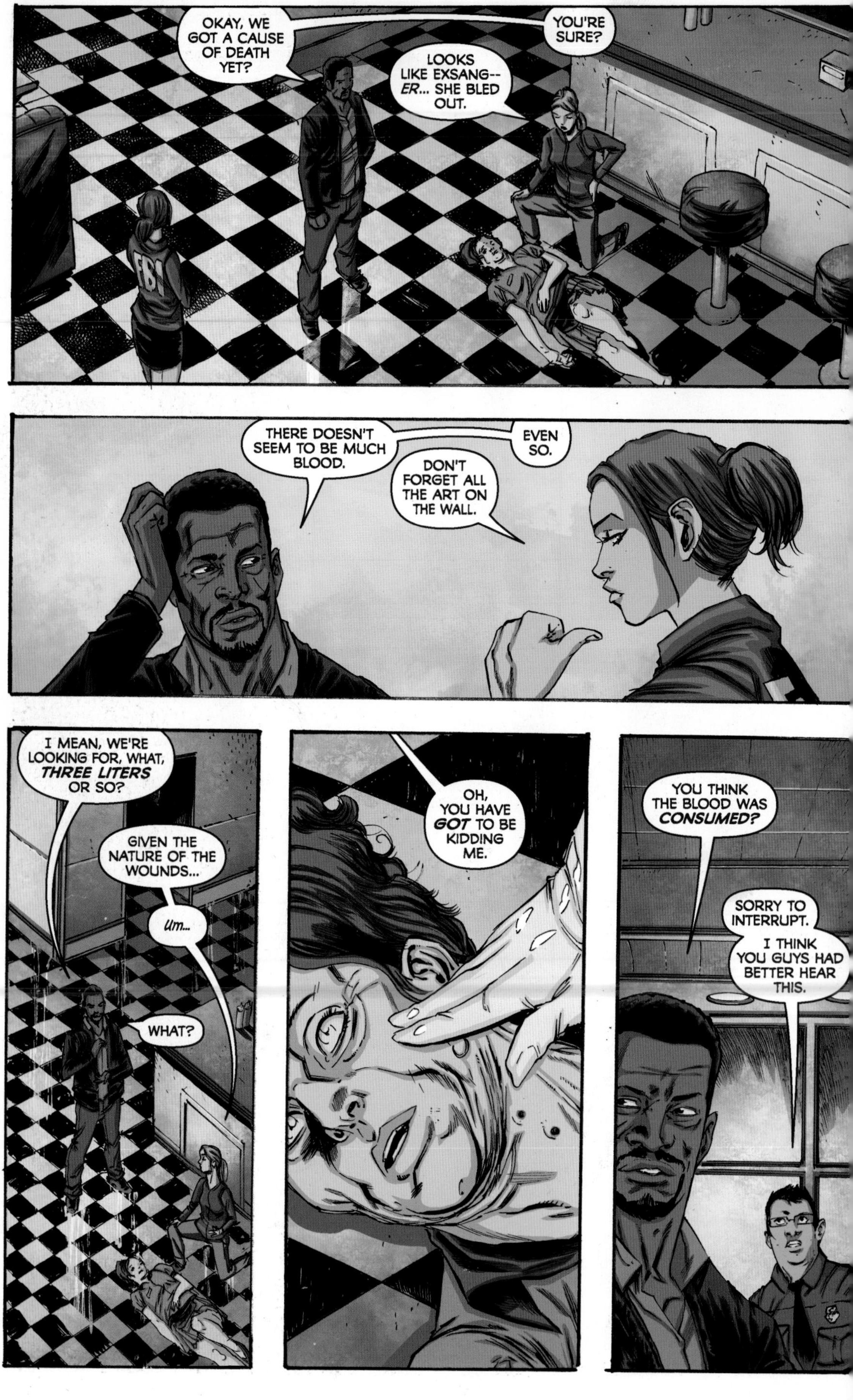
OKAY, WE GOT A CAUSE OF DEATH YET?
LOOKS LIKE EXSANG-- *ER*... SHE BLED OUT.
YOU'RE SURE?
THERE DOESN'T SEEM TO BE MUCH BLOOD.
DON'T FORGET ALL THE ART ON THE WALL.
EVEN SO.
I MEAN, WE'RE LOOKING FOR, WHAT, *THREE LITERS* OR SO?
GIVEN THE NATURE OF THE WOUNDS...
Um...
WHAT?
OH, YOU HAVE *GOT* TO BE KIDDING ME.
YOU THINK THE BLOOD WAS *CONSUMED?*
SORRY TO INTERRUPT.
I THINK YOU GUYS HAD BETTER HEAR THIS.

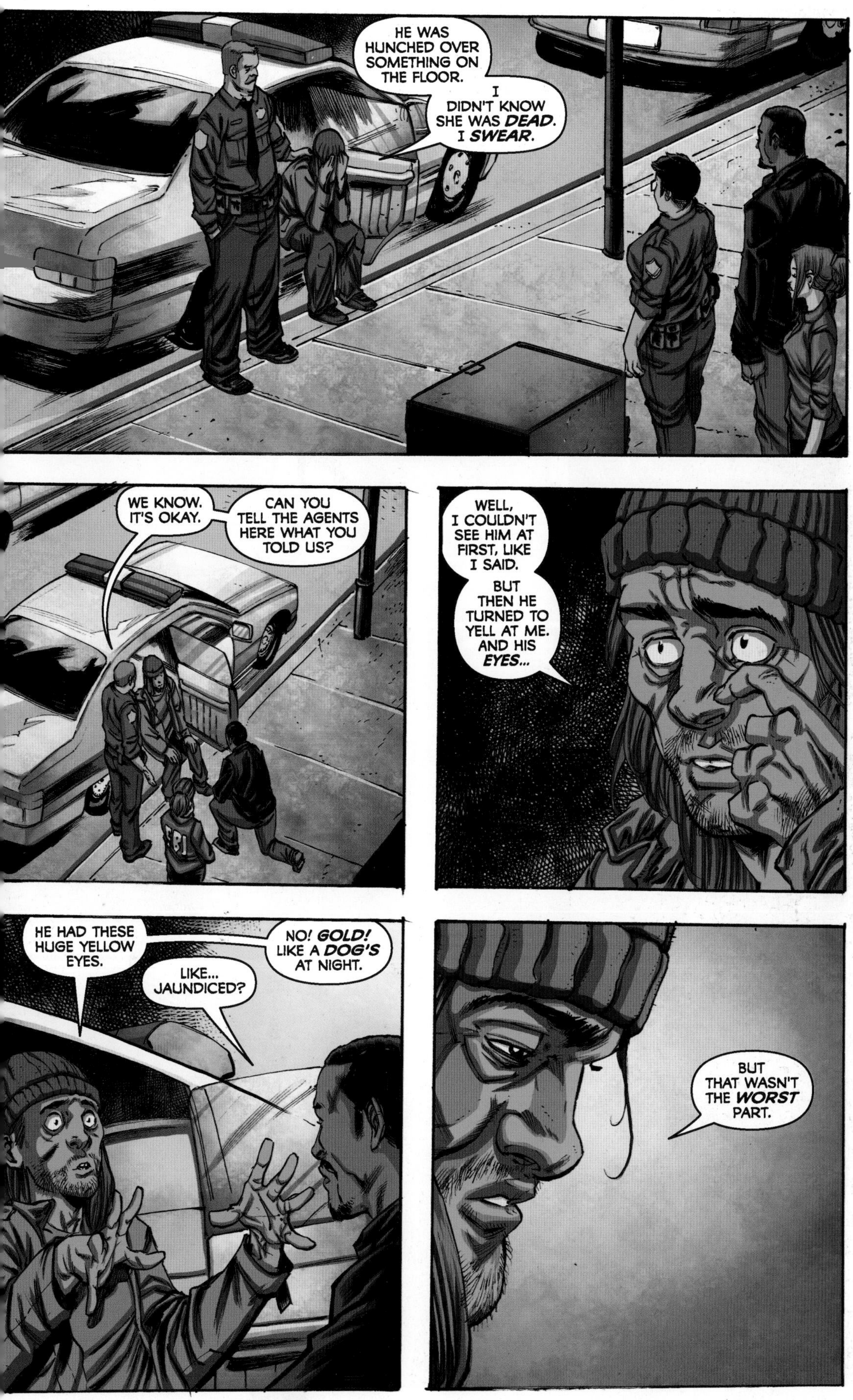
HE WAS HUNCHED OVER SOMETHING ON THE FLOOR.
I DIDN'T KNOW SHE WAS *DEAD*. I *SWEAR*.
WE KNOW. IT'S OKAY.
CAN YOU TELL THE AGENTS HERE WHAT YOU TOLD US?
FBI
WELL, I COULDN'T SEE HIM AT FIRST, LIKE I SAID.
BUT THEN HE TURNED TO YELL AT ME. AND HIS *EYES...*
HE HAD THESE HUGE YELLOW EYES.
LIKE... JAUNDICED?
NO! *GOLD!* LIKE A *DOG'S* AT NIGHT.
BUT THAT WASN'T THE *WORST* PART.

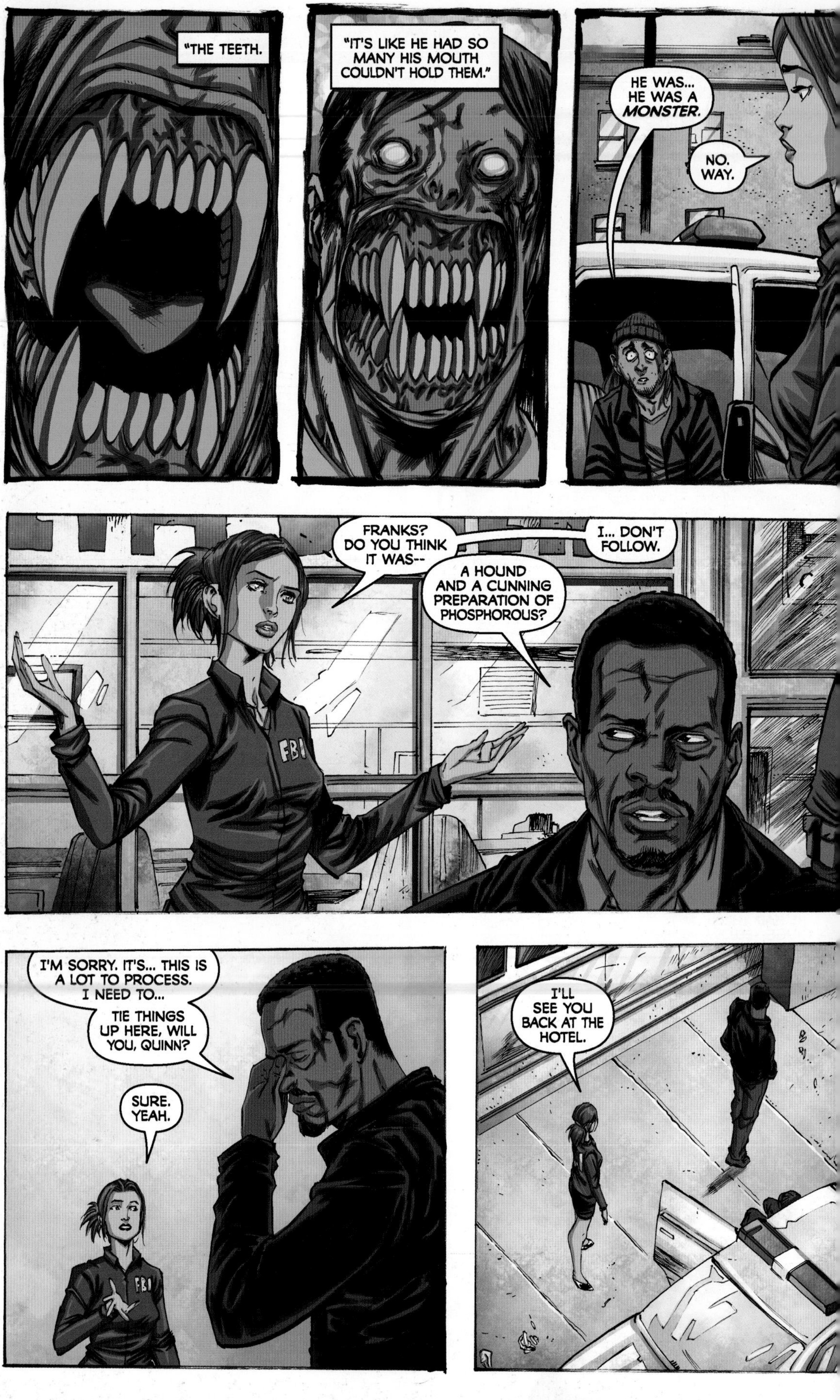
"THE TEETH.
"IT'S LIKE HE HAD SO MANY HIS MOUTH COULDN'T HOLD THEM."
HE WAS... HE WAS A *MONSTER.*
NO. WAY.
FRANKS? DO YOU THINK IT WAS--
I... DON'T FOLLOW.
A HOUND AND A CUNNING PREPARATION OF PHOSPHOROUS?
I'M SORRY. IT'S... THIS IS A LOT TO PROCESS. I NEED TO...
TIE THINGS UP HERE, WILL YOU, QUINN?
SURE. YEAH.
I'LL SEE YOU BACK AT THE HOTEL.

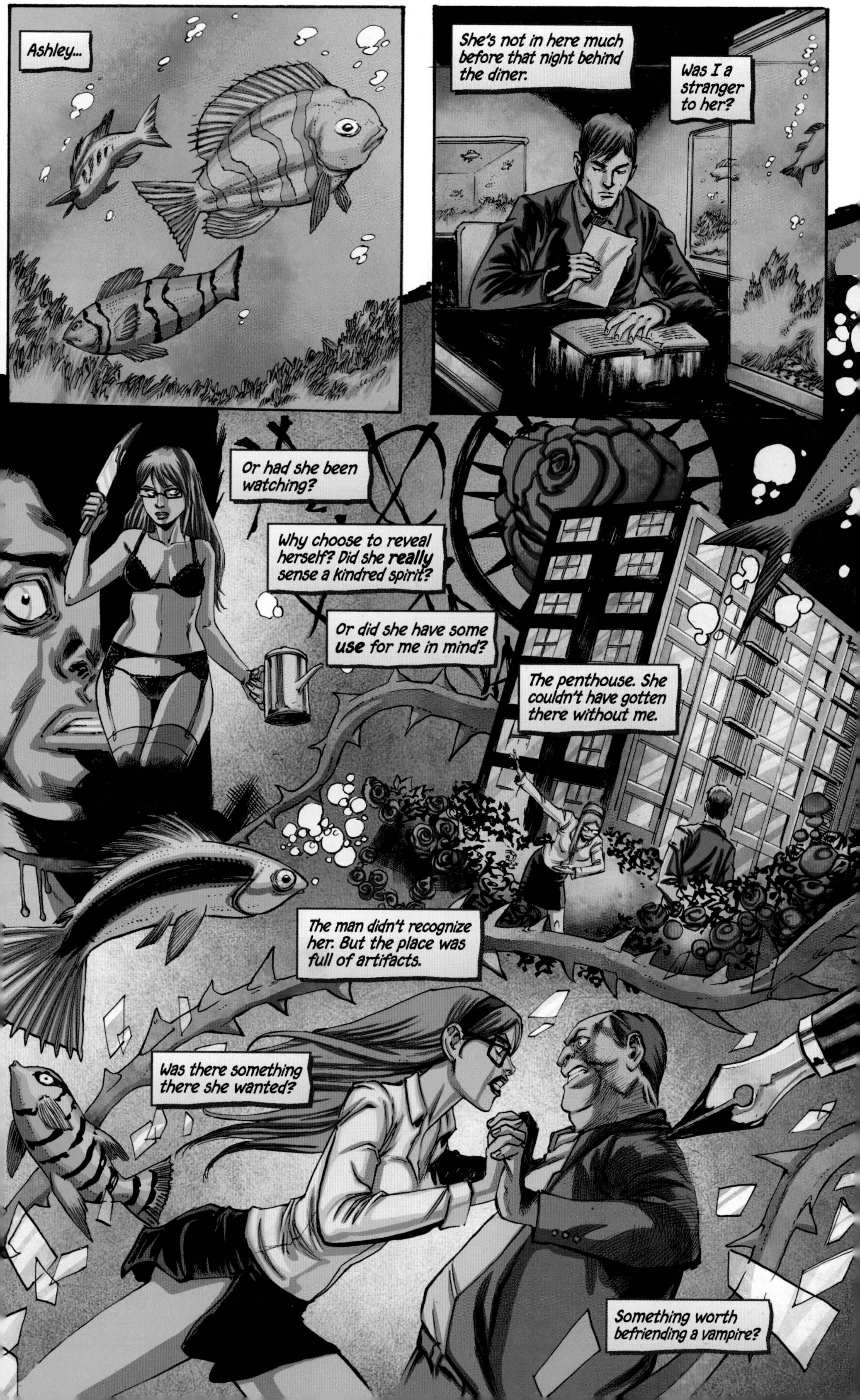
Ashley...
She's not in here much before that night behind the diner.
Was I a stranger to her?
Or had she been watching?
Why choose to reveal herself? Did she **really** sense a kindred spirit?
Or did she have some **use** for me in mind?
The penthouse. She couldn't have gotten there without me.
The man didn't recognize her. But the place was full of artifacts.
Was there something there she wanted?
Something worth befriending a vampire?

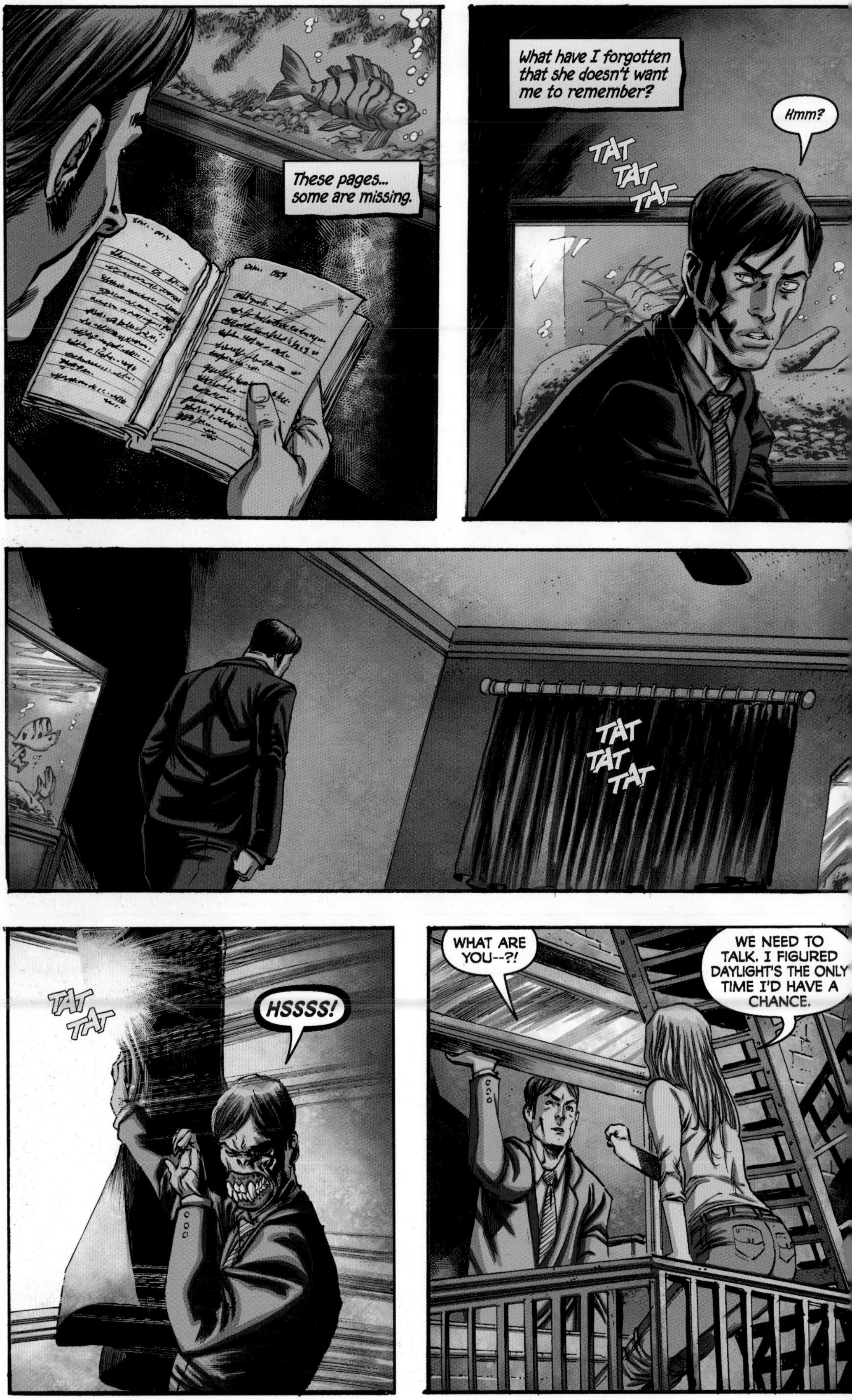
These pages... some are missing.
What have I forgotten that she doesn't want me to remember?
TAT TAT TAT
Hmm?
TAT TAT TAT
TAT TAT
HSSSS!
WHAT ARE YOU--?!
WE NEED TO TALK. I FIGURED DAYLIGHT'S THE ONLY TIME I'D HAVE A CHANCE.

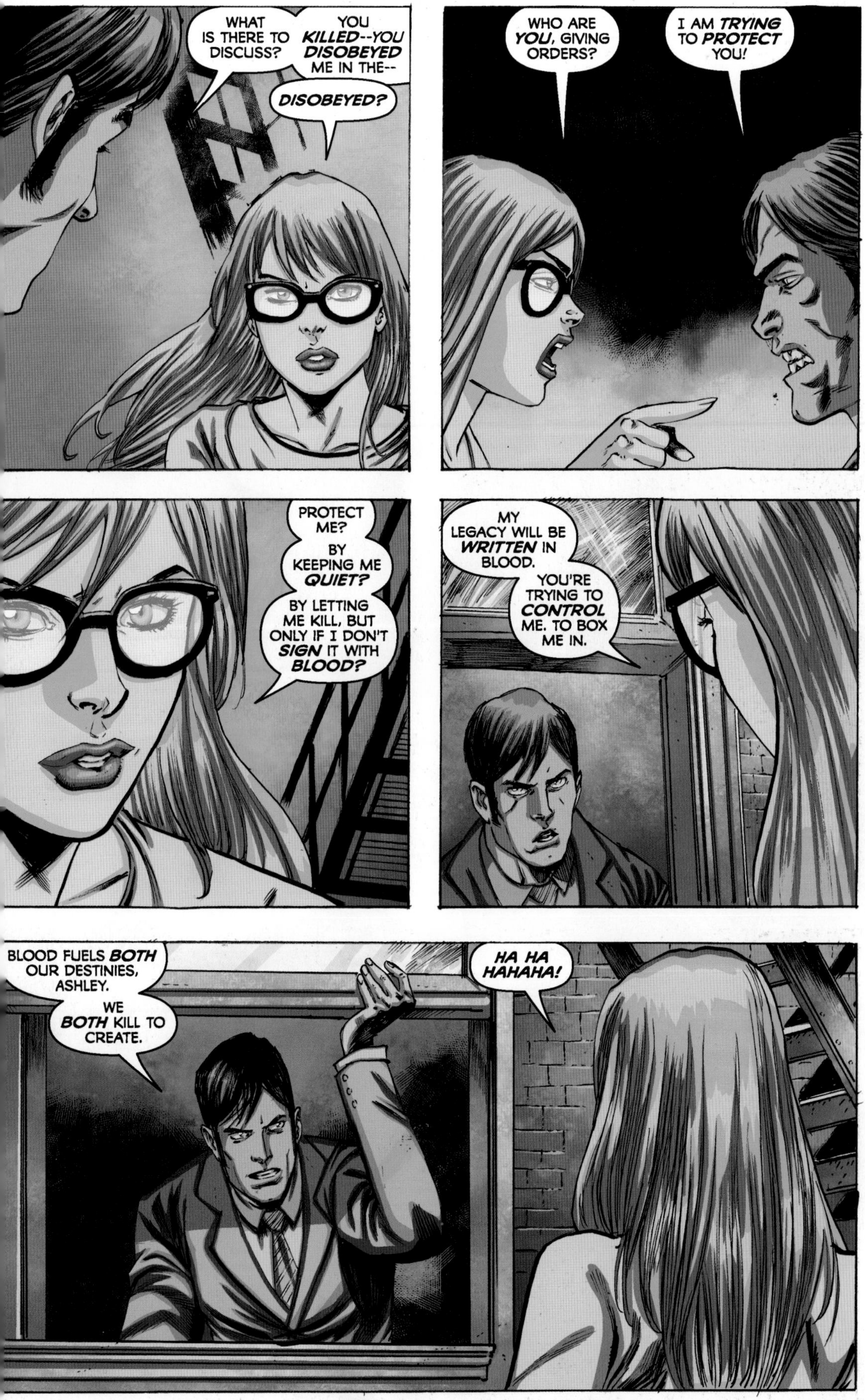
WHAT IS THERE TO DISCUSS?
YOU KILLED--YOU DISOBEYED ME IN THE--
DISOBEYED?
WHO ARE YOU, GIVING ORDERS?
I AM TRYING TO PROTECT YOU!
PROTECT ME?
BY KEEPING ME QUIET?
BY LETTING ME KILL, BUT ONLY IF I DON'T SIGN IT WITH BLOOD?
MY LEGACY WILL BE WRITTEN IN BLOOD.
YOU'RE TRYING TO CONTROL ME. TO BOX ME IN.
BLOOD FUELS BOTH OUR DESTINIES, ASHLEY.
WE BOTH KILL TO CREATE.
HA HA HAHAHA!

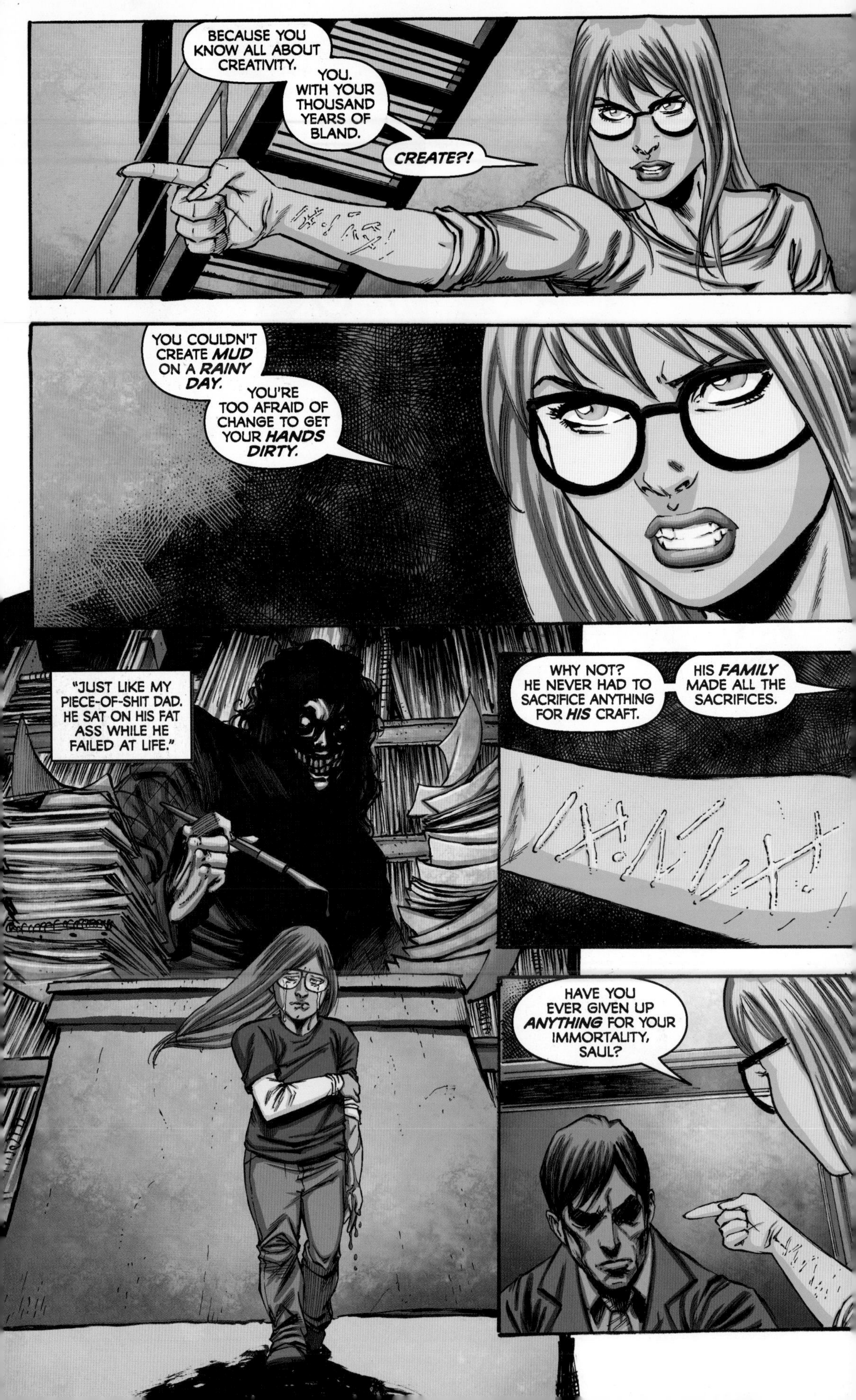

BECAUSE YOU KNOW ALL ABOUT CREATIVITY.
YOU. WITH YOUR THOUSAND YEARS OF BLAND.
CREATE?!
YOU COULDN'T CREATE *MUD* ON A *RAINY DAY.*
YOU'RE TOO AFRAID OF CHANGE TO GET YOUR *HANDS DIRTY.*
"JUST LIKE MY PIECE-OF-SHIT DAD. HE SAT ON HIS FAT ASS WHILE HE FAILED AT LIFE."
WHY NOT? HE NEVER HAD TO SACRIFICE ANYTHING FOR *HIS* CRAFT.
HIS *FAMILY* MADE ALL THE SACRIFICES.
HAVE YOU EVER GIVEN UP *ANYTHING* FOR YOUR IMMORTALITY, SAUL?

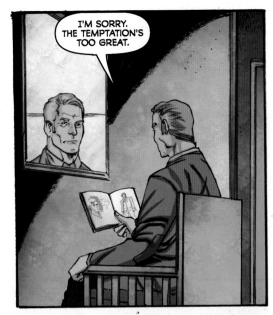

I'M SORRY. THE TEMPTATION'S TOO GREAT.

IT'S TIME TO MOVE ON.

YOU NEED TO *FORGET* ABOUT RICHARD.

AND I NEED TO FORGET ABOUT *YOU*.

GOODBYE, JOY.

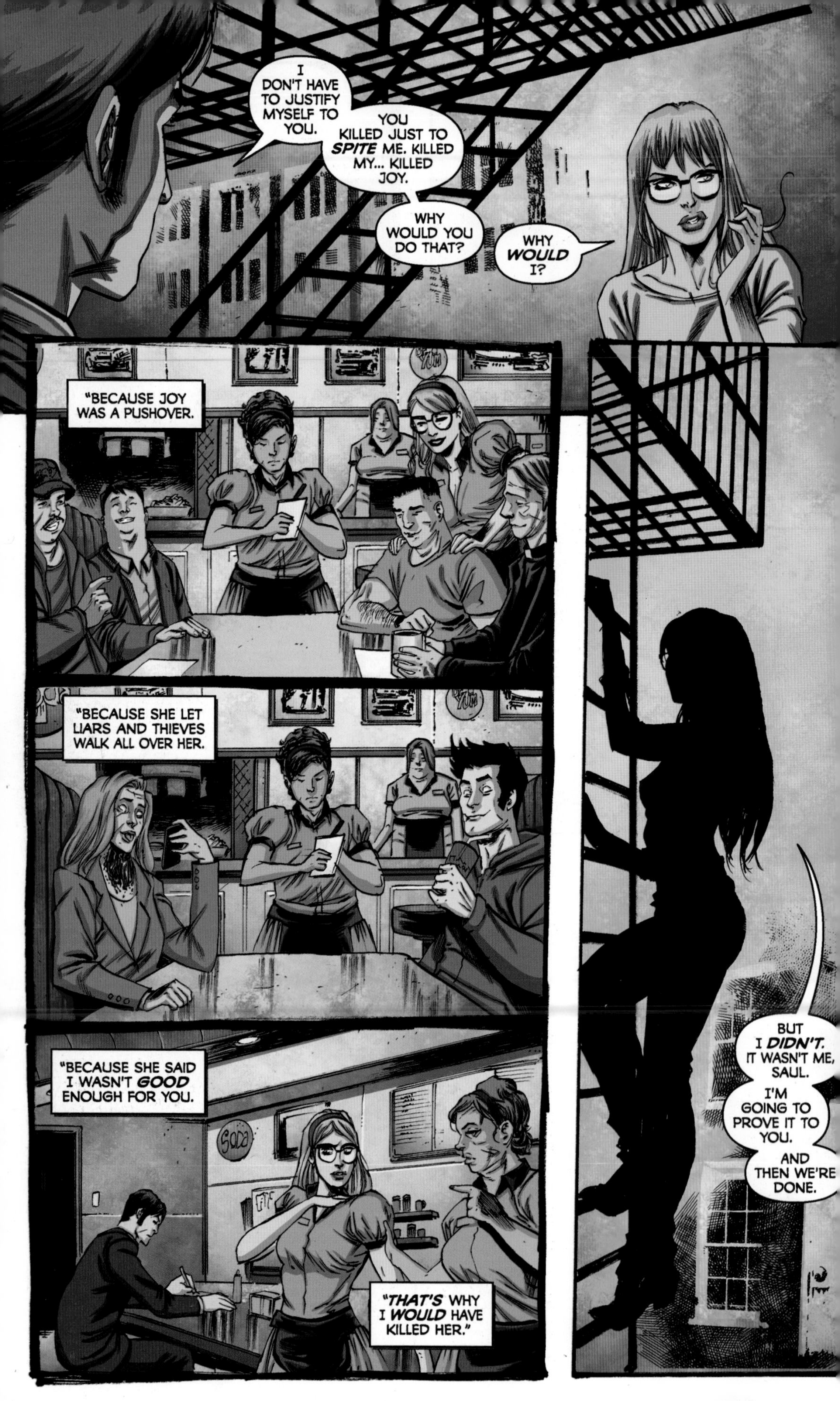
I DON'T HAVE TO JUSTIFY MYSELF TO YOU.
YOU KILLED JUST TO SPITE ME. KILLED MY... KILLED JOY.
WHY WOULD YOU DO THAT?
WHY WOULD I?
"BECAUSE JOY WAS A PUSHOVER.
"BECAUSE SHE LET LIARS AND THIEVES WALK ALL OVER HER.
"BECAUSE SHE SAID I WASN'T GOOD ENOUGH FOR YOU.
"THAT'S WHY I WOULD HAVE KILLED HER."
BUT I DIDN'T. IT WASN'T ME, SAUL.
I'M GOING TO PROVE IT TO YOU.
AND THEN WE'RE DONE.

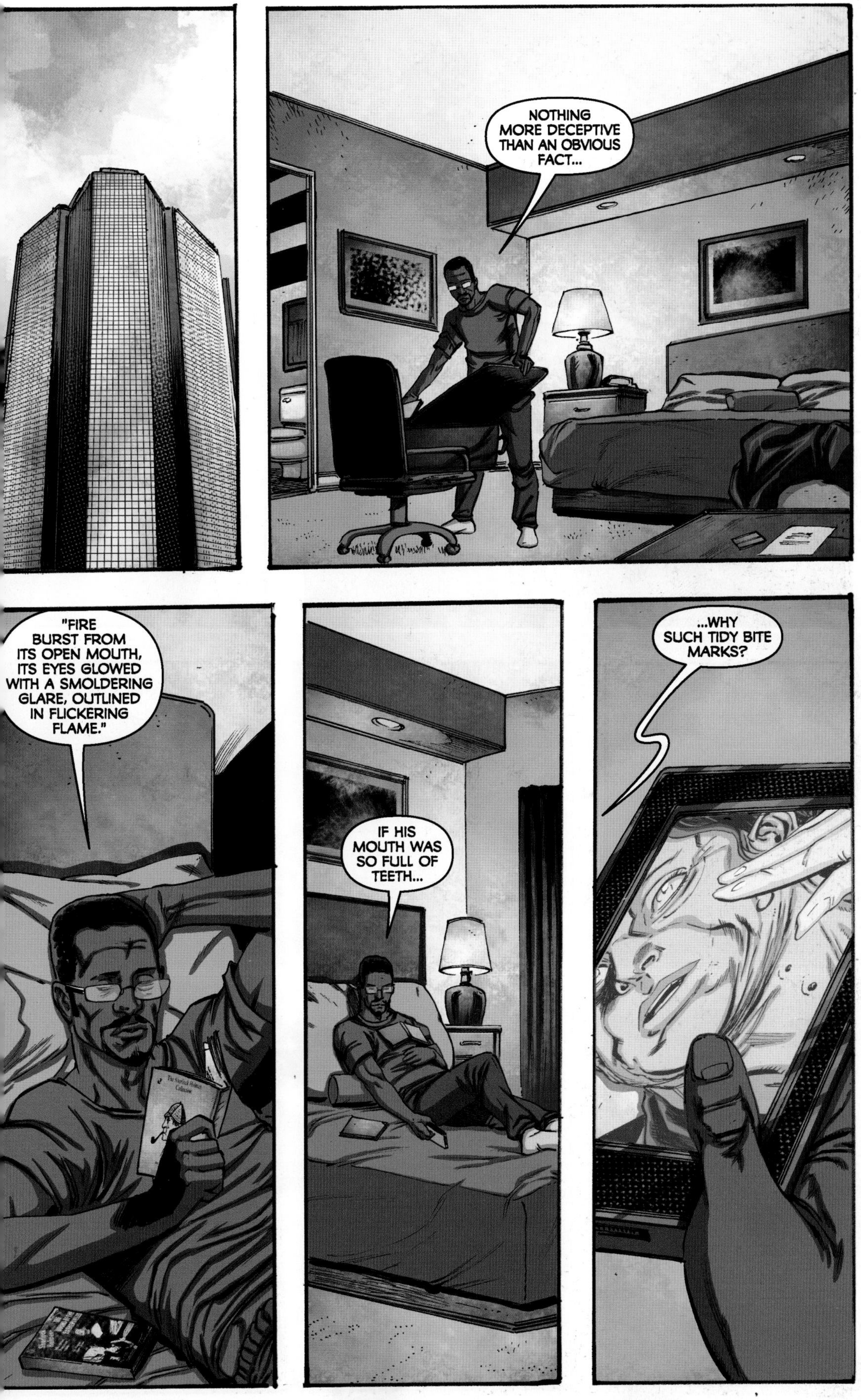
NOTHING MORE DECEPTIVE THAN AN OBVIOUS FACT...
"FIRE BURST FROM ITS OPEN MOUTH, ITS EYES GLOWED WITH A SMOLDERING GLARE, OUTLINED IN FLICKERING FLAME."
IF HIS MOUTH WAS SO FULL OF TEETH...
...WHY SUCH TIDY BITE MARKS?

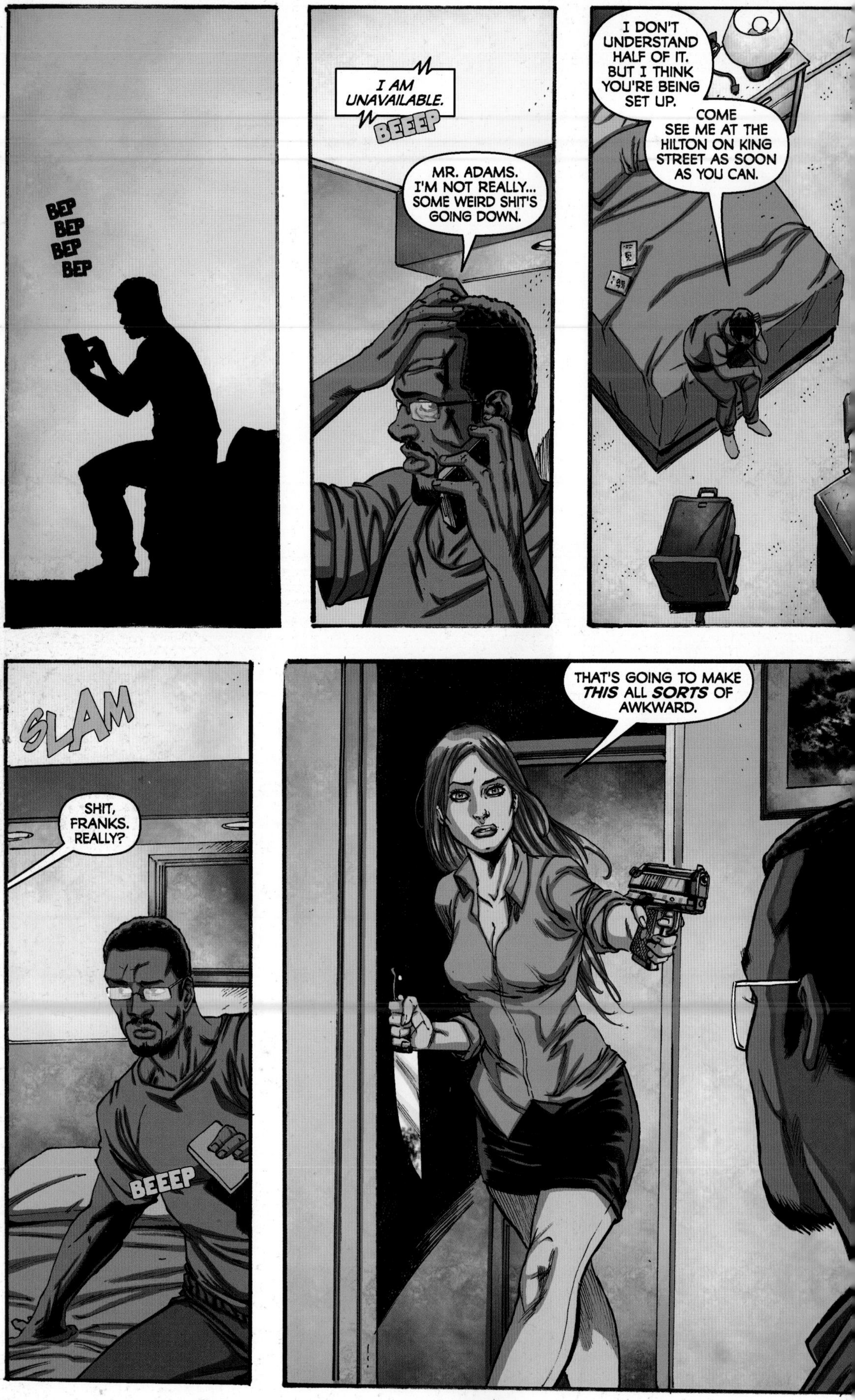
BEP BEP BEP BEP
I AM UNAVAILABLE.
BEEEP
MR. ADAMS. I'M NOT REALLY... SOME WEIRD SHIT'S GOING DOWN.
I DON'T UNDERSTAND HALF OF IT. BUT I THINK YOU'RE BEING SET UP.
COME SEE ME AT THE HILTON ON KING STREET AS SOON AS YOU CAN.
SLAM
SHIT, FRANKS. REALLY?
BEEEP
THAT'S GOING TO MAKE *THIS* ALL *SORTS* OF AWKWARD.

CHAPTER FIVE

AND YET IT MOVES

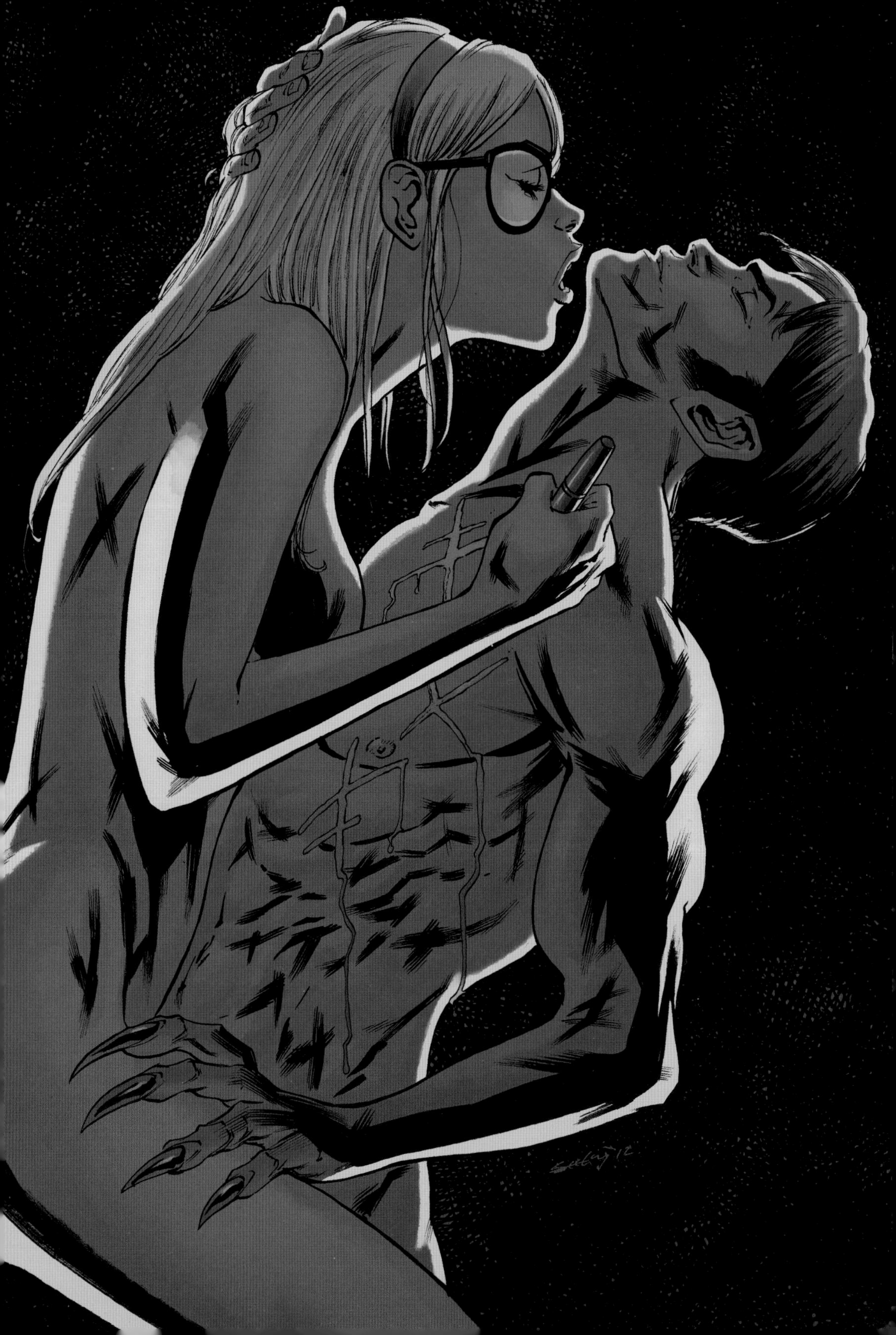

STRIKES

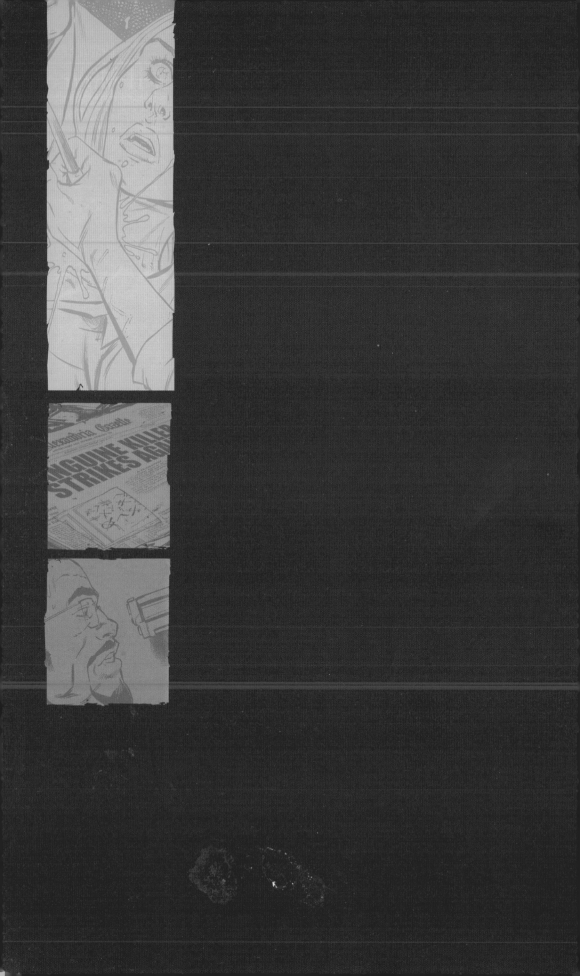

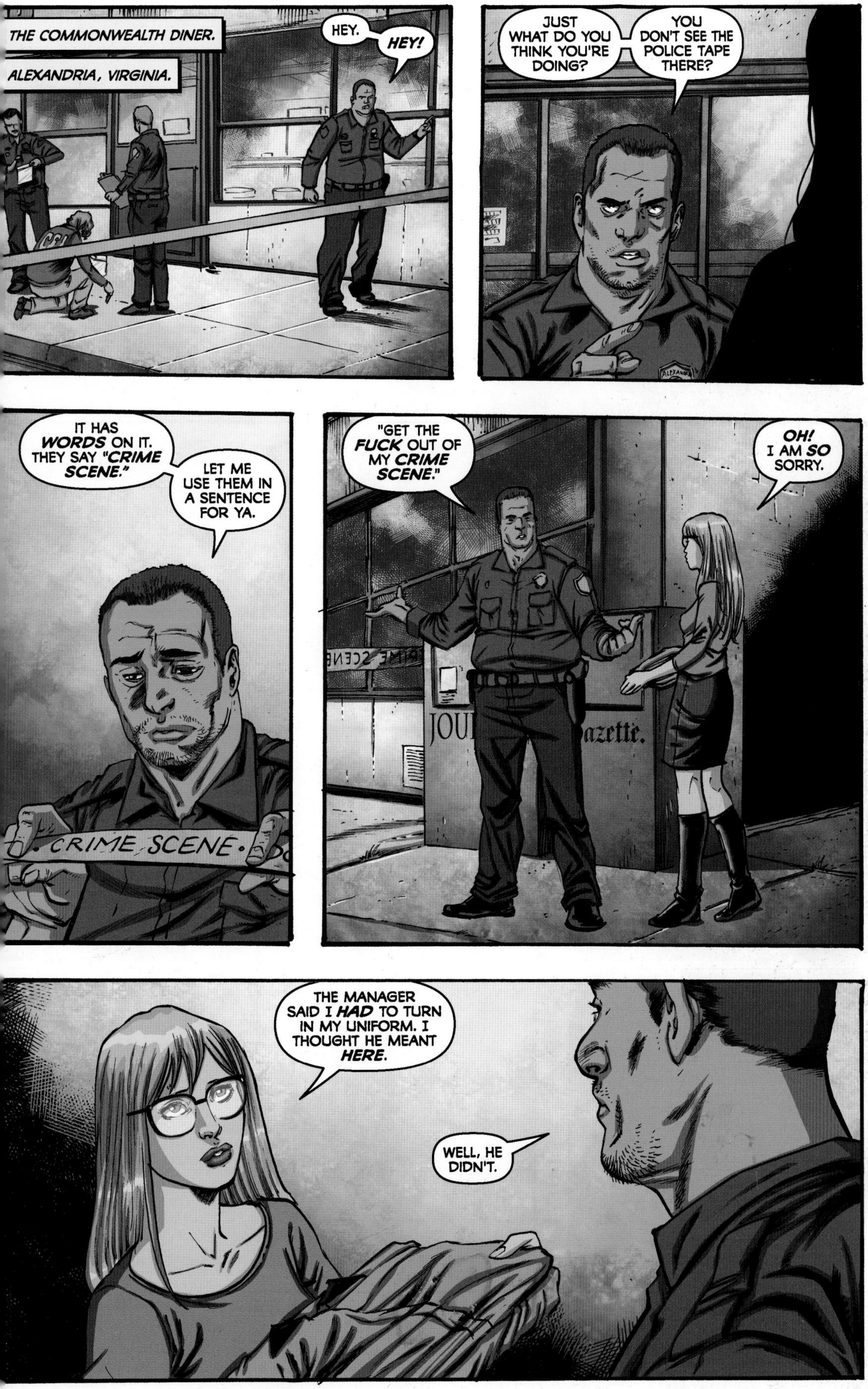
THE COMMONWEALTH DINER.
ALEXANDRIA, VIRGINIA.
HEY.
HEY!
JUST WHAT DO YOU THINK YOU'RE DOING?
YOU DON'T SEE THE POLICE TAPE THERE?
IT HAS WORDS ON IT. THEY SAY "CRIME SCENE."
LET ME USE THEM IN A SENTENCE FOR YA.
CRIME SCENE
"GET THE FUCK OUT OF MY CRIME SCENE."
OH! I AM SO SORRY.
THE MANAGER SAID I HAD TO TURN IN MY UNIFORM. I THOUGHT HE MEANT HERE.
WELL, HE DIDN'T.

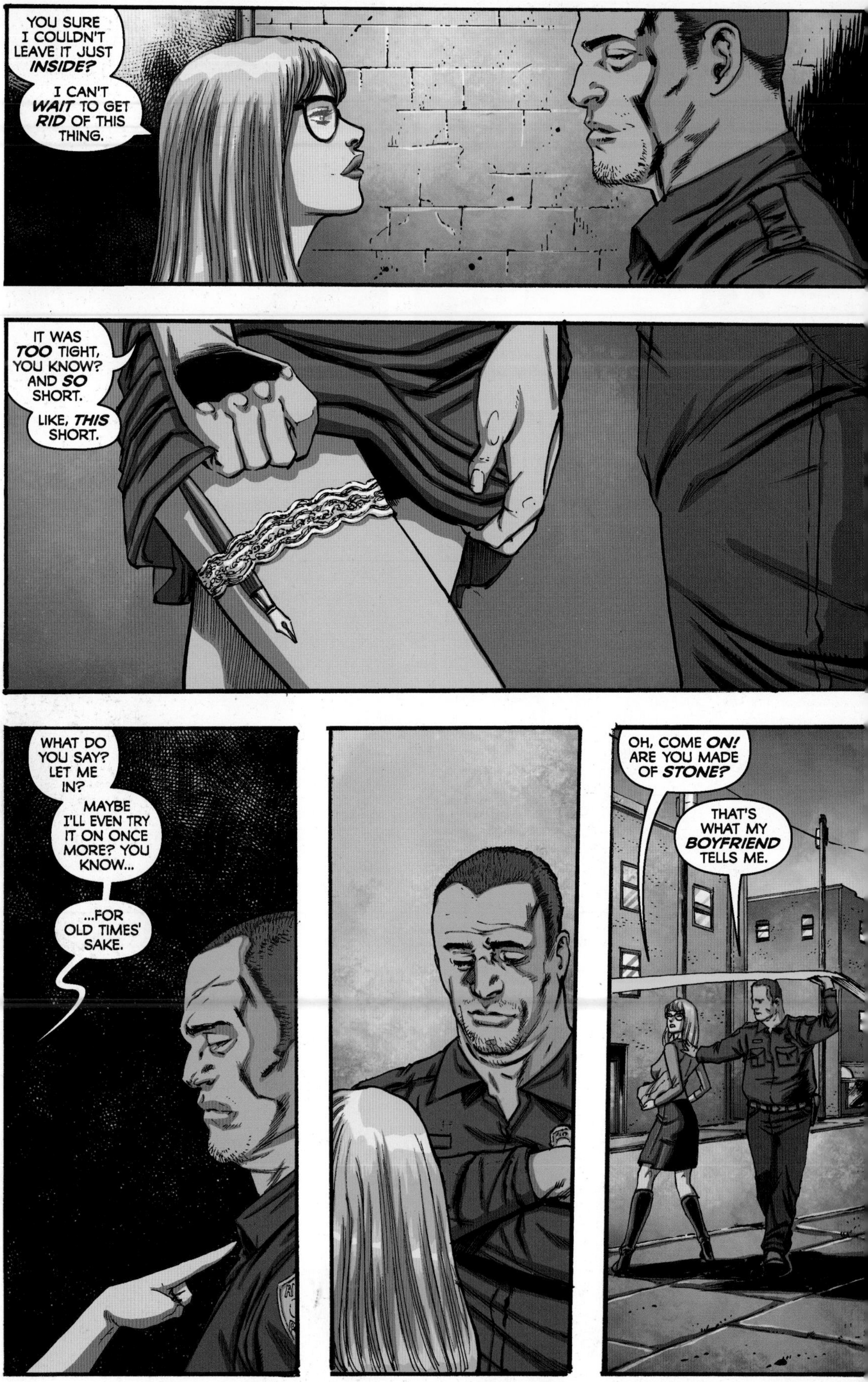
YOU SURE I COULDN'T LEAVE IT JUST INSIDE?
I CAN'T WAIT TO GET RID OF THIS THING.
IT WAS TOO TIGHT, YOU KNOW? AND SO SHORT.
LIKE, THIS SHORT.
WHAT DO YOU SAY? LET ME IN?
MAYBE I'LL EVEN TRY IT ON ONCE MORE? YOU KNOW...
...FOR OLD TIMES' SAKE.
OH, COME ON! ARE YOU MADE OF STONE?
THAT'S WHAT MY BOYFRIEND TELLS ME.

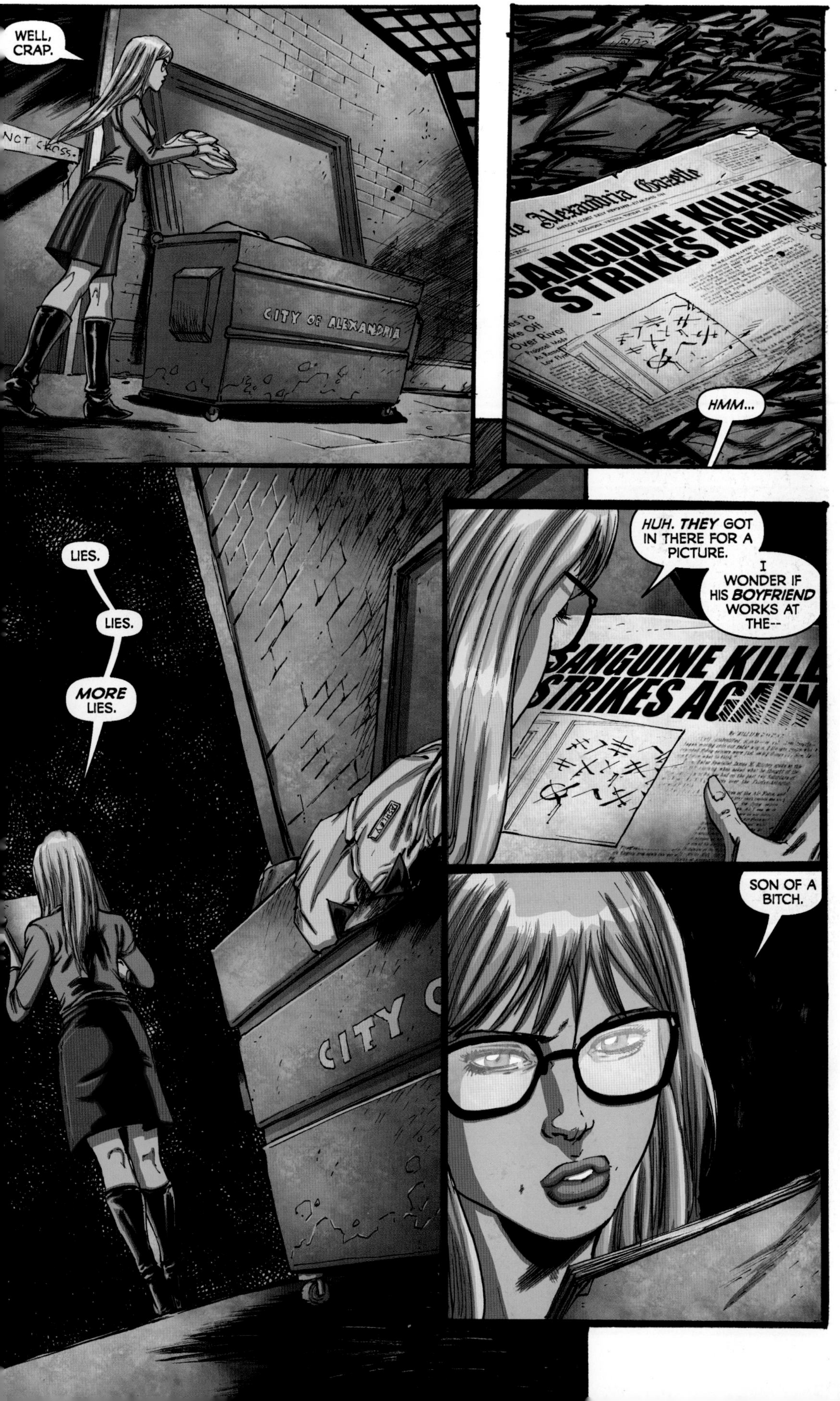
WELL, CRAP.
NOT CROSS
CITY OF ALEXANDRIA
The Alexandria Gazette
SANGUINE KILLER STRIKES AGAIN
HMM...
LIES.
LIES.
MORE LIES.
CITY O
HUH. THEY GOT IN THERE FOR A PICTURE.
I WONDER IF HIS BOYFRIEND WORKS AT THE--
SANGUINE KILLE STRIKES AG
SON OF A BITCH.

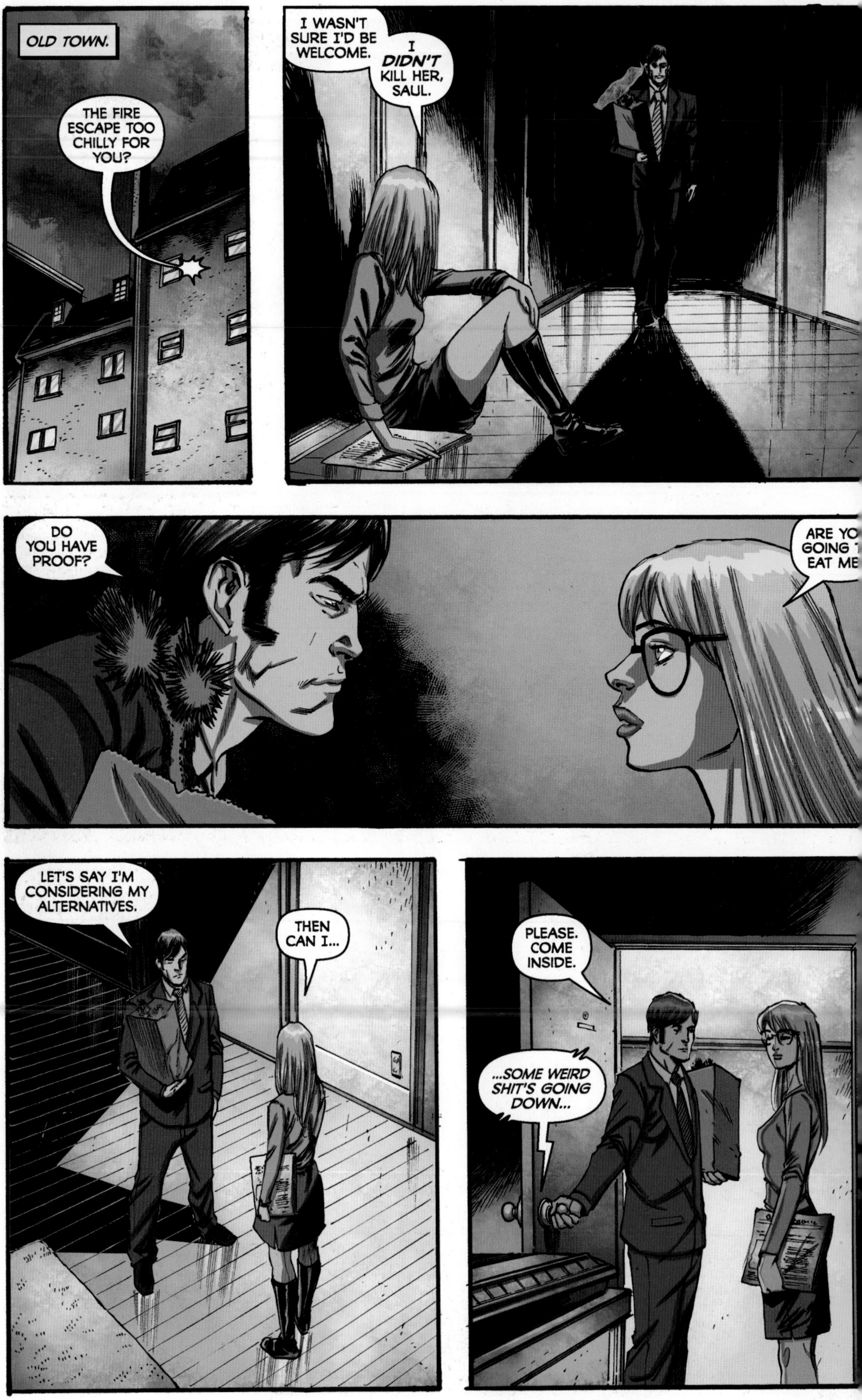
OLD TOWN.
THE FIRE ESCAPE TOO CHILLY FOR YOU?
I WASN'T SURE I'D BE WELCOME.
I *DIDN'T* KILL HER, SAUL.
DO YOU HAVE PROOF?
ARE YO GOING T EAT ME
LET'S SAY I'M CONSIDERING MY ALTERNATIVES.
THEN CAN I...
PLEASE. COME INSIDE.
...SOME WEIRD SHIT'S GOING DOWN...

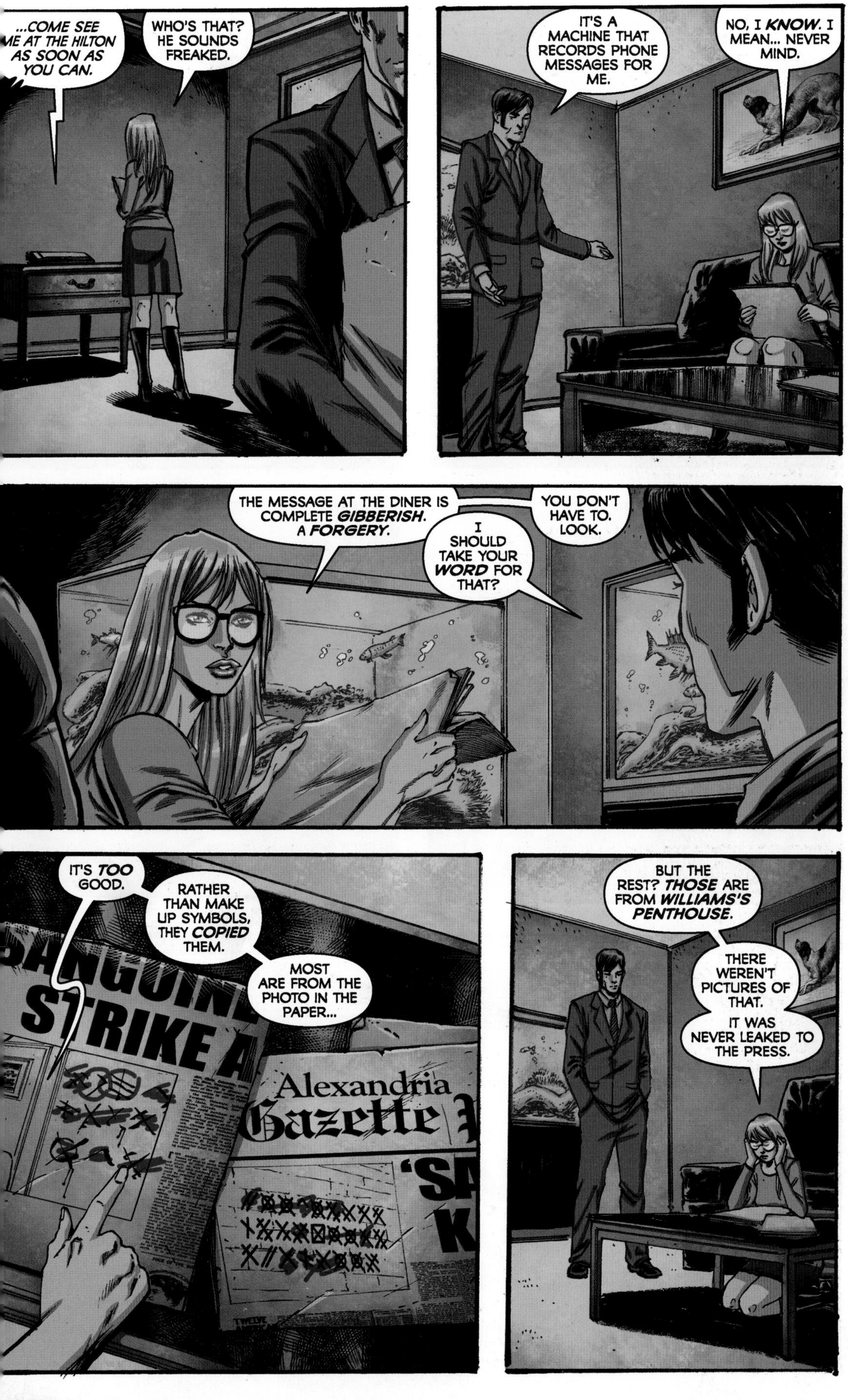
...COME SEE ME AT THE HILTON AS SOON AS YOU CAN.
WHO'S THAT? HE SOUNDS FREAKED.
IT'S A MACHINE THAT RECORDS PHONE MESSAGES FOR ME.
NO, I KNOW. I MEAN... NEVER MIND.
THE MESSAGE AT THE DINER IS COMPLETE GIBBERISH. A FORGERY.
YOU DON'T HAVE TO. LOOK.
I SHOULD TAKE YOUR WORD FOR THAT?
IT'S TOO GOOD.
RATHER THAN MAKE UP SYMBOLS, THEY COPIED THEM.
MOST ARE FROM THE PHOTO IN THE PAPER...
SANGUINE STRIKE A
Alexandria Gazette
BUT THE REST? THOSE ARE FROM WILLIAMS'S PENTHOUSE.
THERE WEREN'T PICTURES OF THAT.
IT WAS NEVER LEAKED TO THE PRESS.

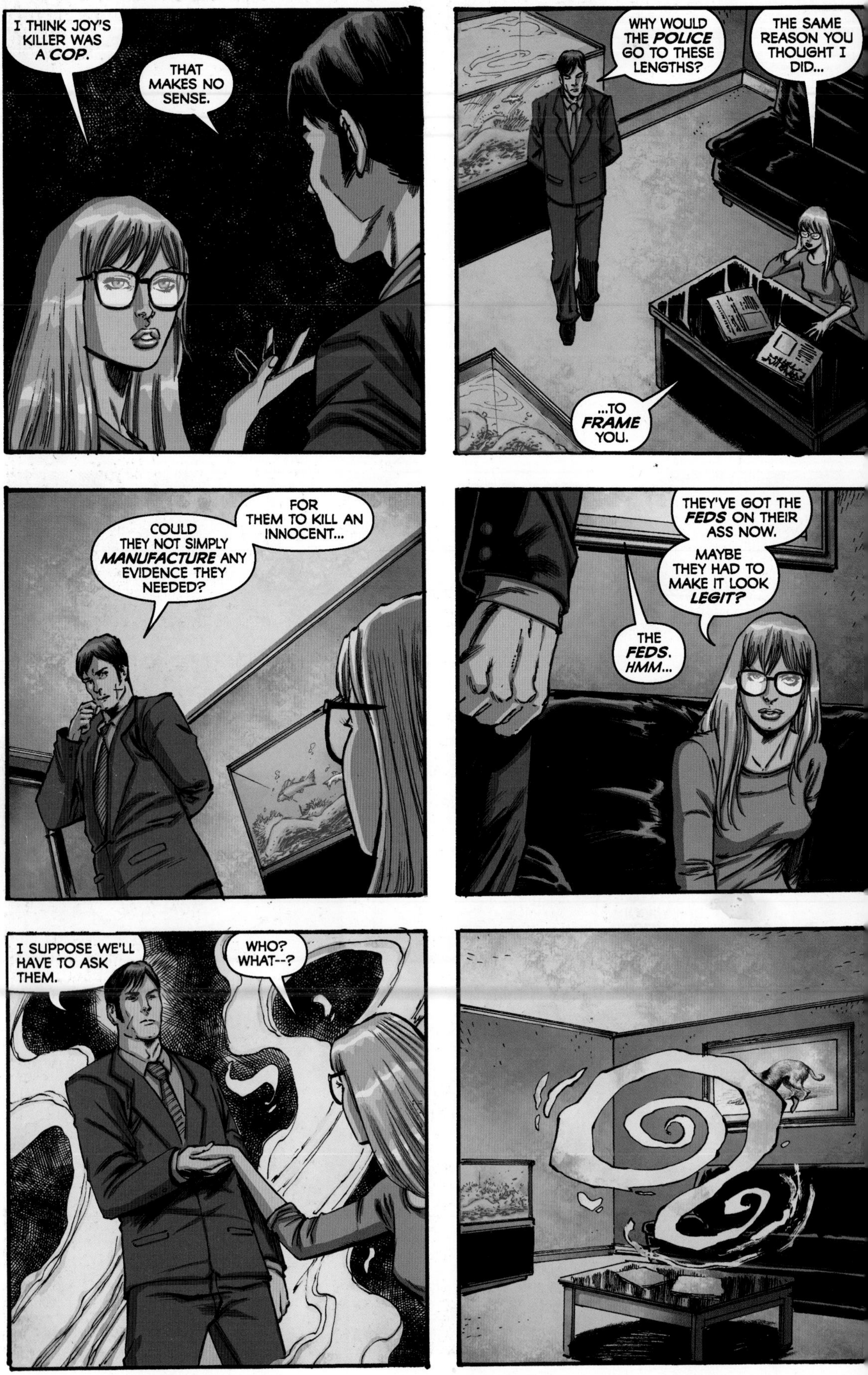
I THINK JOY'S KILLER WAS A *COP*.
THAT MAKES NO SENSE.
WHY WOULD THE *POLICE* GO TO THESE LENGTHS?
THE SAME REASON YOU THOUGHT I DID...
...TO *FRAME* YOU.
FOR THEM TO KILL AN INNOCENT...
COULD THEY NOT SIMPLY *MANUFACTURE* ANY EVIDENCE THEY NEEDED?
THEY'VE GOT THE *FEDS* ON THEIR ASS NOW.
MAYBE THEY HAD TO MAKE IT LOOK *LEGIT?*
THE *FEDS*. HMM...
I SUPPOSE WE'LL HAVE TO ASK THEM.
WHO? WHAT--?

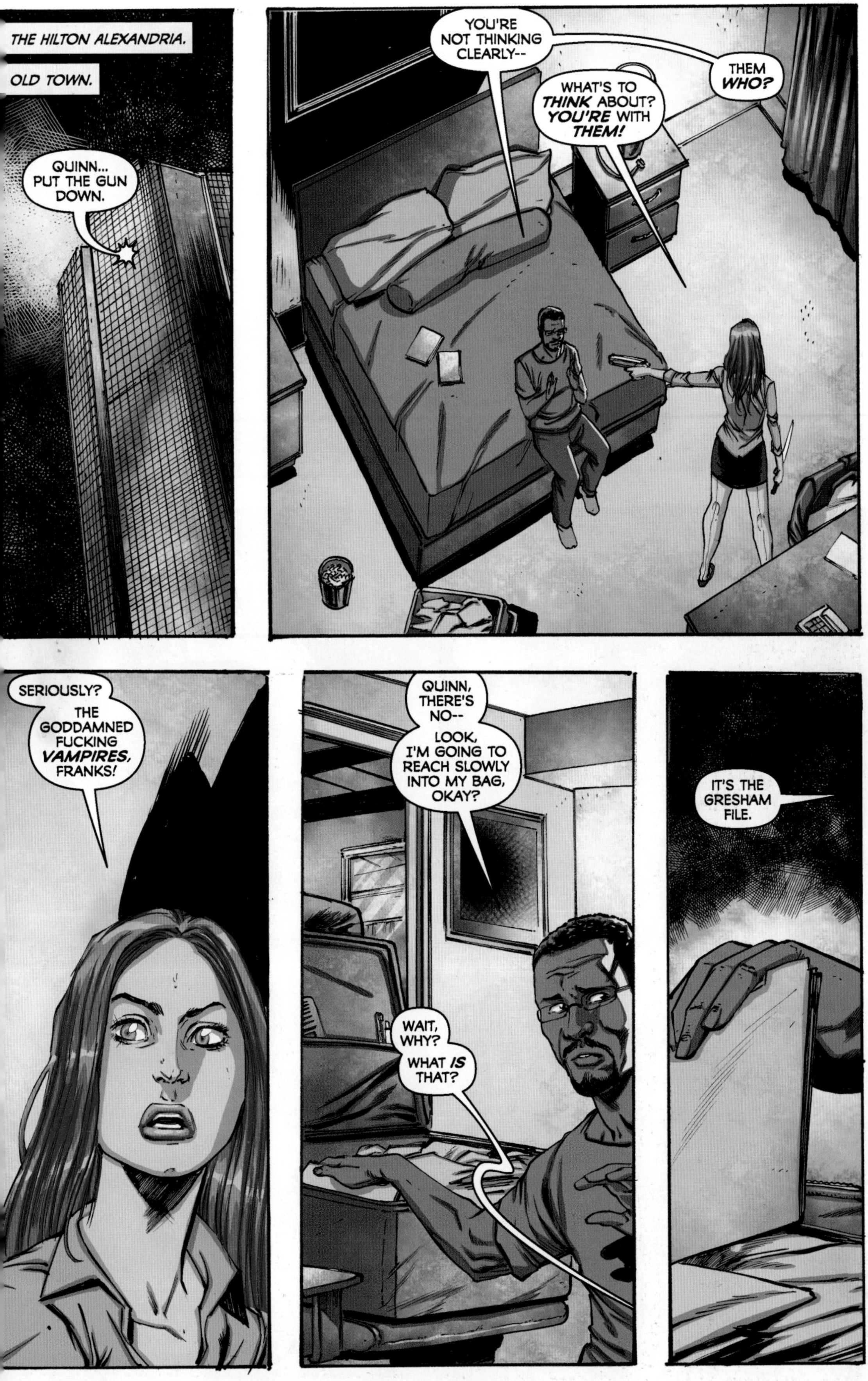
THE HILTON ALEXANDRIA.
OLD TOWN.
QUINN... PUT THE GUN DOWN.
YOU'RE NOT THINKING CLEARLY--
WHAT'S TO THINK ABOUT? YOU'RE WITH THEM!
THEM WHO?
SERIOUSLY?
THE GODDAMNED FUCKING VAMPIRES, FRANKS!
QUINN, THERE'S NO--
LOOK, I'M GOING TO REACH SLOWLY INTO MY BAG, OKAY?
WAIT, WHY?
WHAT IS THAT?
IT'S THE GRESHAM FILE.

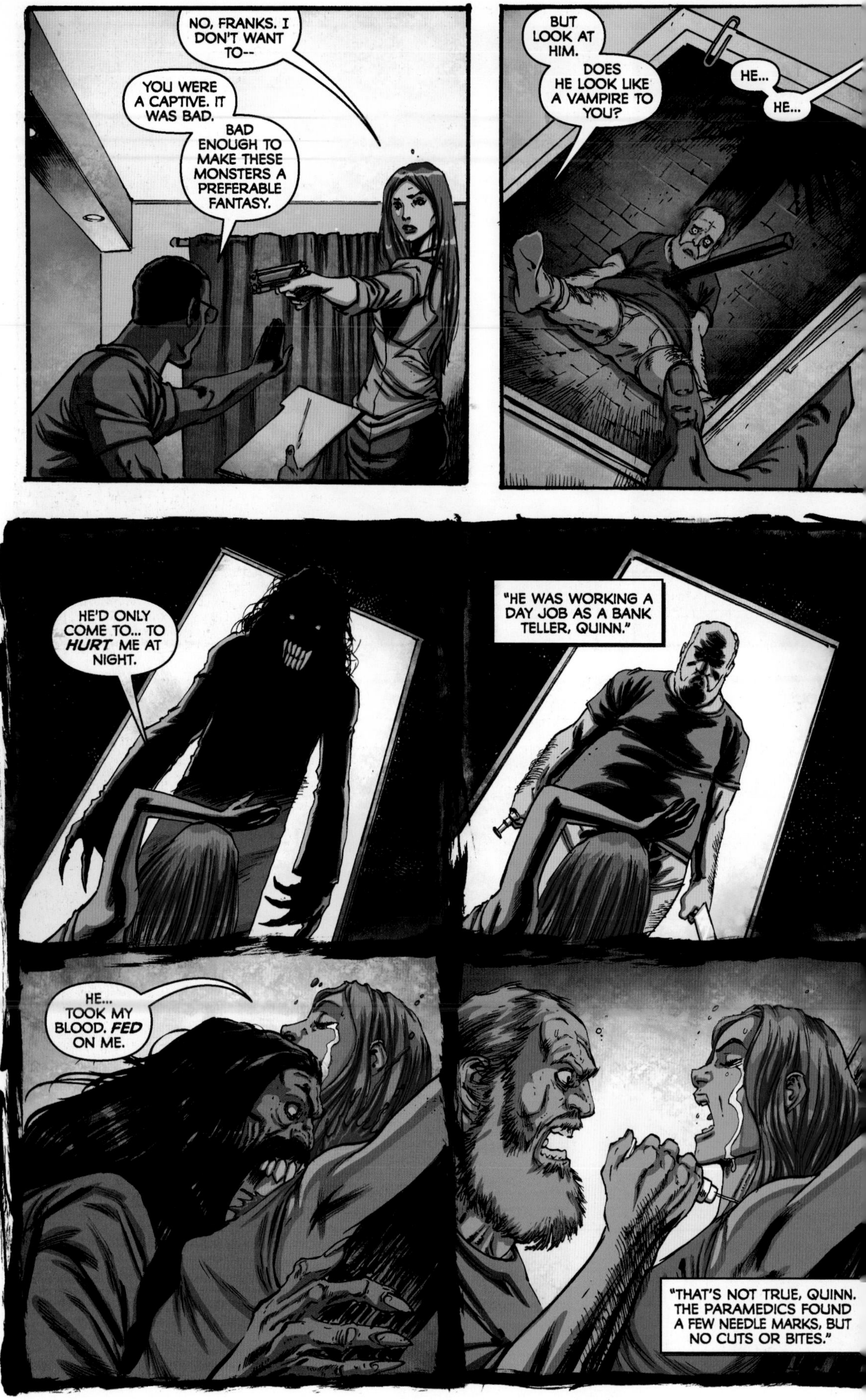
NO, FRANKS. I DON'T WANT TO--
YOU WERE A CAPTIVE. IT WAS BAD.
BAD ENOUGH TO MAKE THESE MONSTERS A PREFERABLE FANTASY.
BUT LOOK AT HIM.
DOES HE LOOK LIKE A VAMPIRE TO YOU?
HE...
HE...
HE'D ONLY COME TO... TO *HURT* ME AT NIGHT.
"HE WAS WORKING A DAY JOB AS A BANK TELLER, QUINN."
HE... TOOK MY BLOOD. *FED* ON ME.
"THAT'S NOT TRUE, QUINN. THE PARAMEDICS FOUND A FEW NEEDLE MARKS, BUT NO CUTS OR BITES."

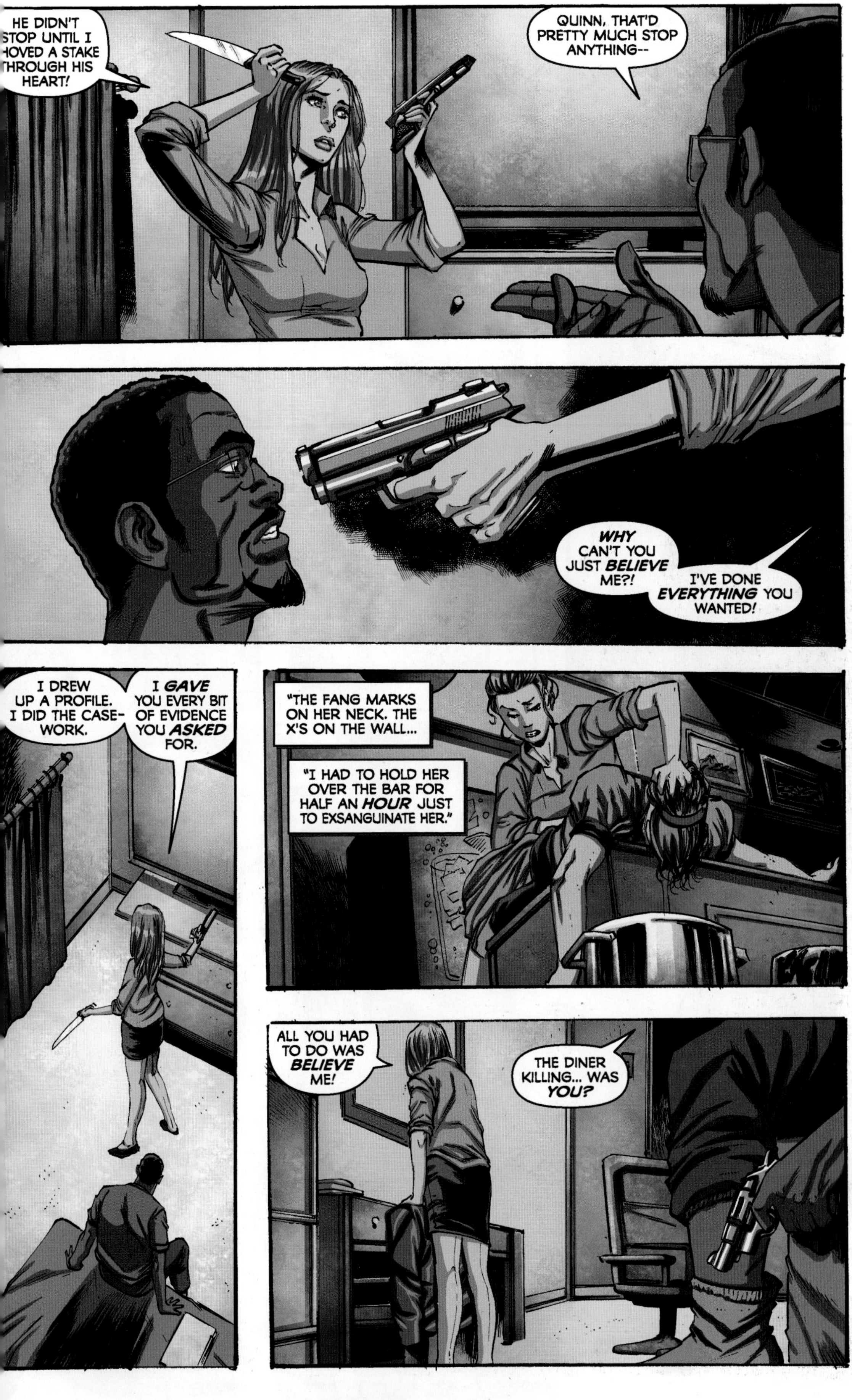
HE DIDN'T STOP UNTIL I SHOVED A STAKE THROUGH HIS HEART!
QUINN, THAT'D PRETTY MUCH STOP ANYTHING--
WHY CAN'T YOU JUST BELIEVE ME?!
I'VE DONE EVERYTHING YOU WANTED!
I DREW UP A PROFILE. I DID THE CASE-WORK.
I GAVE YOU EVERY BIT OF EVIDENCE YOU ASKED FOR.
"THE FANG MARKS ON HER NECK. THE X'S ON THE WALL...
"I HAD TO HOLD HER OVER THE BAR FOR HALF AN HOUR JUST TO EXSANGUINATE HER."
ALL YOU HAD TO DO WAS BELIEVE ME!
THE DINER KILLING... WAS YOU?

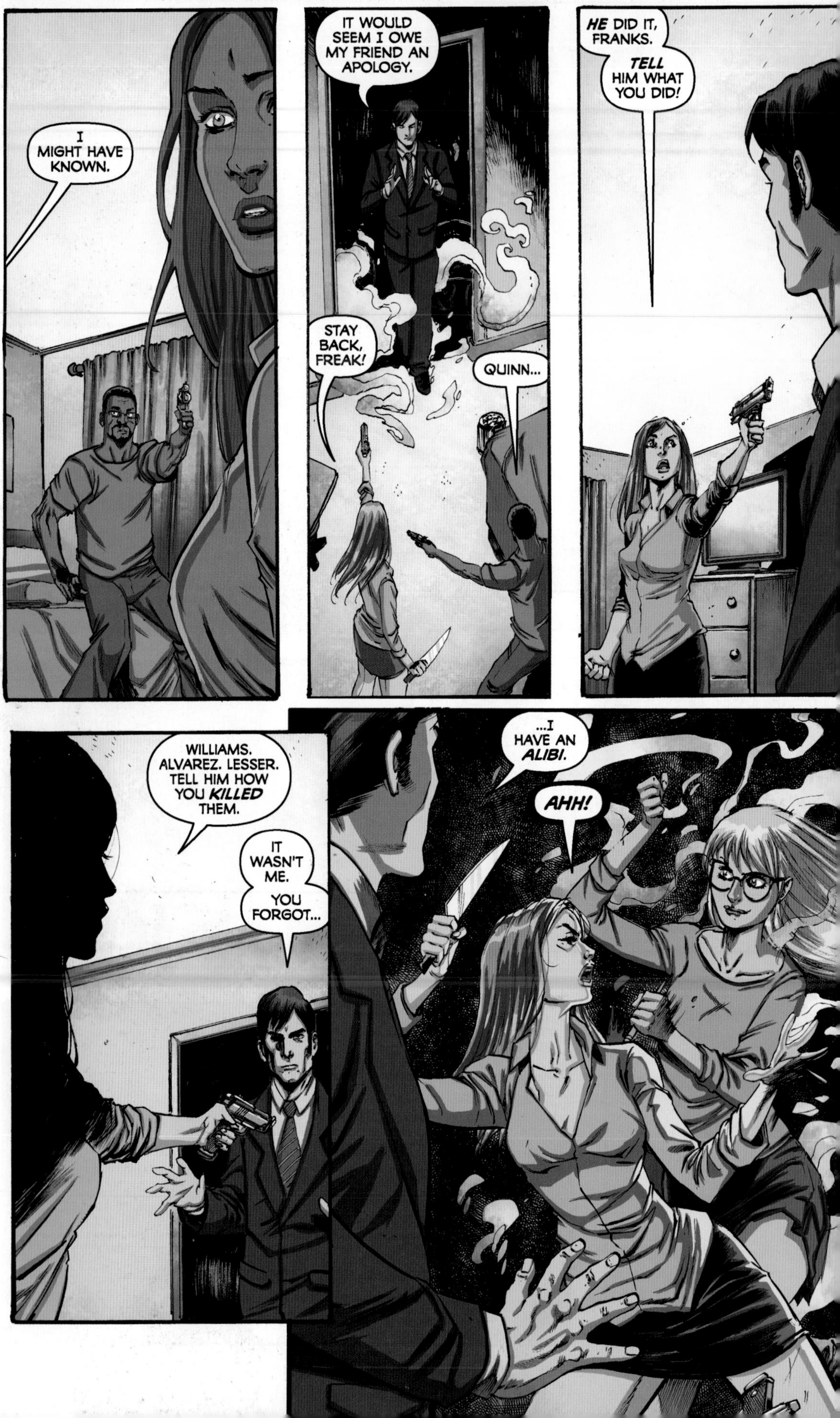
I MIGHT HAVE KNOWN.
IT WOULD SEEM I OWE MY FRIEND AN APOLOGY.
STAY BACK, FREAK!
QUINN...
HE DID IT, FRANKS.
TELL HIM WHAT YOU DID!
WILLIAMS. ALVAREZ. LESSER. TELL HIM HOW YOU KILLED THEM.
IT WASN'T ME.
YOU FORGOT...
...I HAVE AN ALIBI.
AHH!

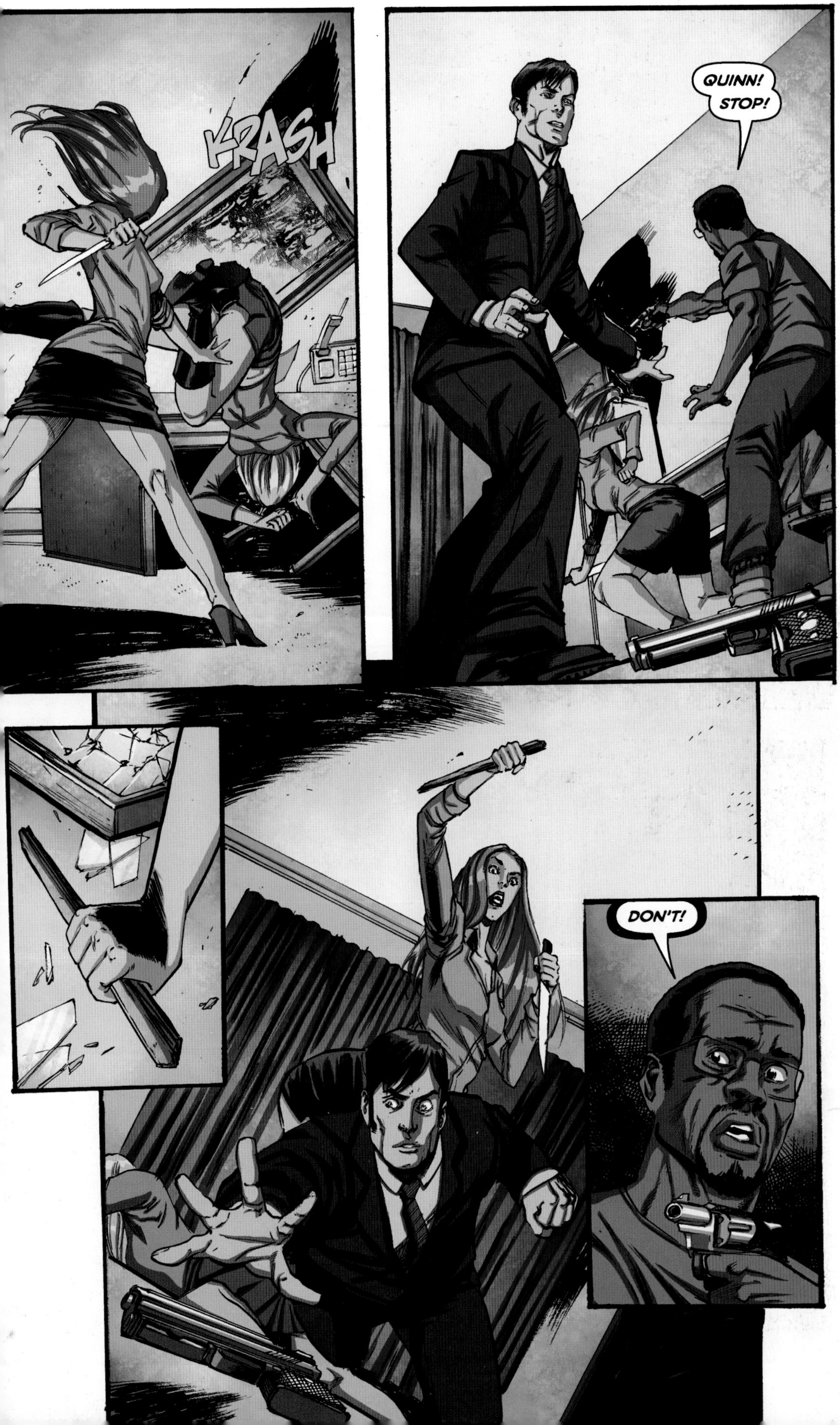
KRASH
QUINN! STOP!
DON'T!

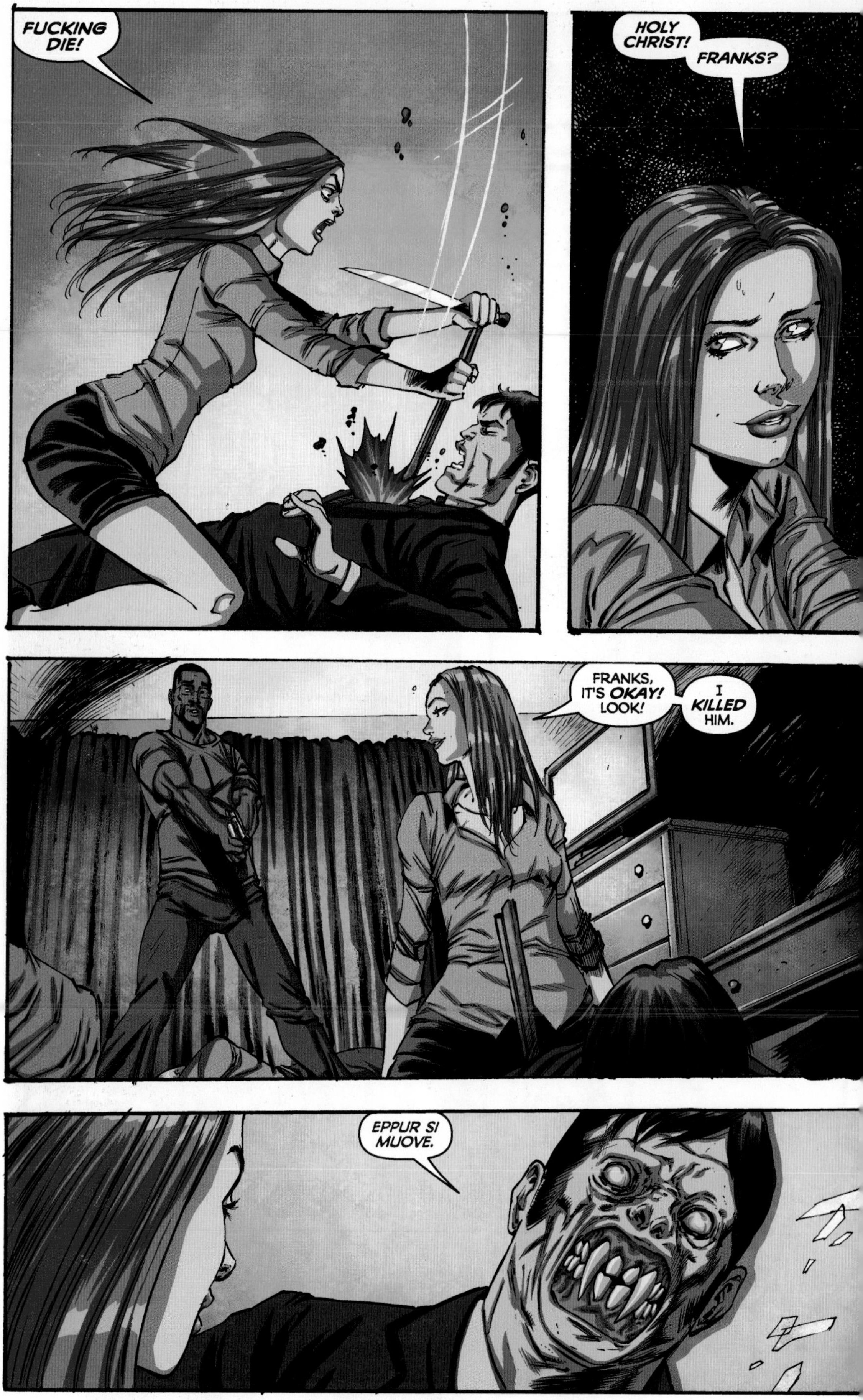
FUCKING DIE!
HOLY CHRIST!
FRANKS?
FRANKS, IT'S OKAY! LOOK!
I KILLED HIM.
EPPUR SI MUOVE.

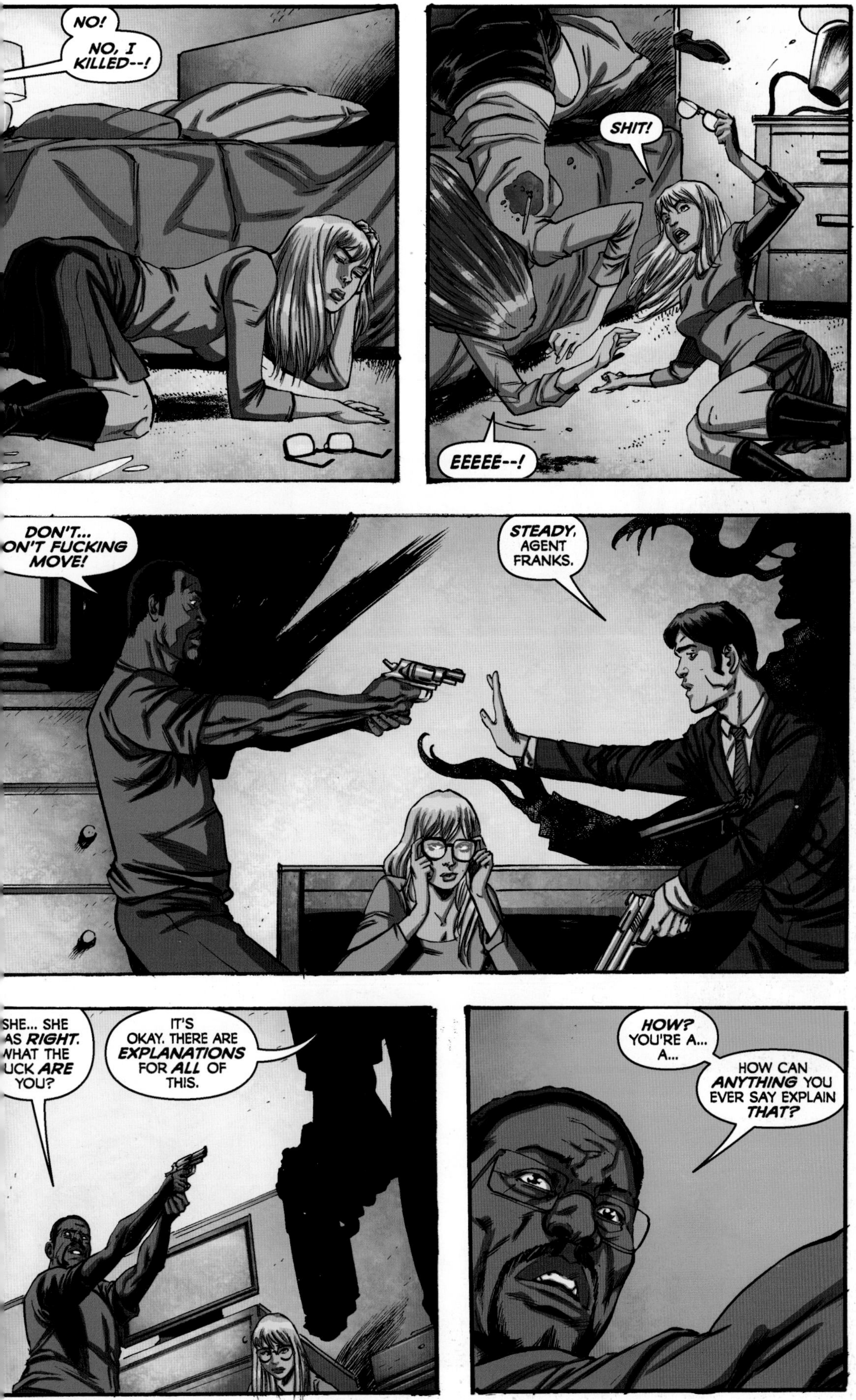
NO!
NO, I KILLED--!
SHIT!
EEEEE--!
DON'T... ON'T FUCKING MOVE!
STEADY, AGENT FRANKS.
SHE... SHE AS RIGHT. WHAT THE UCK ARE YOU?
IT'S OKAY. THERE ARE EXPLANATIONS FOR ALL OF THIS.
HOW? YOU'RE A... A...
HOW CAN ANYTHING YOU EVER SAY EXPLAIN THAT?

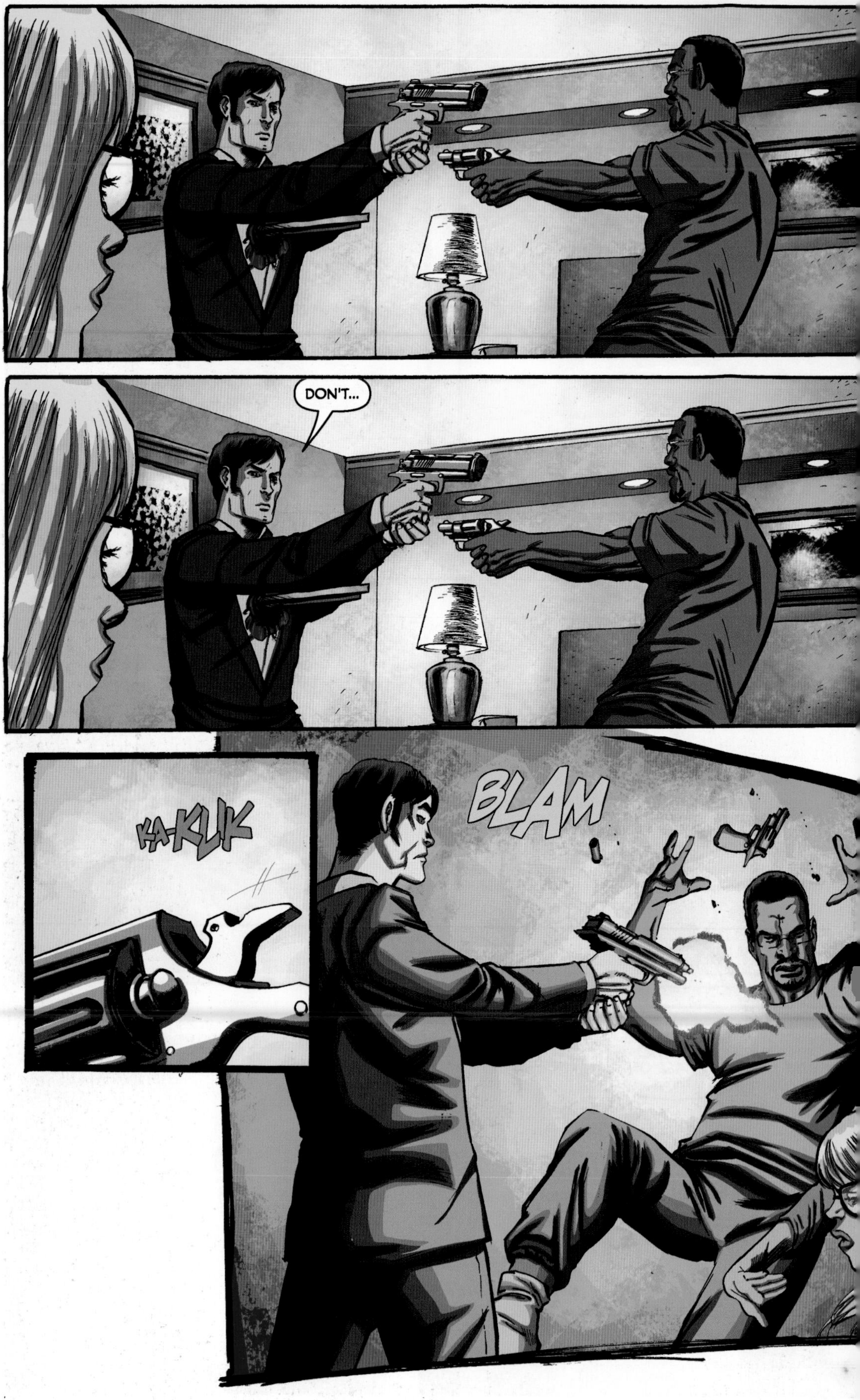
DON'T...
KA-KLIK
BLAM

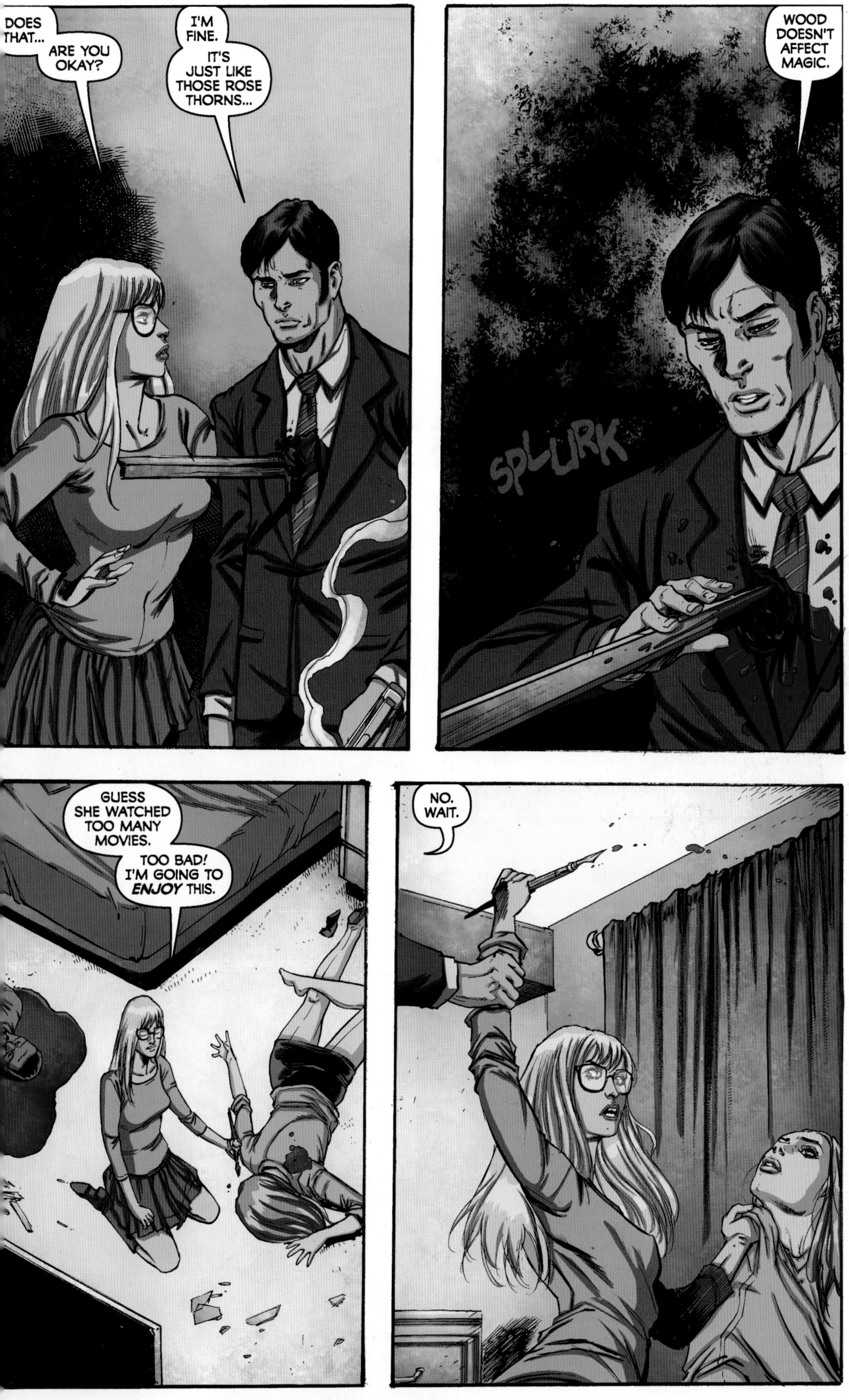
DOES THAT...
ARE YOU OKAY?
I'M FINE.
IT'S JUST LIKE THOSE ROSE THORNS...
WOOD DOESN'T AFFECT MAGIC.
SPLURK
GUESS SHE WATCHED TOO MANY MOVIES.
TOO BAD! I'M GOING TO *ENJOY* THIS.
NO. WAIT.

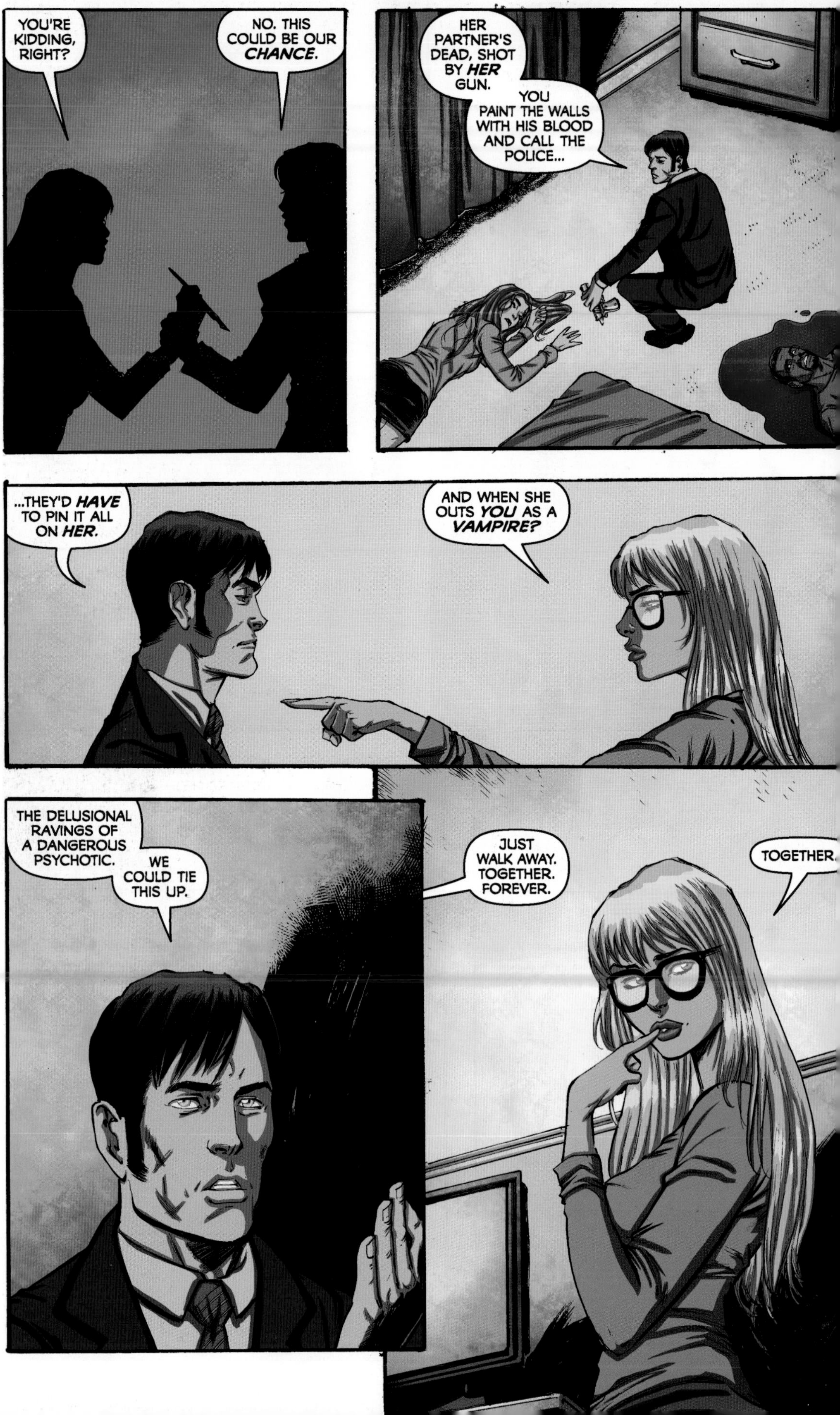
YOU'RE KIDDING, RIGHT?
NO. THIS COULD BE OUR *CHANCE*.
HER PARTNER'S DEAD, SHOT BY *HER* GUN.
YOU PAINT THE WALLS WITH HIS BLOOD AND CALL THE POLICE...
...THEY'D *HAVE* TO PIN IT ALL ON *HER*.
AND WHEN SHE OUTS *YOU* AS A *VAMPIRE?*
THE DELUSIONAL RAVINGS OF A DANGEROUS PSYCHOTIC.
WE COULD TIE THIS UP.
JUST WALK AWAY. TOGETHER. FOREVER.
TOGETHER.

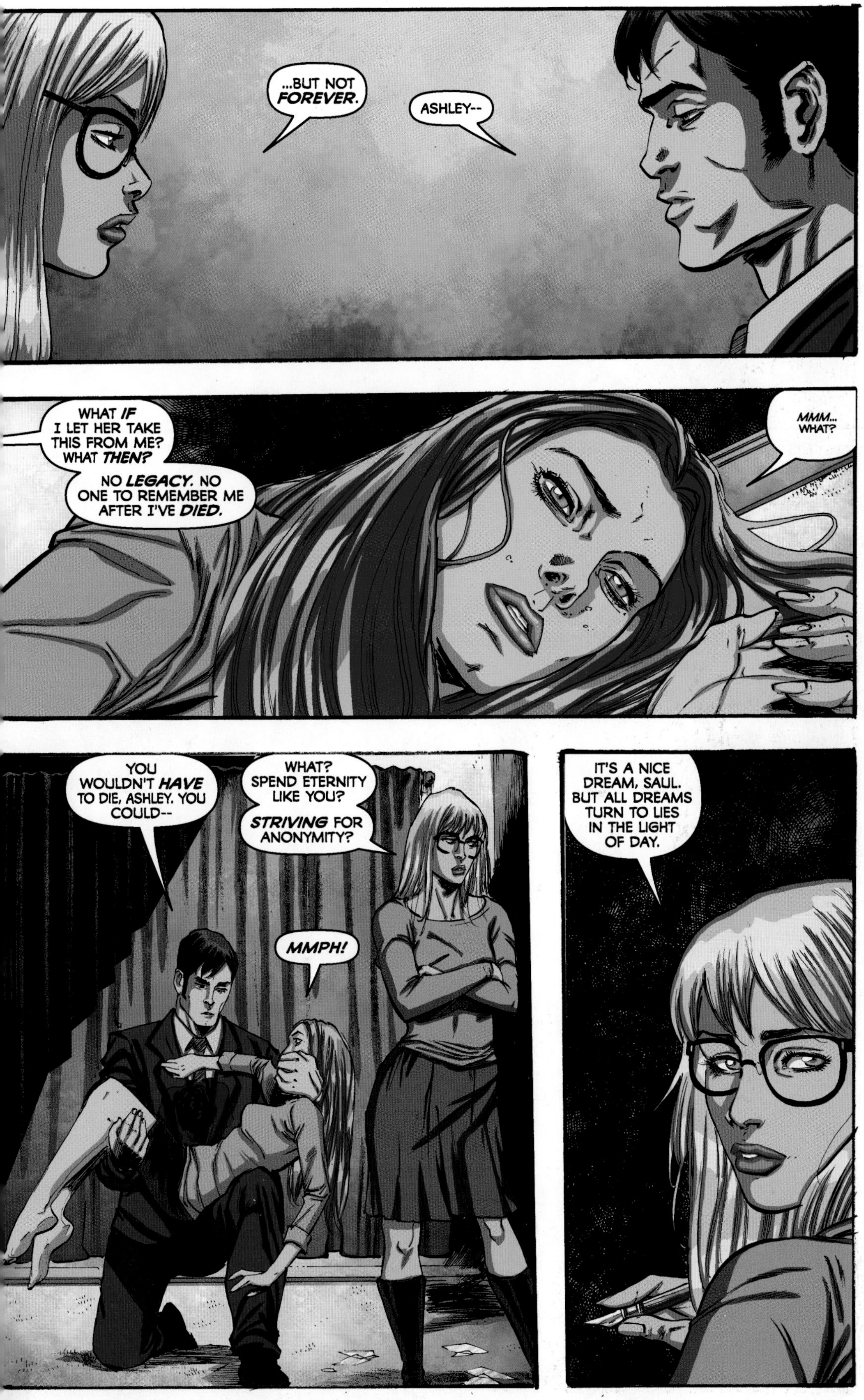
...BUT NOT *FOREVER*.
ASHLEY--
WHAT *IF* I LET HER TAKE THIS FROM ME? WHAT *THEN?*
NO *LEGACY*. NO ONE TO REMEMBER ME AFTER I'VE *DIED*.
MMM... WHAT?
YOU WOULDN'T *HAVE* TO DIE, ASHLEY. YOU COULD--
WHAT? SPEND ETERNITY LIKE YOU? *STRIVING* FOR ANONYMITY?
MMPH!
IT'S A NICE DREAM, SAUL. BUT ALL DREAMS TURN TO LIES IN THE LIGHT OF DAY.

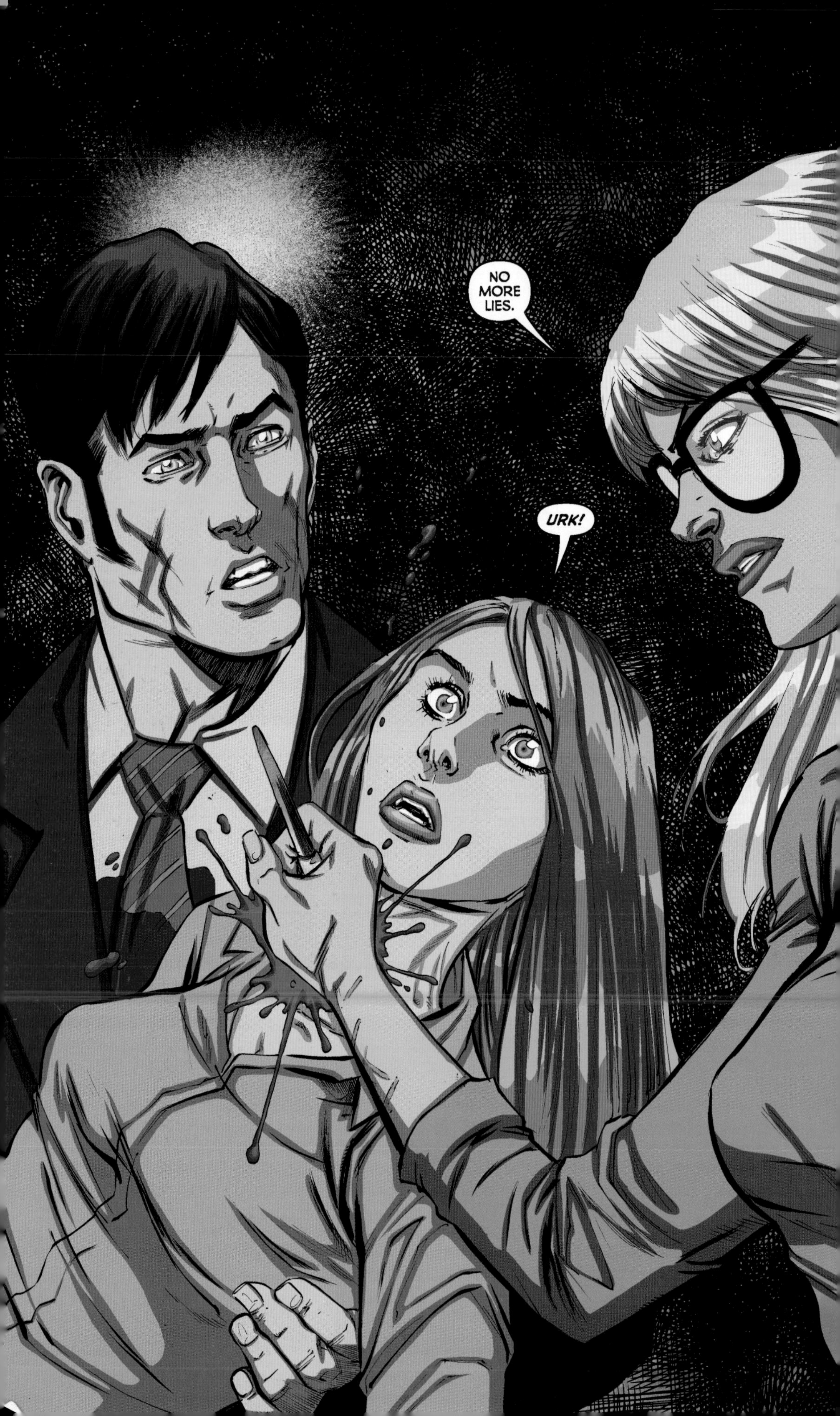
NO MORE LIES.
URK!

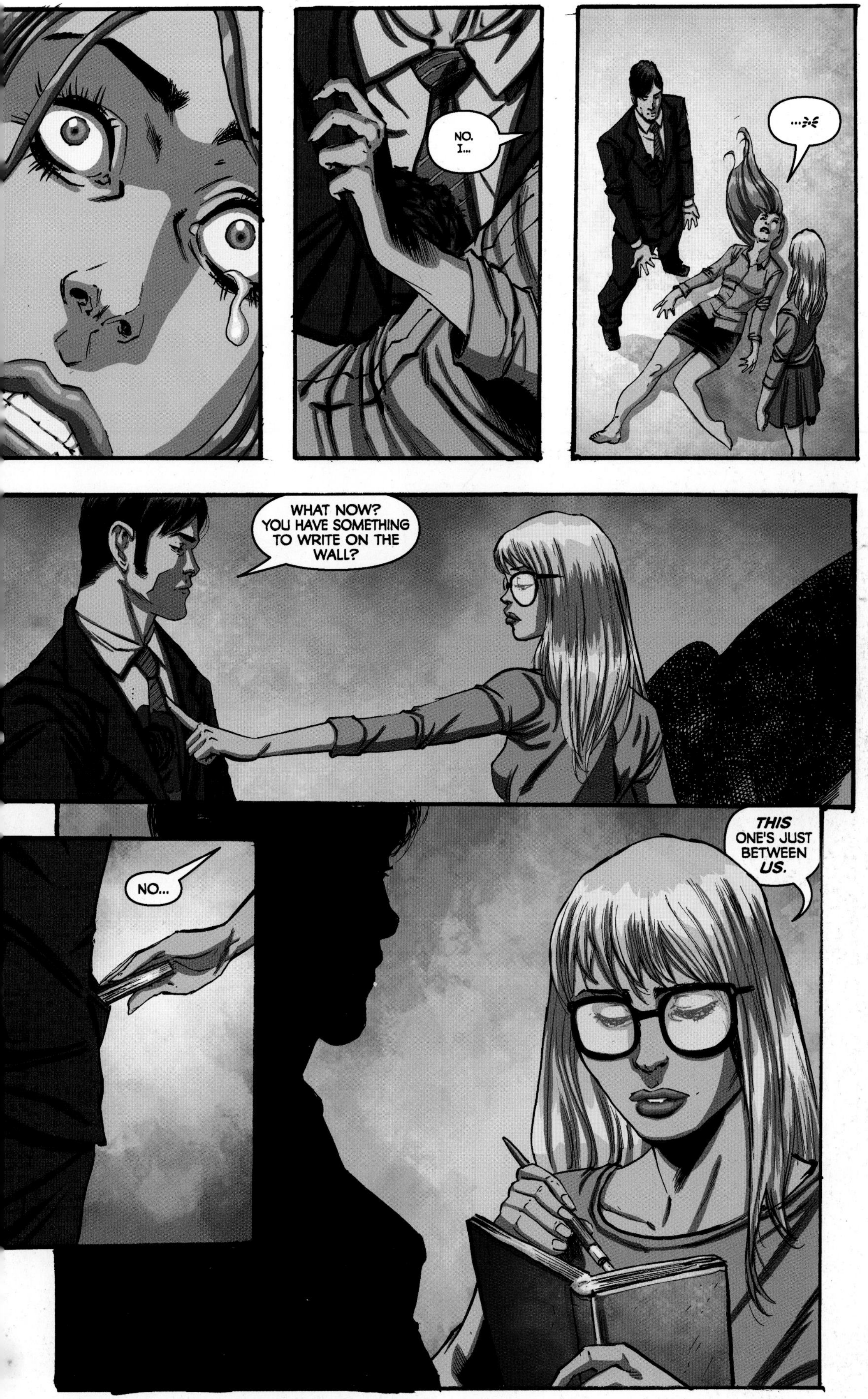
NO. I...
...!!
WHAT NOW? YOU HAVE SOMETHING TO WRITE ON THE WALL?
NO...
THIS ONE'S JUST BETWEEN *US.*

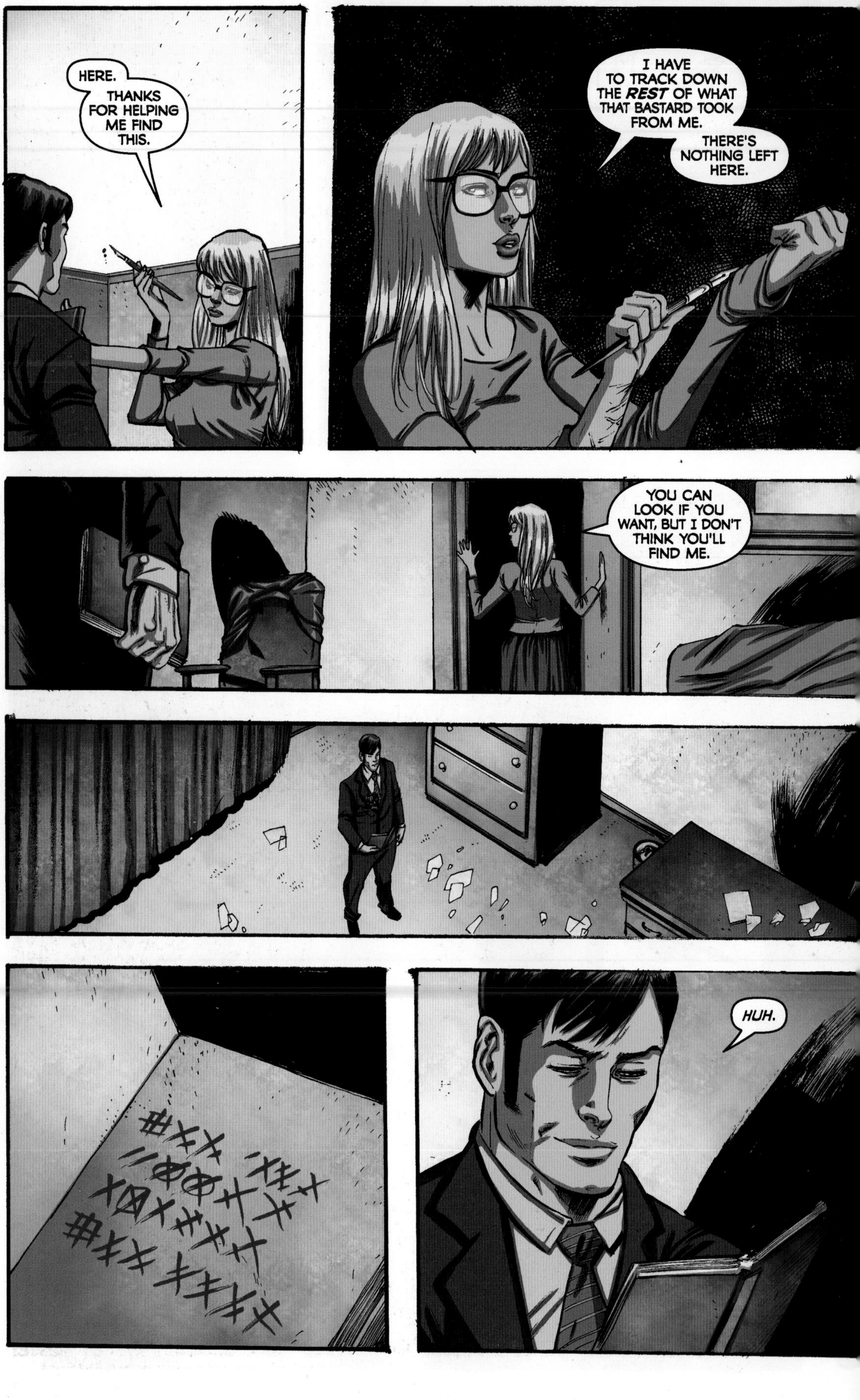
HERE.
THANKS FOR HELPING ME FIND THIS.
I HAVE TO TRACK DOWN THE *REST* OF WHAT THAT BASTARD TOOK FROM ME.
THERE'S NOTHING LEFT HERE.
YOU CAN LOOK IF YOU WANT, BUT I DON'T THINK YOU'LL FIND ME.
HUH.

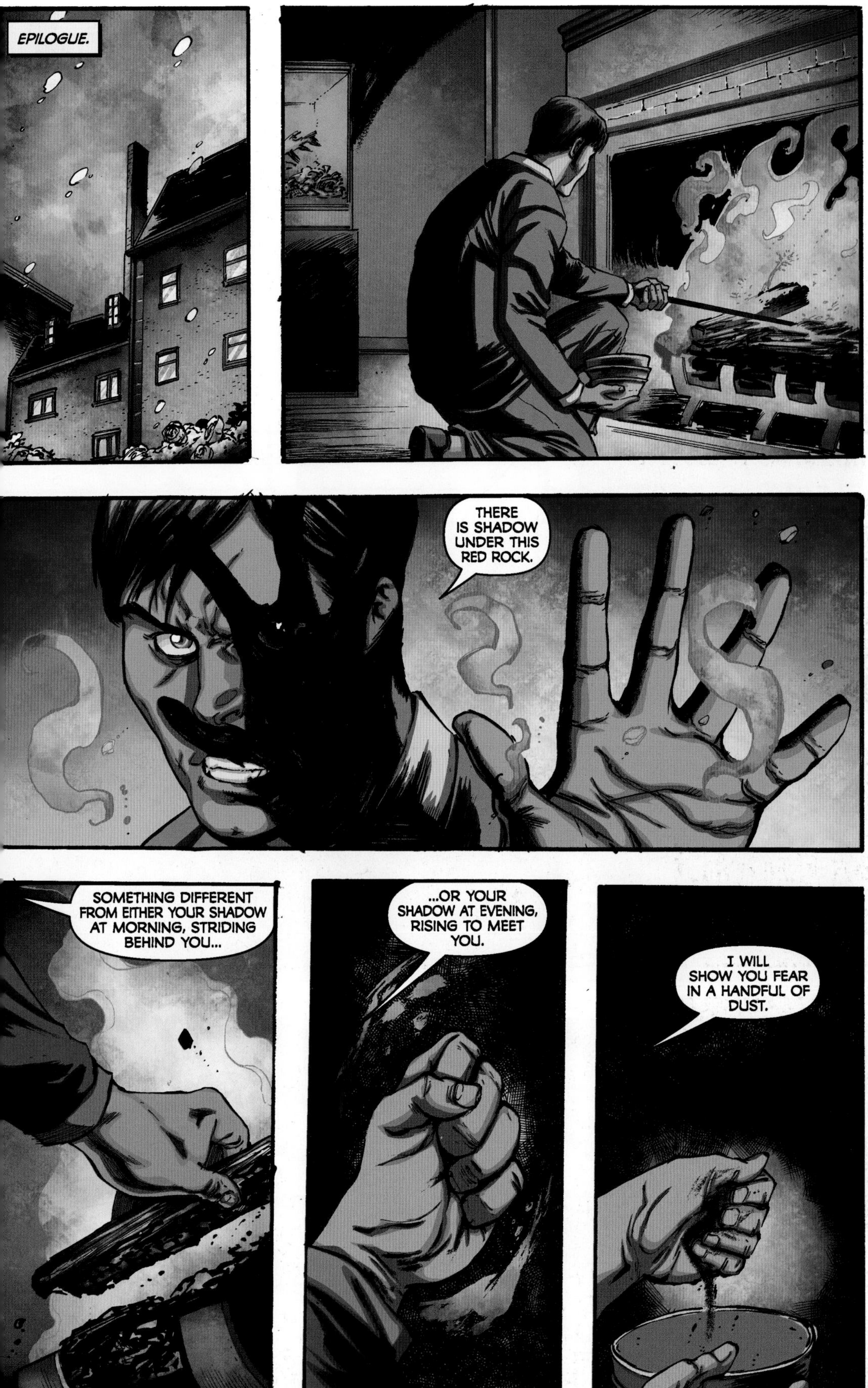
EPILOGUE.
THERE IS SHADOW UNDER THIS RED ROCK.
SOMETHING DIFFERENT FROM EITHER YOUR SHADOW AT MORNING, STRIDING BEHIND YOU...
...OR YOUR SHADOW AT EVENING, RISING TO MEET YOU.
I WILL SHOW YOU FEAR IN A HANDFUL OF DUST.

YOUR ARMS FULL, AND YOUR HAIR WET...
...I COULD NOT SPEAK AND MY EYES FAILED.
I WAS NEITHER LIVING NOR DEAD, AND I KNEW NOTHING.
I LOOKED INTO THE HEART OF THE LIGHT. THE SILENCE.
ÖD' UND LEER DAS MEER.

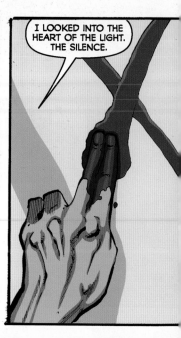

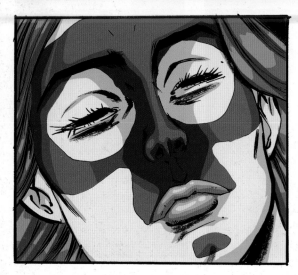

THE END

SKETCHBOOK

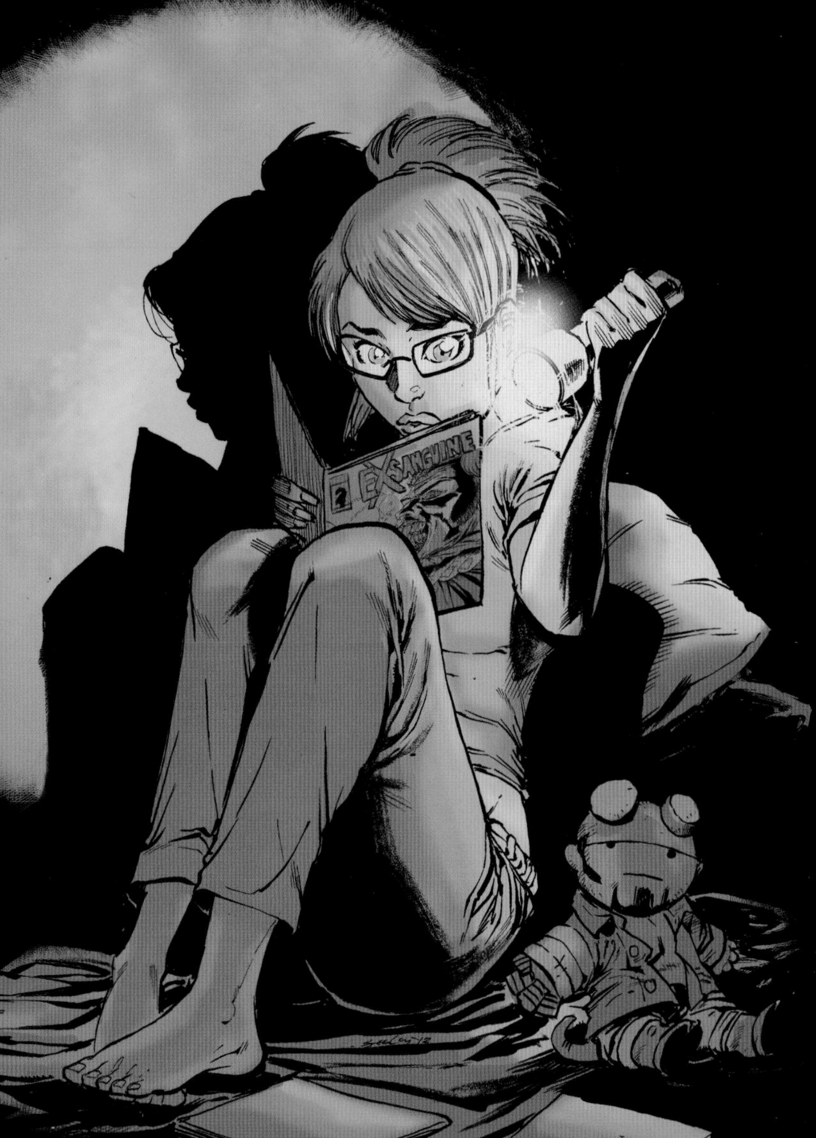
EXSANGUINE

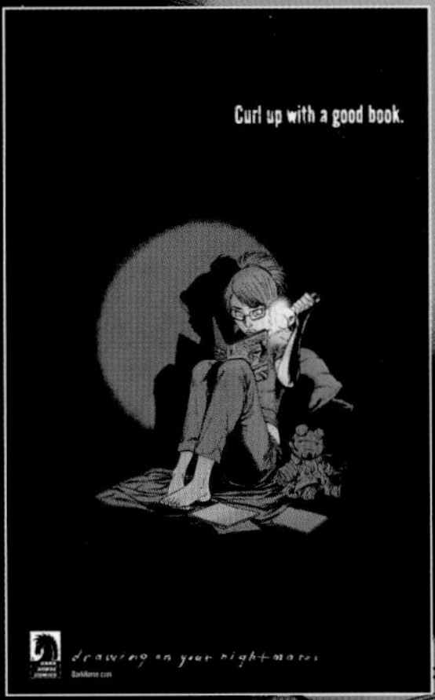
Curl up with a good book.
drawing on your nightmares
DarkHorse.com

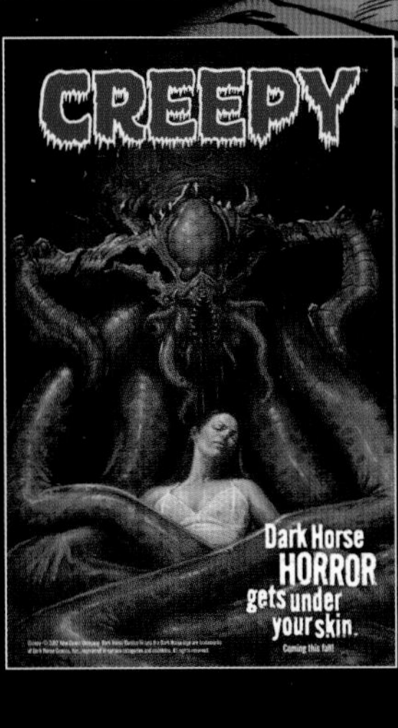
CREEPY
Dark Horse
HORROR
gets under
your skin.
Coming this fall!

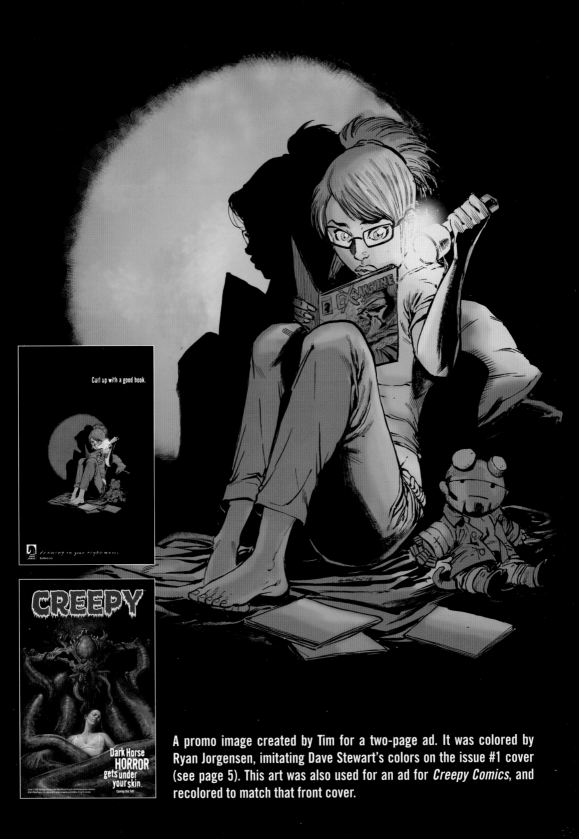

A promo image created by Tim for a two-page ad. It was colored by Ryan Jorgensen, imitating Dave Stewart's colors on the issue #1 cover (see page 5). This art was also used for an ad for *Creepy Comics*, and recolored to match that front cover.

CHARACTER DESIGNS

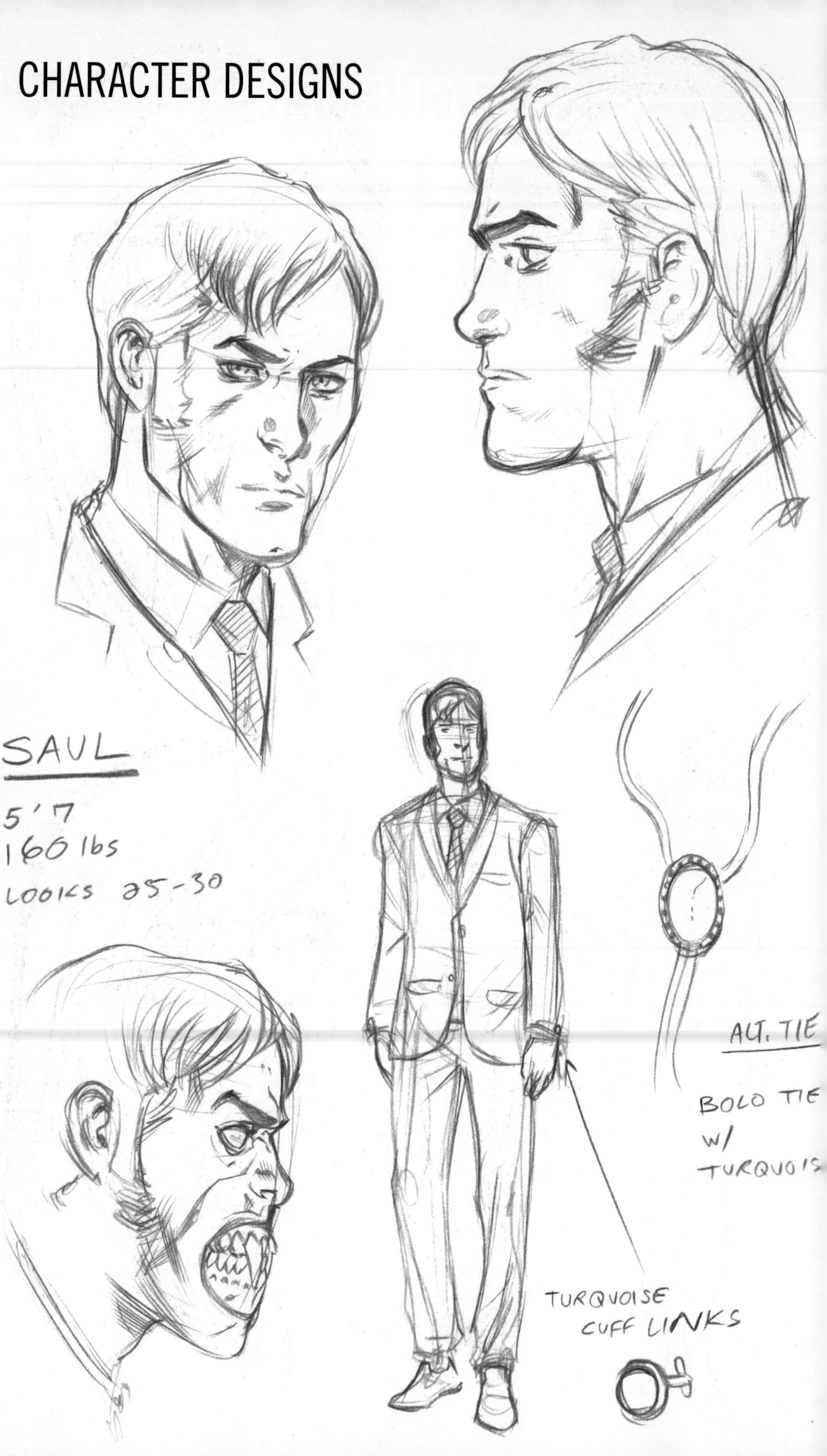
SAUL
5'7
160 lbs
LOOKS 25-30
ALT. TIE
BOLO TIE
w/
TURQUOIS
TURQUOISE
CUFF LINKS

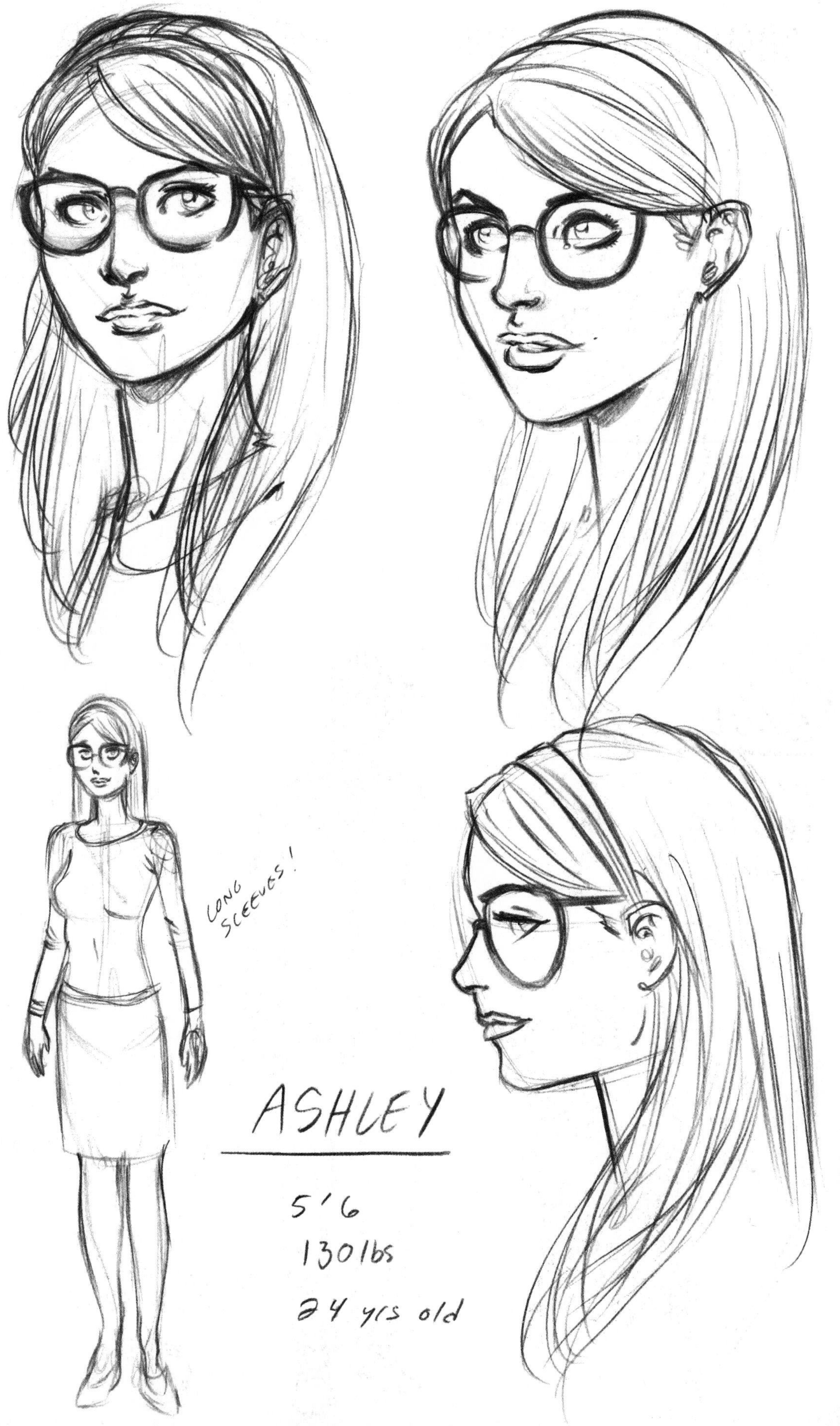
LONG SLEEVES!
ASHLEY
5'6
130lbs
24 yrs old

THE FEDS

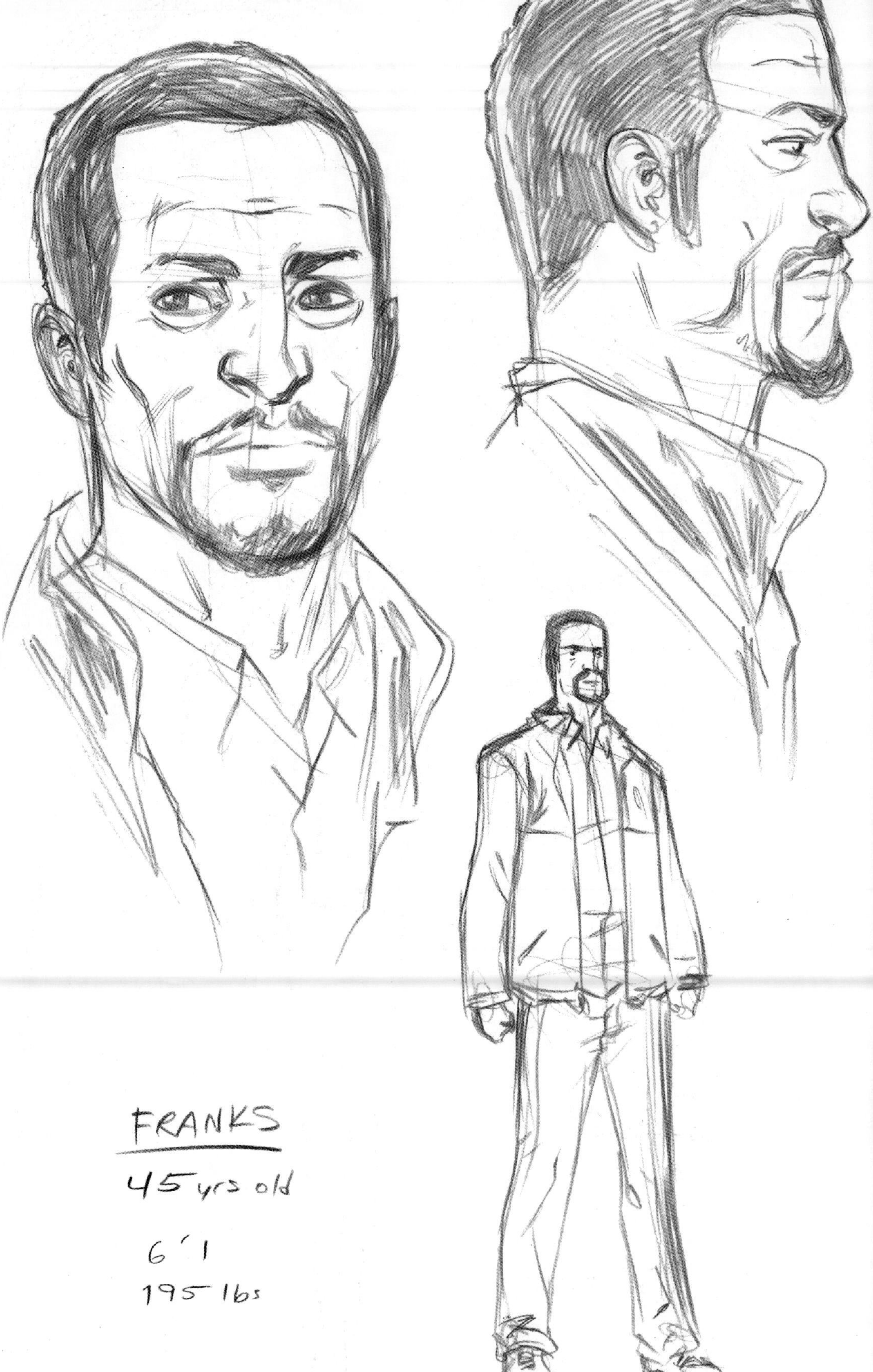
FRANKS
45 yrs old
6'1
195 lbs

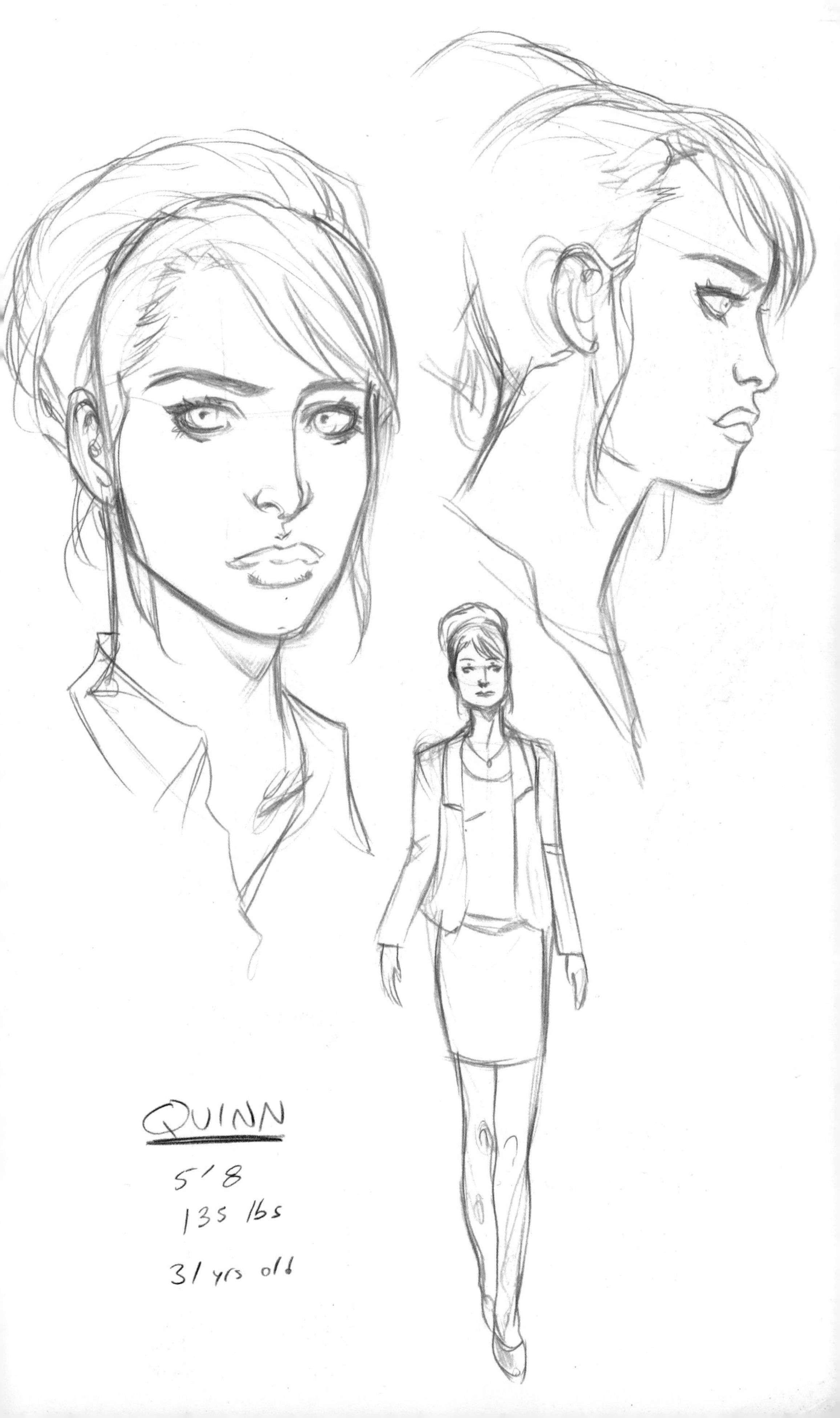
QUINN
5'8
135 lbs
31 yrs old

DESIGN FOR THE SHORT-LIVED P.I.

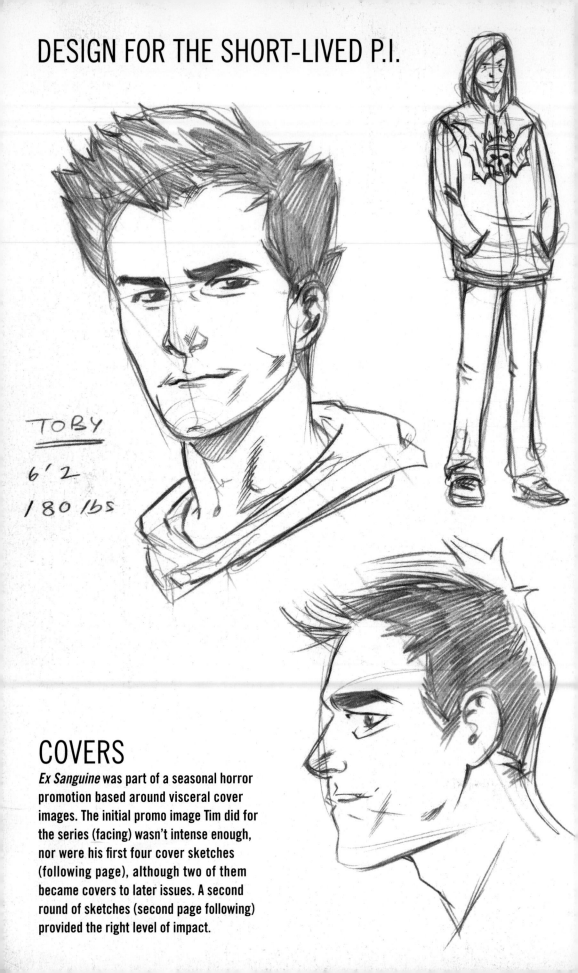

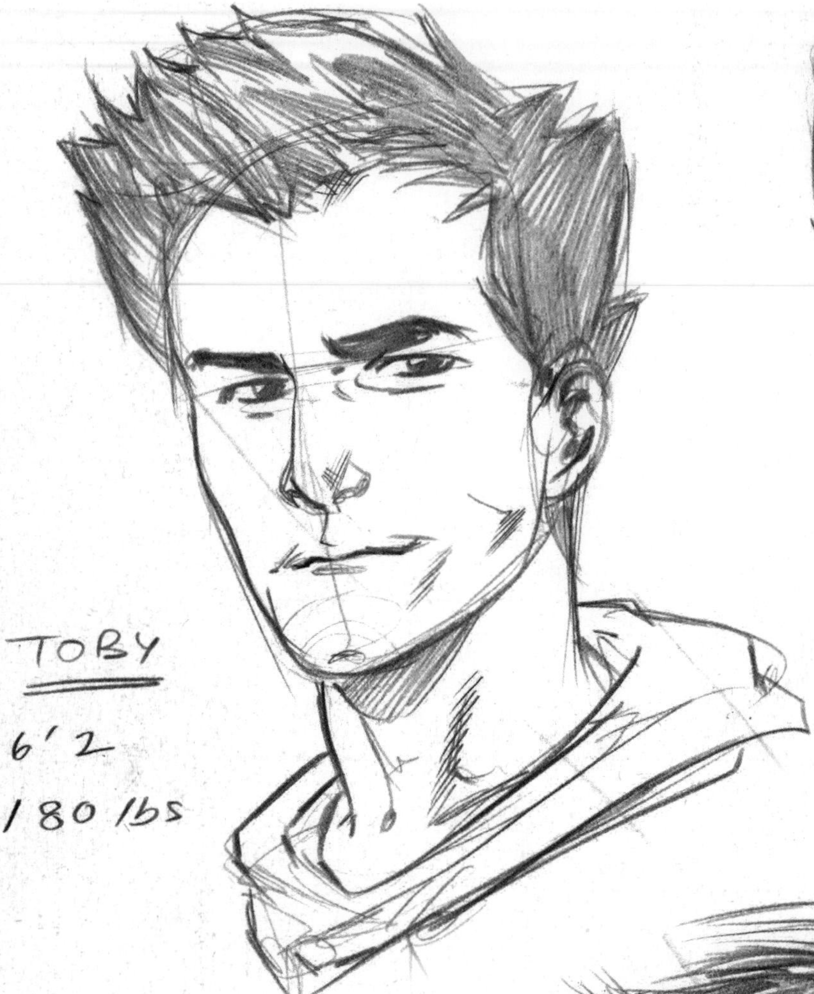
TOBY
6'2
180 lbs

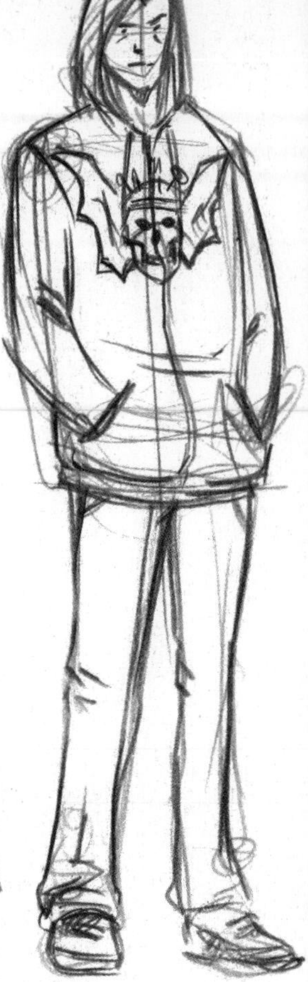

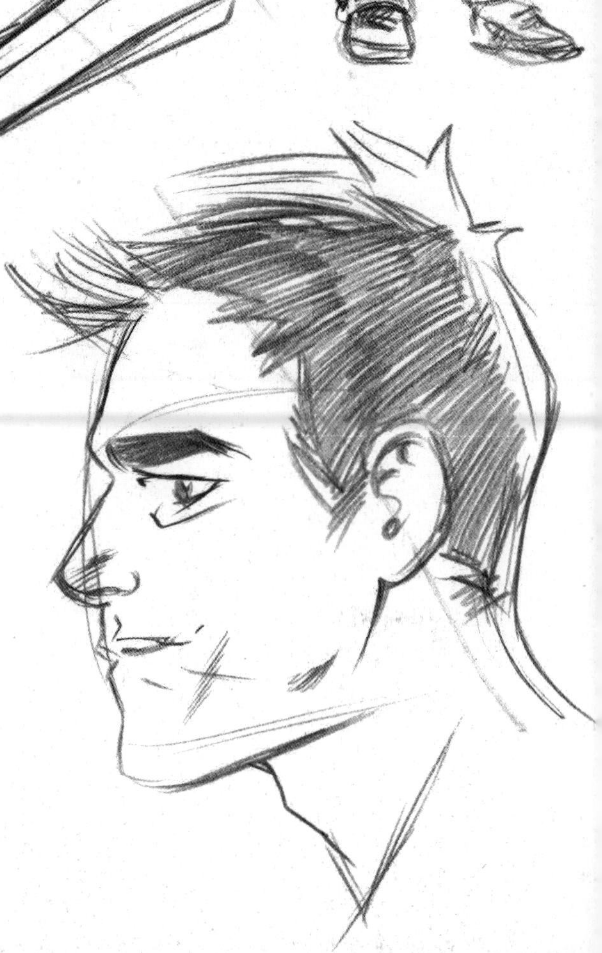

COVERS

Ex Sanguine was part of a seasonal horror promotion based around visceral cover images. The initial promo image Tim did for the series (facing) wasn't intense enough, nor were his first four cover sketches (following page), although two of them became covers to later issues. A second round of sketches (second page following) provided the right level of impact.

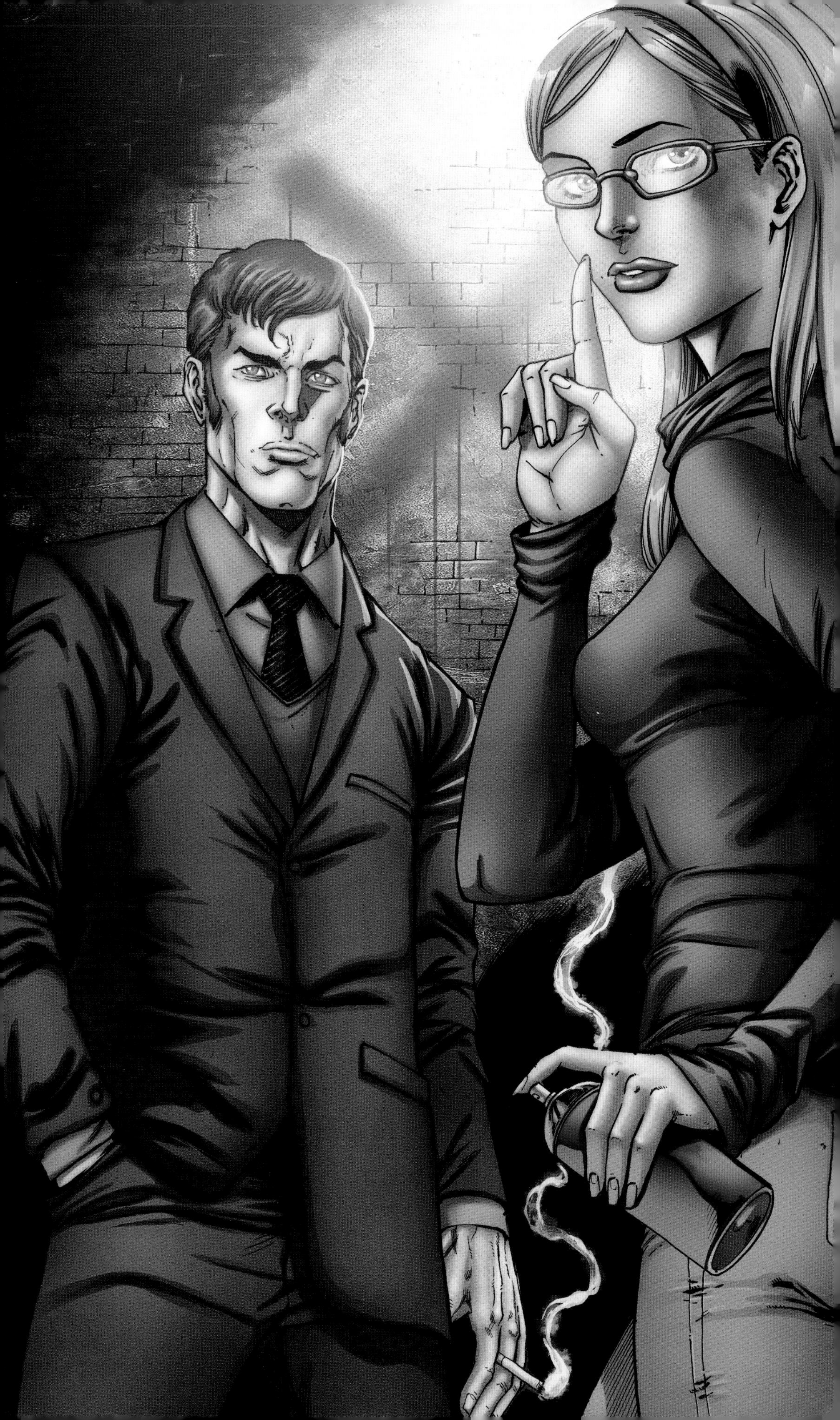

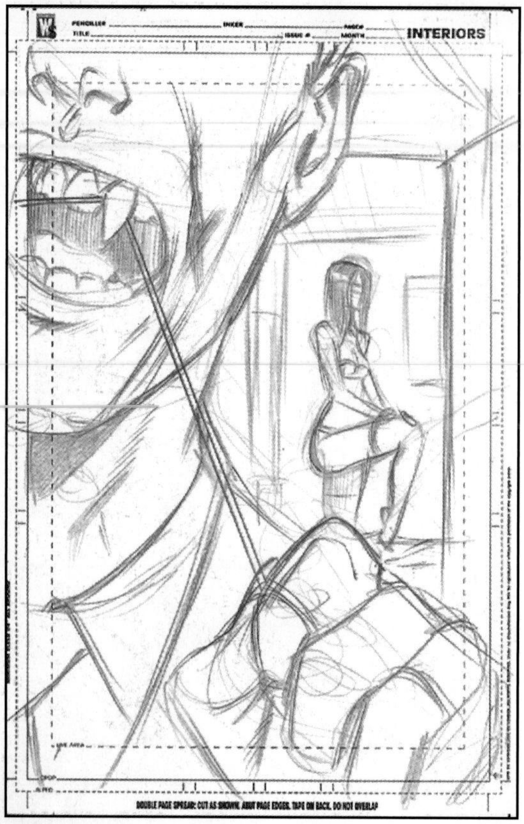
INTERIORS
DOUBLE PAGE SPREAD: CUT AS SHOWN. ABUT PAGE EDGES. TAPE ON BACK. DO NOT OVERLAP

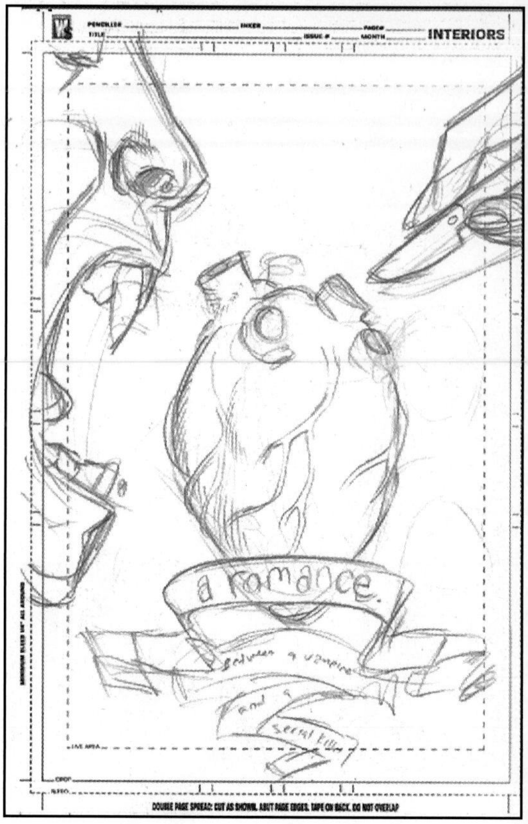
INTERIORS
a romance.
Between a vampire
and a
DOUBLE PAGE SPREAD: CUT AS SHOWN. ABUT PAGE EDGES. TAPE ON BACK. DO NOT OVERLAP

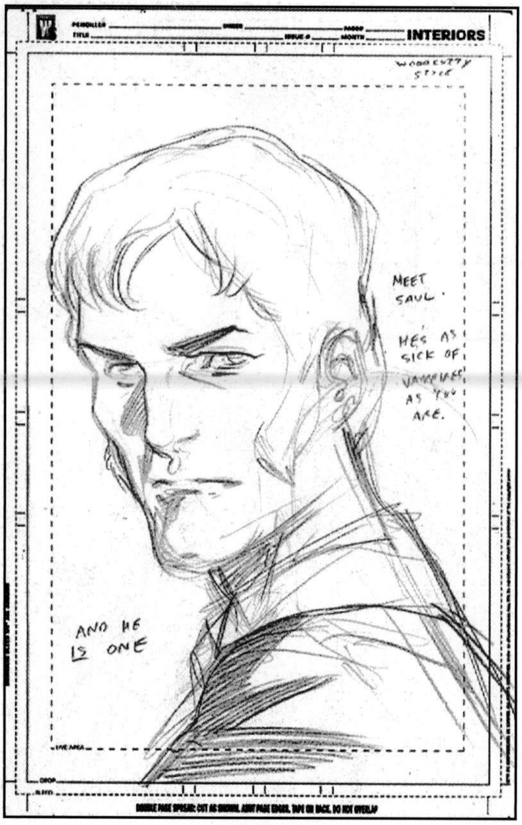
INTERIORS
MEET SAUL.
HE'S AS SICK OF VAMPIRES AS YOU ARE.
AND HE IS ONE
DOUBLE PAGE SPREAD: CUT AS SHOWN. ABUT PAGE EDGES. TAPE ON BACK. DO NOT OVERLAP

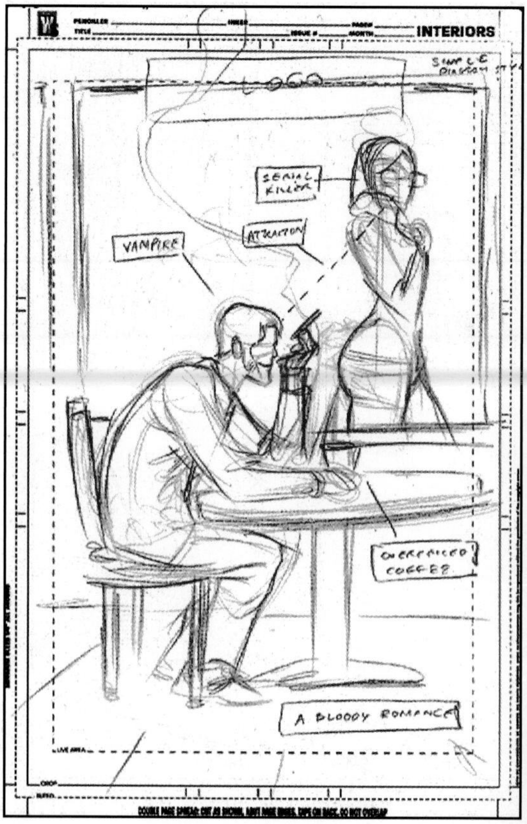
INTERIORS
LOGO
SERIAL KILLER
VAMPIRE
ATTRACTION
OVERPRICED COFFEE
A BLOODY ROMANCE
DOUBLE PAGE SPREAD: CUT AS SHOWN. ABUT PAGE EDGES. TAPE ON BACK. DO NOT OVERLAP

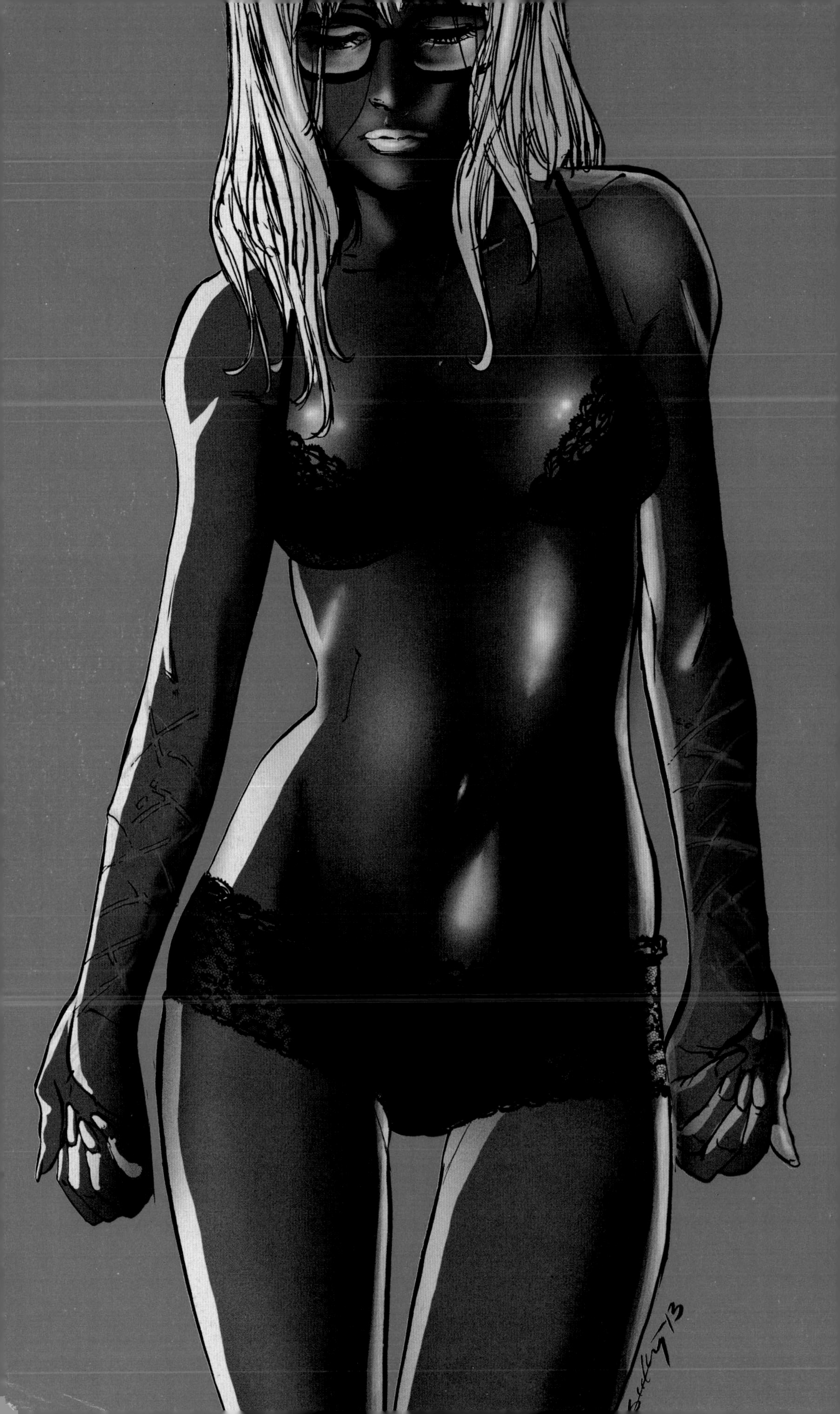

ALSO FROM DARK HORSE

THE OCCULTIST VOLUME 1 TPB

Tim Seeley and Victor Drujiniu

Rob Bailey must balance responsibilities as a boyfriend, as a college student, and as the new wielder of the Sword, an ancient book of spells that has bound itself to him. With a team of hit mages hired by a powerful sorcerer after him, it's trial by fire for the new Occultist, as he learns to handle his powerful magical tome, or suffer at the hands of these deadly enemies. But as he fights for his life, our hero wonders whether he's wielding this enigmatic weapon, or if *it's* the one in control.

978-1-59582-745-6 | $16.99

BUFFY THE VAMPIRE SLAYER: SPIKE—A DARK PLACE TPB

Victor Gischler, Paul Lee, and Andy Owens

Fresh from his latest attempt to get Buffy to act on her feelings for him, Spike, the once-terrifying vampire Big Bad, has fled to the dark side of the moon. His soul-searching trip leads him to a group of dangerous demons and a rude awakening from his reverie, which in turn leads him on an unexpected adventure to . . . Sunnydale! Working in an appearance by the main villains from *Angel & Faith* and a romantic liaison with a succubus, Victor Gischler (*Deadpool*, *Punisher*) brings Spike's character to vivid life, presenting this vampire who chose to have a soul with the hard truth about himself and his pursuit of the Slayer.

978-1-61655-109-4 | $17.99

THE GUILD VOLUME 2: KNIGHTS OF GOOD TPB

Felicia Day, Darick Robertson, Kristian Donaldson, Tim Seeley, and others

Set before the first season of *The Guild*, these hilarious stories delighted fans and newbies alike and introduced plots that influenced the show itself, including season 5's backstory of Tink, originally hinted at in these pages. Featuring a huge variety of comics' best artists, as well as many of the talents key to the web series, and leading directly to the moment Zaboo unexpectedly appears at a startled Codex's front door in episode 1, this collection comprises a true "season 0" of *The Guild*! Collects the one-shots *The Guild: Vork*, *The Guild: Tink*, *The Guild: Bladezz*, *The Guild: Clara*, and *The Guild: Zaboo*.

978-1-59582-900-9 | $14.99

MIKE NORTON'S BATTLEPUG VOLUME 1 HC

Mike Norton

The epic tale of blood and drool begins here! Join Moll and her dogs Mingo and Colfax, as she recounts the legend of "The Warrior and the Battlepug"—a tale of a fearless barbarian, his trusty and freakishly large pug, and evil baby harp seals. This volume collects the first year of *Mike Norton's Battlepug*—the perfect opportunity to get in on the ground floor of the fan-favorite webcomic by Mike Norton, Allen Passalaqua, and Crank!

978-1-59582-972-6 | $14.99

ROBERT E. HOWARD'S SAVAGE SWORD VOLUME 1 TPB

Paul Tobin, Scott Allie, David Lapham, Tim Seeley, and others

From the mind of pulp titan Robert E. Howard comes a slew of thrilling tales of savage heroism and brutal adventure! This collection features larger-than-life Howard heroes, like Dark Agnes, El Borak, the Sonora Kid, and, of course, Conan, and showcases some of today's top creators, like Sean Phillips, Tony Parker, Joe Casey, Paul Tobin, and many, many more! This trade paperback collects all the original material from *Robert E. Howard's Savage Sword #1–#4*, along with a cover and pinup gallery.

978-1-61655-075-2 | $17.99

DARK HORSE HORROR

GETS UNDER YOUR SKIN

"The company known for some of the most prominent horror comics of all time has big plans to keep frightening its readers."—Comic Book Resources

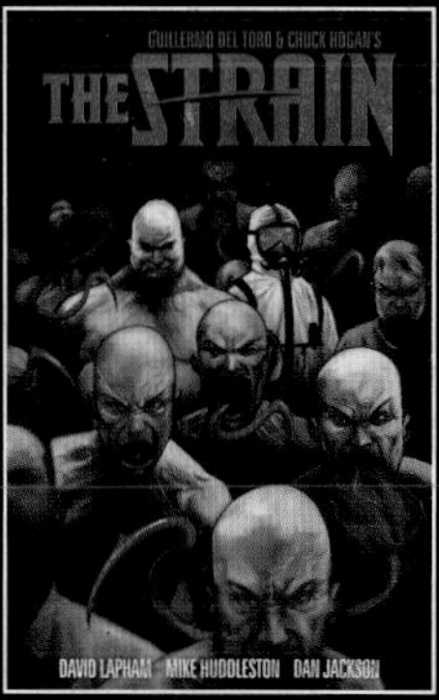
GUILLERMO DEL TORO & CHUCK HOGAN'S
THE STRAIN
DAVID LAPHAM MIKE HUDDLESTON DAN JACKSON

GUILLERMO DEL TORO AND CHUCK HOGAN'S THE STRAIN TPB

David Lapham, Mike Huddleston

When a Boeing 777 goes dark on the JFK runway, the Centers for Disease Control, fearing a terrorist attack, calls in a team of expert biological-threat first responders. Only an elderly pawnbroker from Spanish Harlem suspects a darker purpose behind the event—an undead threat intent on covering mankind in darkness.

Volume 1 | ISBN 978-1-61655-032-5 | $19.99
Volume 2 | ISBN 978-1-61655-156-8 | $19.99

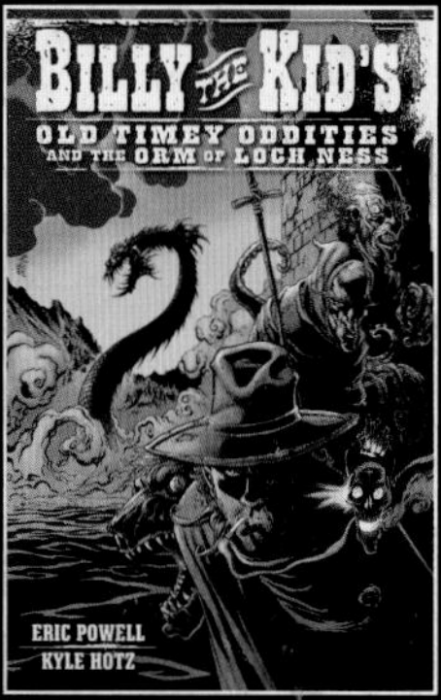
BILLY THE KID'S
OLD TIMEY ODDITIES
AND THE ORM OF LOCH NESS
ERIC POWELL
KYLE HOTZ

BILLY THE KID'S OLD TIMEY ODDITIES TPB

Eric Powell, Kyle Hotz

The world thinks the notorious outlaw Billy the Kid was killed by Pat Garrett, but the Kid is very much alive, the hired gun of Fineas Sproule's traveling spectacle of biological curiosities. Nothing in Billy's career as a gunslinger prepared him for the supernatural terrors he must face with his freak-show cohorts!

Volume 1 | ISBN 978-1-59307-448-7 | $13.95
Volume 2 | ISBN 978-1-59582-736-4 | $15.99
Volume 3 | ISBN 978-1-61655-106-3 | $15.99

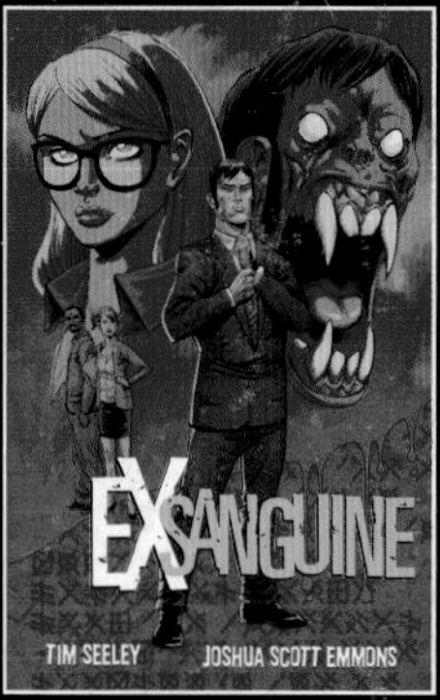
EX SANGUINE
TIM SEELEY JOSHUA SCOTT EMMONS

EX SANGUINE TPB

Tim Seeley, Joshua Scott Emmons

One's a natural-born killer gleefully prowling the night for victims to quench an unnatural blood lust. The other's a vampire. His centuries of existence have left him world weary and detached, until his thirst is reinvigorated when the intricate work of the Sanguine Killer catches his eyes.

ISBN 978-1-61655-158-2 | $17.99

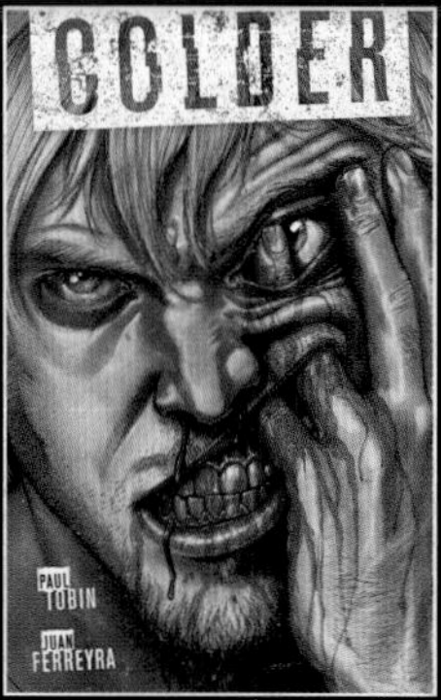
COLDER
PAUL TOBIN
JUAN FERREYRA

COLDER TPB

Paul Tobin, Juan Ferreyra

Declan Thomas's body temperature is dropping. An ex-inmate of an insane asylum that was destroyed in a fire, he has the strange ability to step inside a person's madness and sometimes cure it. He hopes to one day cure his own, but time is running out, because when his temperature reaches zero . . . it's over.

ISBN 978-1-61655-136-0 | $17.99

TO HELL YOU RIDE HC

Lance Henriksen, Joseph Maddrey, Tom Mandrake

A deadly curse plagues a small town, melting the flesh from its victims—the violent revenge four warriors set in motion when their sacred burial grounds were disturbed for the sake of gold miners' greed!

ISBN 978-1-61655-162-9 | $24.99

CRIMINAL MACABRE: FINAL NIGHT—THE 30 DAYS OF NIGHT CROSSOVER TPB

Steve Niles, Christopher Mitten

In this epic crossover with IDW, Steve Niles's greatest characters come together in a final showdown. Cal McDonald only wanted a beer, but what he got was a jaded federal agent and a story about vampires up in Barrow, Alaska. There's a new vamp in LA, and he's hell bent on wiping out mankind.

ISBN 978-1-61655-142-1 | $17.99

AVAILABLE AT YOUR LOCAL COMICS SHOP OR BOOKSTORE! • To find a comics shop in your area, call 1-888-266-4226.
For more information or to order direct visit DarkHorse.com or call 1-800-862-0052 Mon.–Fri. 9 AM. to 5 PM. Pacific Time. Prices and availability subject to change without notice.